THE SUCCESS BLUEPRINT

CelebrityPress®
Winter Park, Florida

CONTENTS

CHAPTER 1

THE MASTER SKILL OF SUCCESS

BY BRIAN TRACY

Your ability to set goals and make plans for their accomplishment is the "master skill" of success. The development of this ability and your making it a lifelong habit will do more to assure high success and achievement than any other skill you can possibly learn.

As with anything, you only *own* the process of goal setting by learning it and then by applying it over and over for yourself until it becomes automatic, like breathing in and breathing out. Your behavioral goal must be to become a continuous goal setter. You must become so clear and focused about what it is you want, that you are doing things that move you toward your goals every minute of every day.

INTELLIGENCE AND SUCCESS

Not long ago, 1500 successful men and women were interviewed to find out what specific qualities they felt they had that had enabled them to rise above 99% of the people in society. One of the qualities they identified was that of "intelligence." But when they were pressed for the definition of intelligence, most of the respondents agreed that intelligence was more a "way of acting" than it was IQ or grades in school.

They concluded that people who were successful acted intelligently. People who were unsuccessful acted unintelligently. Many people from the best colleges with high levels of IQ engaged in unintelligent behaviors. And many people with limited beginnings and blessings engaged in very intelligent behaviors.

So the question then became, "What is, by definition, an intelligent behavior?" The answer is simple. An intelligent behavior is anything that you do that moves you in the direction of something that you have decided that you want for yourself. An unintelligent or "stupid" behavior is anything that you do that moves you *away* from something that you have decided that you want.

For example, if you decide that one of your goals is excellent health and fitness, everything you do to attain that goal is intelligent. Everything that you do, or neglect to do, that takes away from your health and fitness, is, *by your own definition*, a stupid act.

If your goal is to enjoy a high income and become financially independent, everything you do that enables you to increase your personal value and build up your financial resources is intelligent. Any time you do something that moves you away from financial independence, or even when you do something that does not move you *toward* financial independence, you are behaving unintelligently — by your own definition of what you really want.

BECOME MORE INTELLIGENT

Here is a remarkable discovery: Your intelligence is *malleable* over about 25 IQ points. This means that you can increase your IQ by using your mind better. You can become smarter by working on your mental muscles just as you can become physically stronger by working on your physical muscles. And with clear, specific goals that you are working toward each day, you will find yourself acting more and more intelligently in everything you do.

Perhaps one of the most important discoveries of the last 100 years is that you have an automatic, cybernetic, goal-achieving mechanism built into your brain. Human beings are the only creatures on earth that have this particular capacity. Because of this capability, you automatically achieve the goals that you have set for yourself, whatever they are.

This "success mechanism" works night and day, consciously and unconsciously. It both drives you and motivates you toward achieving the goals you have set for yourself. It is almost like a light switch. Once you turn it on, it stays on until you do something to turn it off.

ACTIVATE YOUR SUCCESS MECHANISM

The great problem with most people is that their automatic goal setting mechanism switch is not turned on. Or, if it is turned on, it is focused on achieving goals of limited importance and value. When many people come into work in the morning, their primary goal is to decide what they are going to do at lunchtime. In the afternoon, their primary goal is to decide what they are going to watch on television that evening. For the weekend, their primary goal is how they will enjoy themselves and pass the time. When they pick up the newspaper, their primary goal is to read every sports score that has been accumulated in the nation in the past 24 hours. When they go shopping, their primary goal is to spend everything they have and everything they can charge on credit. They are more concerned with *tension relieving* than with *goal achieving*.

EVERYTHING COUNTS

Here is one of the most important of all success principles: "Everything counts!"

Everything you do adds up or takes away. Everything either helps or hurts. Every action, or inaction, either moves you toward your goals or moves you away from them. Nothing is neutral. Everything counts.

You either win the game of life by deliberate design and by definite activities on your part or you lose the game of life by default, by not playing the game in the first place. You lose the game of life if you fail to switch on your success mechanism and keep it on until you achieve the goals you set for yourself.

Each person also has a "failure mechanism" built into his or her subconscious mind. This failure mechanism is often seen when people seek the fastest and easiest way to get the things they want. Most people follow the line of least resistance. They prefer to do what is fun and easy in the short term rather than what is hard and necessary to assure better results in the long-term.

Every morning when you arise, you are faced with a choice. Do you do what is fun and easy or do you do what is hard and necessary? Do you get up and get yourself ready for the day or do you get up and read the newspaper and watch television?

THINK ABOUT THE CONSEQUENCES

The best way to analyze the importance and value of your behaviors is to think in terms of *long-term potential consequences*. If a behavior is valuable and important, it is something that can have significant consequences in your life. If a behavior is unimportant and irrelevant, it is something that has no consequences at all.

For example, if you drink coffee, read newspapers and watch television, these behaviors will have no consequences for your health, happiness and prosperity, except perhaps negative ones. You can engage in these time-wasting activities for hours. You can become one of the most skillful newspaper readers, television watchers and coffee drinkers in the history of the American republic and it will have absolutely zero effect on your future. Therefore, by definition, these are unimportant, low-value behaviors because they have no helpful consequences.

On the other hand, getting up, exercising, and reading 30-60 minutes each morning, planning your day, and always concentrating on the most valuable use of your time, can have significant consequences for your future. Making a habit of these behaviors will virtually guarantee that you will accomplish vastly more in life than the average person. Every morning, when the alarm clock goes off, you have a chance to choose once again which of these two directions you are going to go. And everything counts.

DISCIPLINE YOURSELF FOR SUCCESS

There is one quality that, throughout the ages, has always been the critical determinant of success or failure, happiness or unhappiness, respect or disrespect, in life. And that is the quality of "self-discipline." The most successful and happy people have always been better disciplined than the least successful and the least happy.

Elbert Hubbard wrote that, *"Self-discipline is the ability to make yourself do what you should do, when you should do it, whether you feel like it or not."*

It is easy to do something when you feel like it, when it is fun or easy or convenient. But it is when the task is difficult and time consuming, and you are tempted to take the line of least resistance, that discipline is required. The wonderful thing is that, the more discipline you exert on yourself, the more you like and respect yourself. You become a better and stronger person. The more discipline you practice, the more you get done and the better you feel.

Self-discipline pays off not only in terms of practical results but also in terms of a positive attitude and higher levels of self-esteem and self-regard.

WORK ON YOUR GOALS EVERY DAY

There is perhaps no area of life where self-discipline is more important than in setting goals and working toward them every day.

In a study done by Dr. Karen Horney in New York a few years ago, participants in high school were taught goal setting. Their results were then tracked over the months and years that followed. What they learned was quite remarkable! The people in the study ended up achieving fully 95% of the goals they set in the program. Think about it! A 95% success rate for goal setters! This is absolutely astonishing, although consistent with all we know about the subject.

They concluded *scientifically* what we have known throughout the centuries. All human action is *purposeful*. Humans set and achieve goals automatically and easily, as long as they work at them. Once you become absolutely clear about what it is you want, and then discipline yourself to do more of those things that move you toward it, your ultimate success is virtually guaranteed.

Here's the question: if goal setting and goal achieving is automatic, and built into your system, why is it that so few people have goals? The estimates, in study after study, are that only about 3% of adults have clear, written, specific goals, accompanied with plans that they work on every day. By the end of their careers, the 3% with written goals eventually earn more in financial terms than the other 97% put together.

People don't set goals for two main reasons. First, they don't realize how important goals are to a successful happy life. Second, they don't know how to set goals. *This* is what we will deal with in the pages ahead.

SEVEN KEYS TO GOAL SETTING

There are seven keys to goal setting. These are general principles that apply to virtually every goal. When you find a person who is not achieving their goals, it is because of a deficiency in one of these seven key areas:

1. **Write Them Down**
   The *first* key is that goals must be clear, specific, detailed and written down. A goal cannot be vague or general, like being happy or making more money. A goal must be specific, concrete, tangible and something that you can clearly visualize and imagine in your own mind.
2. **Make Them Measurable**
   The *second* key to goal setting is that goals must be measurable and objective. They must be capable of being analyzed and evaluated by a third party. "Making lots of money" is not a goal. It is merely a wish or fantasy, which is common to everyone. Earning a specific amount of money within a specific period of time on the other hand, is a *real* goal.
3. **Set Schedules and Deadlines**
   The *third* key is that goals must be time bounded, with schedules, deadlines and sub-deadlines. In fact, there are no unrealistic goals; there are merely unrealistic deadlines. Once you have set a clear schedule and deadline for your goal, dedicate yourself to working toward achieving your goal by that time. If you don't achieve the goal by that deadline, you set another deadline, and if necessary another, and work toward that until you finally succeed. Goal Setting Works.

Throughout the world, many millions of people travel by air each year. Thousands of airplanes with hundreds of thousands of people crisscross the globe every day, touching down in almost every city and town. Air travel is a trillion-dollar industry that affects us all.

The success of the air travel industry, and that of every passenger, is totally the result of systematic, computerized, automatic, national goal setting. When you take a trip, you have a specific city or goal in mind. You decide exactly when you want to fly and how long it will take. You determine the distance to the airport and the time necessary to check in. You calculate how long it will take to fly to your destination and then how long it will take to get to where you are going once you get off the plane. You set a specific schedule for every part of your journey.

Hundreds of millions of people do this every year. They successfully travel from where they are to where they want to go with incredible precision and punctuality. This is goal setting on a mass level. And the same process can work for you on a personal level.

4. Make Them Challenging

The *fourth* key to goal setting is that your goals must be *challenging*. They must cause you to stretch, to move out of your comfort zone. They must be beyond anything you have accomplished in the past. At the beginning, set goals with a 50% probability of success. This makes the process of striving toward the goal slightly stressful, but forcing yourself to stretch also brings out many of your best qualities.

5. Make Your Goals Congruent

The *fifth* key is that your goals must be congruent with your values and in harmony with each other. You cannot have goals that are mutually contradictory. I have met people who want to be successful in business but they want to play golf every afternoon at the same time. It is clearly not possible to realize both of these goals at the same time.

6. Maintain Balance

The *sixth* key is that your goals must be balanced, among your career or business, your financial life, your family, your health, your spiritual life and your community involvement. Just as a wheel must be balanced to revolve smoothly, your life must be balanced with goals in each area for you to be happy and fulfilled.

7. Set Your Major Definite Purpose

The *seventh* key is that you must have a *major definite purpose* for your life. You must have one goal, the accomplishment of which can do more to help you improve your life than any other single goal.

Your life only begins to become great when you decide upon a major definite purpose and focus all of your energies on achieving or obtaining that one single goal. Surprisingly enough, you will find yourself achieving many of your other smaller goals as you move toward achieving your major goal. But you must have a major definite purpose for your life.

In addition to the seven keys to achieving any goal, you must also have a method for goal setting and achieving that you can apply to any goal for the rest of your life.

GOAL SETTING EXERCISE

Here is a powerful exercise that brings everything in this chapter together into a simple process. Take out a clean sheet of paper and at the top of the page write the word "Goals," with today's date.

Then, make a list of at least 10 goals that you want to accomplish in the next 12 months. Write these goals in the present tense, as though a year has passed and you have already attained the goals. For example, if you want to *weigh* a certain amount, you would write, "I weigh X number of pounds by this date." If you want to earn a certain amount of money in the next 12 months, you would write, "I earn X dollars by this date."

Once you have written out your 10 goals, you then review and analyze your list. You ask yourself this question, "What one goal, on this list, if I accomplished it, would have the *greatest positive impact* on my life?" You read through your list of goals and select *one* specific goal. This goal then becomes your major definite purpose for the foreseeable future. This goal becomes your primary organizing principle. This becomes the goal that you focus on every single day.

BEGIN TODAY

Write your goal on a separate sheet of paper, and set a deadline. Analyze your starting position and write out a list of reasons *why* you want to achieve this goal. Identify the obstacles that stand between you and the attainment of this goal. Identify the knowledge and skills that you will need to achieve the goal. Identify the people whose cooperation and assistance you will require.

Make a plan to accomplish this goal, a series of steps organize by sequence, a checklist. You then take action on your plan and do something every day that moves you toward your major goal. You visualize your goal as if you had already achieved it, and you resolve that you will never give up until you are successful.

YOU WILL AMAZE YOURSELF

When you begin to practice these principles in your life, you will be literally astonished at the things that you start to accomplish. You will become a more positive, powerful and effective person. You will have higher self-esteem and self-confidence. You will feel like a winner every hour of the day. You will experience a tremendous sense of personal control and direction. You will have more energy and enthusiasm. As a result, you will accomplish more in a few weeks or months than the average person might accomplish in several years.

When you become a lifelong goal setter, through study and practice, over and over again, you will program the "Master Skill of Success" into your subconscious mind. You will join the top 3% of high achievers in our society and become one of the happiest and most successful people alive.

About Brian

Brian Tracy is Chairman and CEO of Brian Tracy International, a company specializing in the training and development of individuals and organizations. Brian's goal is to help people achieve their personal and business goals faster and easier than they ever imagined.

Brian Tracy has consulted for more than 1,000 companies and addressed more than 5,000,000 people in 5,000 talks and seminars throughout the US, Canada and 70 other countries worldwide. As a Keynote speaker and seminar leader, he addresses more than 250,000 people each year.

For more information on Brian Tracy programs, go to:
- www.briantracy.com

CHAPTER 2

FINDING YOUR PATH TO INDIVIDUAL SUCCESS THROUGH SERVICE TO OTHERS
— HUMANITARIAN LEADERSHIP

BY G. BRYAN CORNWALL, Ph.D., P.Eng.

The Success Blueprint is an enticingly simple concept but creating such a plan requires inquisitiveness, perseverance, and self-awareness. The key tools for designing this blueprint are your personal commitment to continuing development and your intellectual curiosity. After reading hundreds of books and querying hundreds more individuals, there are familiar elements that you can assemble into your own blueprint or map for success.

For many years, I was unable to articulate a coherent definition of success. Looking around, I found that the people I most admired possessed enormous self-awareness but, more than that, they demonstrated a selflessness that transcended material accumulation. As I studied the examples of my mentors, I realized that they were not simply servant leaders. By freeing themselves from the tyranny of external justification, they derived their own validation by giving to others – they became humanitarian leaders.

When I am asked for guidance or to formulate a model, I envision a

27

3 x 3 framework: three outwardly radiating circles of influences each containing three key pointers. The circles are Self, Teams/Tribes, and Society. As one develops mastery of the core concepts, the interfaces between the circles weave a rich tapestry. Like with a beautiful architectural structure, a blueprint is beneficial to help guide you through the plan development.

1. SELF AWARENESS

Any frequent traveler is familiar with the ubiquitous safety admonition: "In the event of unexpected turbulence, put on your own mask before assisting others." As an individual, you are constantly acting within various circles and interacting with varied constituencies. The point is: you must look after yourself before you can look out for others. Only through rigorous self-analysis can you maintain a healthy awareness of your core values and deepest motivations. These attributes form the foundation for the Success Blueprint.

1.1. Committing to Your Personal Values:
The more clearly you understand your core values, the more confidently you can make decisions that affect your life and career. I lived for years fundamentally understanding my own values but not necessarily able to articulate them. I was very fortunate to find jobs that closely aligned with my values. However, as I developed more experience, and upon further reflection found that not all companies behaved with the same values they extol. Early in my career, I left a great paying job with an innovative company because their values were not aligned with who I wanted to represent or how I wanted to conduct myself. The more clearly you understand your values, the more confidently you can make the important decisions that affect your life and career. _Key Inquiries:_ *"What Five Values define me?" and "Am I living my life and making decisions that are consistent with these values?"*

1.2. Setting Goals and Establishing Metrics:
Several summers ago, I was relaxing at a family gathering when a distant cousin came up to me and said: "I hear you are running some crazy 50-mile race in Africa next year." "Really?" I replied, "Where did you hear that?" "Your wife has been talking about it all day." "Well I guess I am now," was all I could reply. In that

moment, a goal barely envisioned became a concrete reality – all because I had mentioned it casually to my "accountability partner" (my wife). Setting goals is important but establishing metrics by which those goals can be measured is even more vital. I have found that the simple act of writing down a goal (and its derivative metrics) is a requisite skill to enabling success. By sharing that goal with a mentor, a friend, or a loved one (your "accountability partner"), you animate the process, and make achieving success far more probable. I was in early middle age – after completing university, running several marathons, and climbing up the corporate ladder – before I adopted this routine. Writing down goals, establishing metrics, and engaging accountability partners has become fundamental to my own Success Blueprint; it was a turning point in my life. Since that chat by the lake with my cousin, I went on to complete "the Comrades" ultramarathon and pursue the larger goal of running a marathon on all seven continents. _Key Inquiries:_ "Have I written my goals for the year?" and "When was the last time I checked my progress toward those goals?"

1.3. Practice Focused Self-Discipline (Work Ethic):

When asked to name the single most important ingredient for success, Brian Tracy once answered, "Self-Discipline." That answer struck me as self-evident, a bit like being asked "What is the single most important activity for life?" And replying, "Breathing." It was only after reflecting on this advice, and adding the adjective "focused," that I began to appreciate the subtle universality of Tracy's comment. Focused self-discipline as manifested by an intense and enduring work ethic affects every circle of interaction: from self to team and tribe all the way up to society. Personally, I believe that self-discipline can be most clearly expressed by an individual's approach to health. When I was a third year engineering student in university, I found myself studying so hard that my physical conditioning reached a private nadir. I happened upon a book about elderly (or so I thought at that time) men who remained active and vigorous physically and mentally through an ongoing commitment to their health. I thought to myself, "Here are these old guys that are in better shape than I am, yet I am in the 'prime of life.' I better change my ways." That epiphany was the catalyst for a lifelong change. No matter how busy I become, I take time for my health and exercise is a daily routine. This focused self-discipline has stood me in good stead recovering from significant injuries and as I successfully battled a brain tumor. *Key inquiries:* *"Choose a respected mentor or colleague who is an example of self-discipline and ask them how they maintain their focus?"* and *"Define metrics that allow you to track your progress toward personal health goals."*

2. WORKING WITHIN TEAMS AND TRIBES

Most interactions – and nearly all successes – occur within collaborative environments. Whether at school, in the workplace, or among the community, team-skills are requisite to the Success Blueprint.

2.1. Building Trust and Demonstrating Loyalty

– Stephen M.R. Covey wrote the most influential book that I have ever read on the concept of "Trust." His work has positively influenced both my personal and professional life. He explains the four cores of credibility with associated questions to ascertain congruence. Two cores are related to character: integrity and intent, and the other two cores are related to competence: capabilities and results. Thirteen behaviors are also described to build trust with an outwardly radiating pattern starting with yourself, then in developing relationships and finally with stakeholders such as organizations, markets and society. Think about examples when you were working really well and enormously productive. Was the environment trusting? Next think about examples at home or work that were taxing and overly burdened with bureaucracy. Was there an absence or lack of trust? Trust is a key to unlock potential and efficiency. Demonstrating loyalty is a fundamental behavior for team success by simultaneously building trust and your own personal credibility.

My 19-year-old son has a good job – some would say a dream job – working at a go-cart and laser tag fun house. However, he has to deal with demanding customers and unfortunately for him, the work culture is not positive. Most of his co-workers hate their job (even though they are too young and too blessed to figure out how lucky they are). When dealing with an angry customer, my son solved the problem with diligence and positive energy. His co-workers asked him why he cared, to which he responded: "I wanted to change the perception of this place. I thought our service would improve our next Yelp rating." I could not be more proud of his loyalty to his employer. Loyalty to the team reinforces personal values, builds trust, and brings obvious benefits to the collective. *Key Inquiries:* "*Does my team understand my intent enough to trust my actions?*" *and* "*What behaviors can I practice that will build trust and not create trust taxes?*"

2.2. Commit to Follow-Through and Execution

– your ability to "get things done" or execute is a key to building confidence with a team and increasing your own self-confidence. The focus and skill required for execution is not a "gift" but can be practiced by anyone willing to exercise disciplined processes including: clarifying goals with metrics, tenaciously following through, and creating accountability for results. In *Execution: The Discipline of Getting Things Done*, accomplished business leaders Larry Bossidy and Ram Charan offer this summary: "Execution is a systematic way of exposing reality and acting on it." When I reflect on the times I have felt most successful, it is when a series of key goals were executed. *Key Inquiries:* "*Are the priorities sufficiently clear to expedite execution and facilitate team success?*" *and* "*Is there a better way to accomplish this goal with better efficiency?*"

2.3. Before Looking Up, Look Down and Around:

At every juncture of my career when I have consciously tried to climb the corporate ladder or look for the short route to an advance in title or salary, I have been disappointed: 100% of the time! It is humbling to reflect back on that sobering statistic. However, when I focused on what was important: doing the job I was hired to do and doing it well, productivity increased. When more focus was directed to the people on the team I was fortunate to lead or in support of other colleagues, productivity again increased. When I "looked down and around" with the genuine intent to serve others rather than looking up at how I could benefit, the team improved and individuals were more productive. They knew that their leader cared about their contributions and their individual success. As a result, I felt more satisfied and this invariably led to other opportunities that were better – both personally and professionally. Most importantly, individual engagement increased and performance improved – a true WIN-WIN-WIN. *Key Inquiries: "What can I do to facilitate the team success as well as the success of the individuals on the team?" and "Am I genuinely thinking about "we," or am I too focused on "me?"*

3. CONTRIBUTING TO SOCIETY

Successful teams become tribes and tribes form the basis of societies. Selfless contributions to a small collective grow and reap personal rewards as the collective evolves and expands. Faithfulness in the small things is what prepares you for leadership in larger venues.

3.1. Share your Experience:

Sharing your experience and success with others through mentoring or teaching is an enormous generosity. When mentoring, it is possible to discern contributions with regular contact. When I was in college I was very involved with the Big Brothers program. "Jason," one of my little brothers, came from a home without a male role model and a family that did not value education. Jason loved sports and gradually came out of his shell as he spent time with me and the varsity basketball team. Years later I learned that he was the first member of his family to graduate high school and go onto college. He had successfully broken the cycle of educational despair! I was so proud of Jason and the future he built for himself. All that it took was someone who cared and showed him the possibilities that were out there if he did his homework. Sharing your experience with others through mentoring or teaching often yields unexpected, delayed results. Just as with Jason, I found great personal satisfaction when one of my engineering students, recently graduated, sought me out to thank me for opening their eyes to the careers and opportunities that are available within their community. *Key Inquiries: "What experiences do I have that I could share with a high school or college student?" and "What can I do to make my community a better place?"*

3.2. Attitude of Gratitude and Counting Your Blessings

– I heard an insightful story about a young professional hockey player who suffered a severe, career-threatening injury. As part of the rehabilitation program, he and twenty other talented, injured players were brought together and asked to list all of the things for which they were thankful. The only exceptions were the obvious ones; they could not list their skills, their families, their friends, or their faith. After twenty minutes of tortured silence, he realized he could think of nothing. He had spent his entire life developing his skills as a player – skills that might no longer be of use. . . What about you? Have you ever listed your "other" blessings? It is not a cliché to say that every day should be seen as the gift it is. Coach John Wooden credits his father with the sage advice: "Make each day your masterpiece." *Key Inquiries:* *"Other than the obvious (career, family, friends, faith), what are the seven things for which I am most thankful?" and "Have you shared this positive energy with at least one person today?"*

3.3. Humanitarian Leadership and the Global Citizen Mindset:

Australian Hugh Evans was twenty-five when he founded the Global Poverty Project with the stated goal to Make Poverty History. In a recent TED talk, he talks extensively about taking on a "Global Citizen Mindset" by thinking more broadly than one's nation of origin. Taking on this mindset expands the personal perspective, enriches the moment, and further develops the Success Blueprint. After suffering in the crucible of infertility, it took some time for my wife and I to heal and adjust to the idea of adoption. We eventually realized that strong plants (and families) can be developed by "grafting", not just grown from seeds. After a domestic adoption process heartbreakingly failed at the last possible moment, we were blessed with two biological children. We subsequently expanded our family twice more through international adoption and have further become supporters of international communities to provide care for abandoned and impoverished children. Please consider reading *The Humanitarian Leader in Each of Us* by Frank LaFasto and Carl Larson – which offers concrete examples and a framework to guide those wanting to make bigger contributions in their own communities and on a global scale. *Key Inquiries:* *"Do I want to make my contribution locally or to an international community, and what will that contribution be?" and "What will I measure at the end of one year of contribution?"*

The Success Blueprint starts with self-awareness (and self-discipline). From there, life's journey leads to team-building and tribe-making before finally measuring true success in our contributions to society. As I have grown and become "successful," I have come to realize that time spent in reflection on my core values, efforts spent working toward collective goals (and the achievements of my teammates), and a selfless giving back to society at large are all interspersed mileposts on this journey.

About Bryan

G. Bryan Cornwall, Ph.D., P.Eng. is a seasoned and dynamic executive with extensive experience leading large teams in Product Development, Research (post-market and clinical trials), Clinical Operations including intra-operative neuromonitoring (IONM), Surgeon Education, Quality Engineering, Regulatory and Quality Assurance (RA/QA/CA). Corporate accomplishments include building and leading multiple departments at a "game-changing" medical device company. Bryan was employed at NuVasive, Inc. from start-up (venture capital-backed with about 20 employees and zero revenue in 1999) to the #3 player in the global spine market, with more than $811M in annual sales and 2,000+ employees in 2015.

Bryan Cornwall's academic background includes a Bachelor of Applied Science in Mechanical Engineering, a Master of Applied Science in Material Science, and a Ph.D. in Mechanical Engineering, specializing in Orthopaedic Biomechanics from Queen's University in Kingston, Ontario, Canada. He is currently pursuing an MBA at the Rady School of Management at UCSD. Bryan has worked in the Medical Device Industry for 20 years and he has more than 14 years of executive leadership experience: being involved in new technology evaluation, strategy development, translation, and cultural proliferation including coaching, mentoring, and education. Bryan continues to demonstrate an academic focus authoring more than 21 peer-reviewed publications, six academic book chapters, and 20 U.S. patents. He also remains active in education being invited to provide engineering lectures at San Diego State University (SDSU), University of Southern California (USC), University of California San Diego (UCSD), Duke University, Queen's University and more.

Bryan has an active and long-standing interest in not-for-profit volunteering and service. His current role is Executive Director of the Society of Lateral Access Surgery (SOLAS), an organization advancing less-disruptive spine surgery to improve patient outcomes. He has also been President of the Big Brothers of Kingston Board of Directors (a United Way organization), the NuVasive Spine Foundation (NSF) and has served leadership roles with Toastmasters International.

In addition to volunteering, Bryan is also an active runner completing more than 20 marathons around the world. He is a member of the "7 Continent Club" completing marathons on six of seven continents including Comrades (the Ultimate Human Race) in South Africa. Bryan and his wife Deeanne of 25 years of marriage, are very proud of their four children from four countries (Canada, United States, China and Ethiopia).

You can contact Bryan at:
- bcornwall@gmail.com
- www.twitter.com/GBCornwall
- https://www.linkedin.com/in/g-bryan-cornwall-phd

CHAPTER 3

TWO LITTLE WORDS THAT WILL TRANSFORM YOU

BY NATSUYO NOBUMOTO LIPSCHUTZ

What is the number one thing that stands between you and your success? Lack of resources, lack of skills, lack of opportunities, or simply lack of luck? Maybe all of these are true. But these are not the number one thing that stands in your way.

By the end of this chapter you'll be empowered to use two words that can transform you—the way you think, the way you act, and the way you script the rest of your life. But first allow me to share a personal story that led to my own transformation . . .

* * *

It was a crisp, dry day in November 2010. I was sitting in the doctor's office with my husband, waiting to hear the results.

"I have good news and bad news," the doctor said in a warm tone of voice. "The good news is that you have one more chance. The bad news is . . . your odds of success are 2 percent." She showed us the genetic test data. Every single test item was marked "99 percent abnormal."

"Honestly, I've never seen such a high percentage of abnormality," the doctor said. "If the next round of your fertility treatment shows the same result, you may want to rethink about getting pregnant."

Imagine injecting yourself with something that feels like molten lava spreading across your belly for fourteen consecutive days. Friends asked me if the needles were painful. No, it wasn't the needles. My body didn't hurt so much. It was my mind that was in a lot of pain. Day by day, I was feeling less and less like a human being and more and more like those hormone-injected livestock we hear about.

My thoughts ran in a perpetual loop: "No, it can't be right! Why me?! I hate this . . . this is so humiliating! No!" I kept thinking NO every single day of my fertility regimen.

When I heard "99 percent abnormal," I took the doctor's words quite well, or so I thought.

When I got home, however, all of a sudden the feeling of despair crept in. It felt like the door toward success and hope had just slammed shut in front of me. I threw myself on a bed and couldn't stop crying. Ninety-nine percent abnormal? Odds of success only 2 percent? How could it be?

Something was definitely standing in the way of my dream of having a child. Where did I go wrong? Had I used up all the luck in my life already?

A number of years ago, the National Science Foundation estimated that our brains produce as many as fifty thousand thoughts per day, 70-80 percent of which are negative thoughts. That means we have about three thousand thoughts per hour when we are awake, or fifty thoughts per minute—almost one thought every single second. Most of our lives are spent in what I call – The World of NO.

But wait, this is when you are in an average situation. If you were faced with a very negative situation, your thoughts could be 99 percent negative. You can only imagine how much damage that would cause, right?

This is it. The number one thing that stands between you and your success is your thoughts.

"No, I can't do that." "No, I'm not good enough." "No, I don't like that." "No, I don't think so." "Yes, but . . ."

Even if everybody in the entire world is saying "yes you can" but you are saying "no I can't," who do you think is going to win? You. And you just gave up your success right there. The only way to reprogram this conversation in your head – so that it aligns with the success you want to achieve and the person you want to be and the life you want to live – is to transform your thoughts from The World of NO to The World of YES.

I know, but that's not easy, Natsuyo, you may say.

No, it's not. Unless you have a powerful, magical tool. Is there such a thing? What if I told you that, YES, there is? And that with this magical tool you could turn off that World of NO as easily as flipping a switch and direct all your thoughts into the positive World of YES? Imagine unleashing your full potential. Miraculous, yes?

When I first discovered such a switch, however, I didn't realize it was so powerful.

My friends may laugh at me now, but I used to be a *hako-iri-musume* as we say in Japanese. It means a gently-raised princess in a little pretty box. I had nothing to complain about. My parents gave me everything I needed, if not more. But I wanted to see the world. I wanted to see what was beyond that little pretty box I was in. So back in 1993, when I was a junior in college in Japan and saw a poster about an exchange program, I said to myself, "YES! I want to see the world. YES, I'm going to do this!" My World of YES propelled me across the ocean to an exciting new world—albeit it was St. Louis, Missouri.

But one month after arriving, I was struggling. I had lost all confidence: in my English, in my social abilities, and in my decision to come to this so-called "world." I felt so intimidated and embarrassed to speak with anyone, socialize with anyone, and expose myself to anyone. My World of YES quickly turned into The World of NO.

One Friday night, my dormitory hosted a party for freshmen. Now that was the last place where I wanted to be! As I was sneaking back to my room, someone grabbed my arm. It was Nate, a floor-mate who had been drinking like a fish.

"Hey, where are you going?" he blurted. "You are always so anti-social."

That was a verbal knife to me.

My frustration was at its peak, I was losing confidence in myself, and I even started to regret my decision to come to America. Maybe it was too early. Maybe I should have mastered English first . . . I felt like a water-filled balloon, ready to explode. And the drunken freshman Nate popped it.

I burst into tears in front of everyone. What a party spoiler. I hated myself even more.

"Um . . . no, no . . . my English not good!" was all I could manage to say before crying again.

Now you wouldn't think a drunken freshman would ever have anything helpful to say to anyone, would you? Well, he actually did. And this is what he said:

"SO WHAT?"

When I heard "So what," something miraculous happened. My negative thoughts disappeared. Poof!

"My English is not good." SO WHAT?

"It's embarrassing." SO WHAT? No one cares. Only I do.

"Well, people will judge me." SO WHAT? Poof!

THOSE TWO LITTLE WORDS!

So simple and yet so profound, this switch called "SO WHAT" transported me back to The World of YES and set me on a new course of action.

The next day I started to keep my door open so people could pop in and say hi. I started to knock on their doors to have a little chat. Fast-forward twenty-three years and look at me now! I spoke at a TEDxTalk event, I won Toastmasters International Speech Contest two years in a row, and now I'm a co-author of a bestselling book. That's the success I couldn't even have dreamed of. When you hear me speak, you may still detect a trace of a foreign accent, but . . . SO WHAT?

The number one thing that stands between you and your success is your thoughts.

If you are aiming to achieve a breakthrough, and your thoughts are blocking the way to your success, whether it's your fear, self-consciousness, lack of confidence, or perfectionism, simply ask yourself "SO WHAT?" Not once, not twice. As many times as it takes until The World of NO starts to make a way out. It is nothing but your own thoughts that are limiting your growth, success, and potential.

Ironically, I learned this important life lesson from that drunken freshman, Nate. But at that time I still had no idea that the shift in my mindset could be so powerful it would even bring a miracle.

When I was going through that fertility treatment and heard "99 percent abnormal," I realized that something else was very negative. You guessed it right. My thoughts.

Every single day I was contaminating my mind with all those NOs. The doctor said I had only one last chance, which seemed almost impossible. I needed a miracle. I needed to get my World of YES back. More injections? SO WHAT? Feeling like livestock? SO WHAT? Poof! YES, I HAVE ONE MORE CHANCE!

I started to visualize my future baby girl and talk to her every day: "YES, I WILL read you fairytales every night. YES, I WILL push you in a swing high into the sky. YES, I WILL hold your little hand whenever you need me. All the pain and hardship of my regimen . . .? SO WHAT?!"

Two months later I started the second and final round of the treatment. I lived in The World of YES every day during that time and asked myself "SO WHAT?" every time any negative thought came up in my mind.

The final result came back. The moment of truth.

It was 99 percent... normal! YES!

The doctor said, "This is *so* abnormal to be *so* normal! This is a miracle!"

Narrow New York City streets were deeply covered with snow, but my feet felt as light as a feather. My life was transformed.

Now I have a beautiful five-year-old daughter, Leena. What greater success could I ask for?

Those TWO LITTLE WORDS switched my perspective and result from 99 percent negative to 99 percent positive—and brought me a miraculous success. They transformed my life. Leena is the very proof.

This simple yet powerful tool can cause a tremendous shift in your mindset and get you moving toward success.

In fact, this "SO WHAT" principle can be applied beyond your personal success because it is a tool that helps you look at things from different perspectives and takes you deeper into what's really important.

When I was a summer intern at McKinsey & Company, "Where is the SO WHAT?" was the frequently-used maxim.

McKinsey's clients were high-level management at large companies, and they hired us to ensure the success of their businesses. As trusted advisors, we needed to provide "synthesis = summary + insight." Not a mere summary of data. So from day one we were trained to ask ourselves, "SO WHAT?" at least five times to get valuable synthesis.

I now have my own strategy consulting firm called ASPIRE Intelligence, as well as a global public speaking consultancy called Breakthrough Speaking.

I use this "SO WHAT" principle whenever I help clients transform from "good" to "great."

Sometimes the enemy of the great is the good we settle for. The "good" could stand between you and your success in business. I often witness it when consulting for my clients, whether it's about their strategy or speeches.

For example, one of my clients at Breakthrough Speaking is a global IT company, and the original message in their sales presentation was this:

"We produced many number ones in the world." Good pitch. But not great. What's the implication of this message to the potential client? Are you trying to gain trust from stakeholders? Or are you boasting about your track record so you can justify your high prices, or so you can intimidate your competitors? What are you bringing to the table? What's in it for the client?

Let's apply the "SO WHAT" principle here to see how you can transform this good sales pitch into a great one.

"We developed many number ones in the world."
  • SO WHAT? (what does this mean?)
"So we can provide many of the world's number one technologies and products."
  • SO WHAT? (what's in it for the audience?)
"So our leading-edge technologies will help your company succeed."
  • SO WHAT? (how does that benefit the audience?)
 "Your company can be one step ahead of the competition."
  • SO WHAT? (then what happens?)
"With our leading-edge technologies, you can not only get ready to fight the competition, but stay ready to beat the competition all the time."
  • SO WHAT? (what's the most important takeaway for the audience?)
"You will become and stay number one."

By asking "SO WHAT?" you can see that the message changed from "I/we focused" to "You focused," which resonates with the audience far better.

This question gives deeper insights. It gives the potential client a deeper connection with you. It cuts all the unnecessary strings that are keeping you from achieving "it," whatever success *it* might be for you.

The switch that I call "SO WHAT" transforms you from good to great, whether you are seeking great success in your personal life or in business.

This magical switch is within you. If you are aiming for a great success and your thoughts are getting in your way, simply ask yourself "SO WHAT?" Not once, not twice. But as many times as it takes until your thoughts are redirected from The World of NO to The World of YES. Then nothing in life will be impossible for you.

A word of caution though. You may become so overly positive and such a high achiever that people may get jealous and want to compete with you.

Well. . . TWO WORDS . . .

SO WHAT!

About Natsuyo

Natsuyo Nobumoto Lipschutz is the *Managing Principal, ASPIRE Intelligence* and also the *Executive Consultant* for *Breakthrough Speaking™*.

An entrepreneur, management consultant, certified speech coach, competitive ballroom Latin dancer, and mother, Natsuyo Nobumoto Lipschutz harnesses the power of thoughts for positive changes in life, society, and business.

Born and raised in Tokyo, Natsuyo began her career in New York, aspiring to help grow Japanese companies and individuals globally. Today she is the managing principal of a management strategy consulting firm, ASPIRE Intelligence, and the program developer and executive consultant of a global public speaking consultancy, Breakthrough Speaking™.

Natsuyo received her MBA degree from the New York University Stern School of Business, and a BA degree in cross-cultural communication in business from the Waseda University School of Commerce. She also attended Washington University in St. Louis as a full-scholarship exchange student during her undergraduate studies.

Prior to establishing ASPIRE Intelligence (New York) in 2004, Natsuyo held a position at ITOCHU International Inc. (New York) as a sales and business development manager in the Steel and Pulp & Paper Departments. She also served as a management consultant for McKinsey & Company (Tokyo).

As the founder and managing principal of ASPIRE Intelligence, Natsuyo provides strategic and analytical business consulting services in the areas of marketing intelligence, brand strategy, business development, and organizational development for Japanese-US cross-cultural businesses. Natsuyo has conducted numerous corporate workshops in the areas of cross-cultural communications, global leadership, facilitation skills, diverse team building, logical thinking, cultural integration, and more.

The credo of ASPIRE Intelligence is "Sei-Wa-Kon," which was a gift from Natsuyo's late father and the former honorary chairman of Akebono Brake Industry, Yasusada Nobumoto. "Sincerity, Harmony, and Spirit"—with genuine Sincerity, ASPIRE supports its clients, business partners, and communities. With a sense of Harmony, ASPIRE steers its course of action. With high Spirit, ASPIRE holds to uncompromising standards.

Natsuyo is a two-time first-place winner of the Toastmasters International Speech New York Division Contest (spring 2013 and 2014). Additionally, she is currently the only Japanese World Class Speaking™ certified coach. She has been an avid competitive ballroom Latin dancer since 2004 and is a multiple-time finalist at United States Dancesport Championship.

Natsuyo resides in New York with her husband, Robert, and daughter, Leena. She often travels around the United States and Japan to share her knowledge in consulting and global public speaking.

To book Natsuyo for your next event, corporate workshop, or private coaching, contact ASPIRE Intelligence at info@aspireintelligence.com and Breakthrough Speaking at info@btspeaking.com.

For further information, visit the company websites:
- ASPIRE Intelligence: http://www.aspireintelligence.com
- Breakthrough Speaking: http://www.btspeaking.com

CHAPTER 4

EXPOSED – 5 SECRET SUCCESS PRINCIPLES
— TO EFFORTLESSLY ACCELERATE YOUR CAREER AND INCOME IN THE NEXT 12 MONTHS OR LESS

BY KATIE-JEYN ROMEYN

"Sorry mum, I can't make it home this time... no mum, everything's fine... I just can't get the time off work, that's all." I lied in the bravest voice I could muster before I put the phone down and curled up on the lounge, the buzz of the air conditioner my only company.

What had I done?

A minimum wage job working on the front desk for a mining company in remote Roxby Downs, South Australia, was no place for a 20-something female in a very male-dominated environment 2,000km from home.

It was the biggest mistake of my life. It also turned out to be the best thing that ever happened to me. From this seemingly hopeless situation I created a way for a woman to quickly get ahead in a corporate workplace. Today, through my company, **Coach on Collins**, I help other women create the life they want and the recognition they deserve.

We all experience failure on the path to success

Back to Roxby Downs… I was in the most junior of admin roles, on the minimum wage and working minimum hours. As a contractor, I had no special entitlements and lived pay cheque to pay cheque. I couldn't even scrape together $700 for the airfare home to my family and friends. Trapped? Yes, and in truth, I was at rock bottom both financially and emotionally, for which I felt ashamed.

The good news for me, and for anyone in the workplace who feels stuck or that they deserve more, the power of a simple spreadsheet changed everything.

Fast forward just 10 years and my career had accelerated so fast I had become an executive of an ASX-listed resources company, St Barbara Limited. To progress through those multiple levels in this short timeframe was extraordinary and record breaking in the industry, whether for a man or a woman.

Here are the two key decisions, some five years apart, that drove me forward.

I. Money Matters

My saviour came, like I said, in the form of a spreadsheet. And it was a big 'aha' moment. Not long after that depressing phone call home, I was asked to update salaries for all of the mining engineers and geologists on site. The remuneration numbers were huge.

One thing stuck in my mind: I wanted what they had. Not the almost subsistence existence I was living. In that moment I made my first key decision, to create economic independence and to live life on my terms. And it was the most powerful moment of my life to that point.

II. Help Others Win

My next key decision, half a decade later, was about other people, not me. Because I had experienced some negative workplace cultures, I was determined to create an ***employer of choice***. A bold vision considering I was not at a senior level at the time of the decision.

The baseline to create an employer of choice was to provide people with *equal opportunity* and *reward for their performance*. Sounds easy but difficult to achieve because it's no secret, the global corporate environment is unbalanced in terms of opportunities and remuneration for women compared to men. A pay equity gap exists, which must change.

At St Barbara I broadened our strategies from improving business performance through people to also include levelling the playing field. This consistent and powerful combination helped St Barbara become an award-winning company, and also underpinned my own success. Because I helped everyone and the organisation win, I progressed faster and further than I thought possible for me. All of this is why I now empower individual women to disrupt the pay equity gap for themselves.

The pay equity gap explained

Conventional wisdom says the pay equity gap is no big deal because it's based on averages: most women leave the workforce to have children and don't chase opportunities as much as men, so of course there is a gap! The world has changed and that thinking does not stack up to any scrutiny or fairness test.

Consider it this way...

Imagine there is a national announcement that every employed person was going to be given a $700,000 bonus. There you are, thinking about the difference $700,000 would make to your life.

Now, imagine if *every woman* was excluded from receiving the $700,000. How would you feel?

Not great. Well that's *precisely* what is happening today:

- On average, a woman earns approximately $700,000 less than her male counterpart over the course of her career.[1]

- 1 in 3 women will retire with no superannuation at all and around 90% of women will retire with inadequate savings to fund a 'comfortable' lifestyle.[2]

The national Workplace Gender Equality Agency reports the overall pay equity gap for Australia is 17.3%.[3] This means, on average, for every $1 a male earns, a female only earns 83¢. Or put another way, a woman on average would be required to work an additional 63 days in a year to earn the same as a man.[4]

Whilst these figures are specific to Australia, similar trends are evident in EVERY Western economy. *But it doesn't have to be that way for you. It won't be that way.* If you are reading this, you are ready to take action. What I have to share with you in this chapter, when applied consistently, will create amazing results for your career and income, and faster than you might think.

Decide what you want, you might just get it

At St Barbara, we implemented effective people policies and systems including best-practice remuneration strategies. The aim was to ensure employees were treated consistently based on performance and were valued at all levels of the business. The strategy benefited the company and all employees, which resulted in the outstanding reduction in the pay equity gap from a staggering 43% in 2007, to 11.4% in 2014. All of which led to St Barbara winning state and national awards as well as the prestigious Workplace Gender Equality Agency *Employer of Choice* citation.

Turn adversity into opportunity

You see, I firmly believe adversity is life's gift to me. To lead a company to close the pay equity gap and accelerate my career in record time, I had to regard all obstacles as opportunities, and address all conflicts.

No, it wasn't easy. However, the lessons learned now help me to empower other women to *disrupt the pay equity gap on the individual level*, so they too can accelerate their career, increase their income and live life on their terms.

Live life on your terms

That's your aim. The *5 Secret Success Principles to Effortlessly Accelerate Your Career and Income in the Next 12 Months or Less* outlined in this chapter helped me move from being at the mercy of my employer, to "that chick" who defied all odds, my own self-doubt and plenty of detractors along the way, to creating my *employer of choice* vision and now doing what I want. They are now available to you.

SECRET SUCCESS PRINCIPLE 1 – Being Paid What You Are Truly Worth begins with Your Decision that Money IS a Key Measure of Your SUCCESS

Not surprisingly there is a connection between success and money. Women, who accelerate their careers and business, have made the decision to value money. And, I mean *really* value money. They consistently take actions to increase their income so they can measure their success. When money comes in, their tendency is to *invest* rather than spend. They also have a different *conversation* with money. One of respect for what money can offer.

Those who struggle with money often have attitudes such as:

- Money doesn't motivate me
- Money doesn't matter, it's not important
- I'll just take what I can get and try to be happy with it

Imagine having these *same* attitudes towards your significant other. Would they enjoy being around you? Would they want to stay with you? No. The same applies with money.

**Secret Success Exercise #1 - What Would You Like Your Salary to be in a Year from Now?

*What specifically is that number? Write it down NOW and date it. Then do this every single year and after every single change in salary. **What we focus on we get. If we want something to grow, we must grow it with our laser-like focus.***

SECRET SUCCESS PRINCIPLE 2 – Getting the Career You Want Begins with the Magic of Clarity

For a map to be useful, it requires a point A (where you are now) and a point B (where you want to be). Defining point B helps you stay focused and strategise *exactly* what needs to be done, by whom, and by when—so you can get there.

To get clear in your thinking sometimes all it takes is for someone to ask you the right questions. We all know everyone benefits from a fresh set of eyes. I help you clarify and *organise* your many thoughts into something concise so you have a clear vision for your career.

**Secret Success Exercise #2 – Your Magic Wand

Answer this one question: If you could wave a magic wand, what would your dream career look like in five years? Write it down in as much detail as possible. ***Once we know what we want, we are halfway there!***

SECRET SUCCESS PRINCIPLE 3 – Bust Through Your Roadblocks so You DON'T Compromise on Who You Are

We all face roadblocks, both external and internal. Here's a dose of REALITY: to accelerate your career and increase your income you must do whatever it takes to overcome adversity and conflict. You must be strong and have the courage to back yourself.

> Zig Ziglar said: *"If you will be hard on yourself, life will be easy on you. But if you insist upon being easy on yourself, life is going to be very hard on you."*

Most people, when faced with adversity or conflict, shy away from it. But in fact, adversity and conflict are there to help you succeed.

Here is what I discovered…

You will know you are being easy on yourself when you have an ongoing unresolved issue, or avoid a conversation. You may tell yourself it is easier to just not say anything, convince yourself it isn't important, or not worth the bother. Well, it is. Sweeping issues under the carpet is what holds us back from greater success.

When people ask me: "What do you do?" I say, "Whatever it takes." When you practise and understand this principle alone, your career and life accelerates.

**Secret Success Exercise #3 – Sweep it UP from Under the Carpet

Identify 3 issues from your professional and personal life you continually avoid (sweep them under the carpet and the mound keeps getting bigger and bigger). For each, write the answers to these 5 questions:

1. What am I most afraid of and trying to avoid?
2. How can I turn this into an opportunity?
3. How is this helping me in ways I have yet to identify?
4. What is the quickest way to resolve this?
5. How will my life be different when this is resolved?

Then do whatever it takes to action them! **Adversity is your opportunity to shine, so get excited!**

SECRET SUCCESS PRINCIPLE 4 – You ARE Worth It, So Live it!

Invest in yourself – you ARE worth it. Everyone has the resources to invest. You are already *spending* money on *something*. The key is to *redirect* that spending so it becomes *an <u>investment</u> in you and your future.* There is nothing more important than to invest in your mindset. It is what sets you apart from your peers. It did for me. Investing in self-development and coaching to amplify my mindset, improved my self-belief and boosted my confidence in what I could achieve. Results followed.

To do this I connected with people who lifted me up. People who could see what I could not see… people who would challenge my limitations. If you want to go beyond where you are, you must have different conversations with new people.

**Secret Success Exercise #4: Your Future Gratitude

Ask yourself: What can I do today that my future self will thank me for?

To get where you want to be, you must invest in your mindset. This is where an external partner with "insider knowledge" will accelerate your results. **Your life only gets better when you do. Work on you, and life will work for you.**

SECRET SUCCESS PRINCIPLE 5 – The Triple G – Givers Get Growth and Win

It's common for new clients to share with me, "I am good at my job." This is a start, but not enough to accelerate your career. My question that follows is: "What are you doing outside of your job to grow and contribute beyond that?" Because the truth is: being "good at your job" is not enough to get ahead fast.

My intention has always been to help everyone I work with succeed, which is beyond the scope of any role description. I help them be great and "win". The more you give, the more you win. The more people you empower, the more you grow, and so does your career and life.

**Secret Success Exercise #5: What are you prepared to give?

Ask yourself: What have I contributed today outside my role description to help someone else win?

If you haven't helped someone 'win' in the last 24 hours, write down one thing you will do tomorrow. Then do it. Continue to look for ways to win every day. Make it your ritual. Everyone wants people on their team who help them win. Be that person. **How you show up anywhere, is how you show up everywhere.**

Let's Create Successful Change Together!

Accelerating your career, and quickly increasing your income, is an ongoing process. It never stops. You must start it again and again consciously, and with intent. Over and over and over.

I acknowledge you for the courage to step into your own power. I wish you well in creating the career and life you want. And, please share this book with anyone you know who will benefit from it.

Together, we will disrupt the pay equity gap one individual at a time. As we do that, we create a ripple for every other woman in your organisation, in your country, and around the globe.

End Notes:
1. "Gender Pay Gap Statistics March 2016" Workplace Gender Equality Agency | pg. 2 | (www.wgea.gov.au)
2. "Super gap has women fearful about life after retirement" | Shannon Fentiman, Queensland Minister for Communities, Women and Youth | 6 March 2016.
3. "Gender Pay Gap Statistics March 2016" Workplace Gender Equality Agency | pg. 2 | (www.wgea.gov.au)
4. Gender Pay Gap Statistics August 2015" Workplace Gender Equality Agency | pg. 4 | (www.wgea.gov.au)

About Katie-Jeyn

Katie-Jeyn Romeyn helps leaders fast track their career success. Through her company, **Coach on Collins**, she assists professionals, managers and senior executives to create change and accelerate into higher-level opportunities and roles where they become significant influencers and contributors to their chosen field.

Known as a "disruptor," she brings to private practice a wealth of corporate and operational experience in how to get ahead in a male-dominated field. She is widely regarded for shaking things up so her clients progress rapidly rather than remain dormant in their various stages of success.

No stranger to adversity, Katie-Jeyn's rapid rise up the corporate ladder had humble beginnings in a low-paid administration role at a mining company in an isolated country town, Roxby Downs, South Australia. Within 10 years she secured an executive position at an ASX-listed resources company, St Barbara Limited. A battle with the debilitating Crohn's Disease, which involved 9 surgeries in 11 months, was but a speed bump on her path to success.

During her 15-year mining career, Katie-Jeyn worked with the likes of WMC Resources, Rio Tinto, BHP Billiton, and more recently St Barbara where she rose to Executive General Manager for People and Business Services. She credits this rapid rise to the implementation of a series of Secret Success Principles. The 5 Secret Success Principles outlined in this chapter reveal just some of the "insider knowledge" Katie-Jeyn imparts to her clients for their rapid results.

Katie-Jeyn holds qualifications in Executive Education in Compensation Committees from Harvard Business School and is a graduate of the University of South Australia with a Bachelor of Management, focusing on Human Resource Management. She also holds an International Master Practitioner of Coaching from The Coaching Institute, Melbourne, Australia. The work she led has been recognised nationally with numerous business and industry awards including:

Employer of Choice for Gender Equality
Workplace Gender Equality Agency – 2014
Employer of Choice for Gender Equality Citation – St Barbara Limited

Women in Resources National Awards – 2014
Excellence in Diversity Programs and Performance – St Barbara Limited

Women in Resources Awards
Chamber of Minerals and Energy Western Australia (WA) – 2014
Outstanding Company Initiative - St Barbara Limited

Business Achievement Awards
Workplace Gender Equality Agency (formerly the EOWA) - 2011
EOWA's Director's Award - St Barbara Limited - Winner
Outstanding EEO Practice in a Non-Traditional Area – St Barbara Limited – Finalist
Diversity Leader for the Advancement of Women – Katie-Jeyn Romeyn – Finalist

Katie-Jeyn is continuously inspired to create positive changes to the business environment through corporate and individual initiatives, all of which create success for others.

According to Katie-Jeyn, "*Life is more fulfilling when you step into your own power, help others win and live on your own terms by creating economic independence.*"

For information to accelerate your career faster, go to:
- www.AccelerateYourProfessionalCareer.com.au

CHAPTER 5

A PEAK PERFORMANCE LIFE
— WHERE SCIENCE AND SPIRITUALITY MEET

BY DR. KEERTHY SUNDER
~ Chief Medical Officer of Mind & Body
Treatment and Research Institute

What would you do with limitless cognitive potential?

Inspired by science, tradition, and compassionate care, I've dedicated my professional life to helping people achieve and thrive at their personal best. We've all played witness to the struggles that come from the human condition in our lives. For me, it was my loving and delightful mother, a woman who struggled with achieving her best despite her post-partum depression. It unraveled her, tugging away at her emotional, physical, and spiritual seams. She faced extraordinary challenges and all we wanted was for her to succeed in overcoming them. It was never easy or ideal, but it was a heartbreaking reality.

How many of us are not living a peak performance life?

Through my mother's struggles, I noticed how her warning signs and symptoms played against each other, creating a relentless struggle. When she suffered from bouts of Bronchial Asthma, her moods would fluctuate. If she was feeling depressed, it spurred on Asthmatic events. It was tough for those who loved her to watch this rollercoaster, and

59

absolutely tougher on her. I wondered, was it preventable? I learned that it was and I saw a possible solution about how I could not only help her, but also take an innovative lead in helping other people who longed for a peak performance transition that lead them from a place of struggle to a place of actualization – whether they were an athlete, student, a homemaker, or a professional.

I was a practicing OB/GYN first, inspired to help women experience good pregnancies and birth experiences. To do that, I had to pay attention to more than a changing body; I had to focus on their changing mental state of awareness, as well. It fascinated me, leading me to further pursue my training in Psychiatry to explore the mind and body connection. Ultimately, I saw that I needed to fuse my Western Medicine know-how with my Eastern Practices awareness that I'd bore witness to growing up in India. This fusion was inclusive to the:

- *Biological self:* balance of energy, hormones, immune integrity markers, neurotransmitters and brain electrical activity
- *Psychological self:* mastering of emotional and cognitive capacities
- *Spiritual self:* building resilience through positive pathways to conscious and unconscious thought

These components, when working in harmony and conjunction with each other, hold the answers we need to begin experiencing sustainable peak performance.

Our bodies hold unlimited potential to do great things, but to experience this, we need to understand its internal processes.

At the Mind & Body Treatment and Research Institute, we focus our work on achieving success in the biological, psychological and spiritual self, all of which lead to a more exceptional self by:

- Developing and expanding performance in males and females of all ages
- Looking below the surface and diving deep to explore specific challenges and opportunities
- Targeting and accessing different modalities toward continued peak level performance

We create a framework through using a multidimensional approach that processes the biological structure—the body and the mystical component, which is called the psyche.

Our psyche is subjective, while also being highly impactful on our physical selves (e.g., the heart and the brain). Through its components, it has immense influence on our ability to perform at our highest level and experience fulfillment throughout our lives—consistently and continuously. This psychological piece is also significant, in that it processes emotions, feelings, thinking, actions, behaviors, and sound decision making. Even our ability to exercise our will is contained in the psyche. This is why it's so critical to our body's overall health and responsiveness in our chosen environment.

Through mindfulness, we can achieve balance by addressing the psyche, which helps to bridge the psychological and spiritual component of our lives. This helps us to recognize our innate intelligence about our body and how to detect what is happening from within us. We all have this ability, even if we don't actively practice it.

What happens when we don't actively practice mindfulness of our body and its symptoms? We usually seek out the help of an expert, or someone who's willing to give us some "friendly advice" based on their perspective.

We are all unique in body and mind, which means that our solutions are individual—customized to us, in specific.

The biological component of our bodies is so important, because it directly impacts our psychological selves and even our spiritual alignment. *Think of our body as a temple; it is the only one that we have and we must take care of it.* Most of us have no problems attending and tending to a church, synagogue, or a spiritual center; however, we hesitate to treat our body wonderfully, refusing to embrace what it tells us and seeking out ways to take better care of it. An off-balance body reveals signs and finding the source of the problem is important. Often enough, it's not what our symptom leads us to believe. For example: when we experience a headache or brain fog, this could be a reaction to gluten present in wheat or dairy sensitivity.

There is no singular, effective approach to answers. At our clinic, when we meet with patients, we go through many layers, including:

- Hormones
- Biochemistry
- Immune Markers
- Brain Electrical Activity

The body is a complex symphony consisting of many instruments playing at the same time. A finely-tuned conductor will be able to find the strengths and weaknesses of each section. Many times, the source of the problem is found by discovering the communication patterns of electrical activity in the brain. What type of energy exists? Our energy (qi, chi, prana) is expressed through our body and by paying attention to it we can find connections between our biological and psychological beings.

Do you have any data that monitors how your energy is being expressed in your body? Few people do, which means that it is nothing more than luck if they have sustained peak performance.

Many of us do try to give our bodies and lives balance. We strive for good relationships, a healthy diet, fitness, and aim for a good night's rest. I meet people daily who embrace these components—and they are important—but they seldom understand the ideology behind them. Through understanding the condition of our markers, we gain specific information that helps us make positive adjustments. These markers include:

- Sugar levels: too much sugar in our diet is a health risk and indicator of diseases such as Diabetes. Checking for surrogate markers for your sugar control through Glycated Hemoglobin provides us valuable information about your risk for depression and dementia.
- Vitamin D: although classified as a vitamin, it's true nature is that of a hormone that is intricately linked to estrogen and testosterone levels, making it deeply connected with who we are and what our fundamental energy level will be.
- Hormones: dysregulation of sexual, adrenal, and thyroid hormones are often symptoms of conditions that stem from the gut and a breakdown of the gut-brain barrier.

If you were to take a step toward peak performance today, it should be to find out what your level of Vitamin D is, as it is highly impactful to your health.

Having peak performance requires having your hormones checked on a regular basis (semi-annually to annually), as they can change sporadically and without warning, often from small adjustments in our body that we cannot physically feel taking place. Changes in the seasons also impact this, necessitating adjustments of dosing during winters and summers.

Do you know what the one symptom is that is often an indicator that your body is having an adverse reaction to an imbalance?
The answer: inflammation of the joints or organs.
The leading cause of this type of inflammation is leaky gut.

Leaky gut is serious, and impactful. Many people haven't heard of this before they visit with my team. Here's an overview as to what it is, and what it entails:

> This concept is known in Eastern traditions (Ayurvedic Medicine) and it is centered around the importance of an appropriate diet suited to a particular body constitution. In particular, a plant-based diet is highly recommended to assist in alleviating problems that are related to the small and large intestines. When a problem arises where the intestinal barrier cannot contain the food particles the particles create a cascade of inflammation, resulting in a "leaky gut." When the gut-brain barrier is compromised, it leads to many conditions and symptoms, either temporary or acute, including:
>
> - Inflammation of the joints and organs
> - Autoimmune disorders

Conditions such as what are mentioned above impact the psychological and spiritual self as well, because they are stressful and life-altering. We move less, feel worse, and often withdraw from the very activities that make it a joy to be human.

What we consume for food should never cross the gut barrier and make its way into the blood stream—ideally. When it does, something is wrong. Where we can learn to prevent the onset of leaky gut is through the acknowledgement and recognition of certain variables in our life, mostly within our control. Contemplate these questions:

- How often are you stressful, and how do you conquer that stress?
- Are there certain foods you eat that upset your stomach or drain your energy?

Food, in particular, can be challenging. More people have food sensitivities and allergies that they are not even aware exist. The most common adverse reactions to food come from milk and dairy, nitrates in vegetables, peanuts and tree nuts, and gluten. Often times, when these foods cross the gut barrier, they will produce a tremendous immune reaction because the immunity markers try to fight it (antibodies). They are foreign bodies to the system, and as a result, inflammation occurs.

We can never really succeed without balance in our lives. My greatest successes come from those I meet, and help to find integrated solutions that make them better.

It's very important for us to recognize that the food we consume, the water we drink, and our environment impact our ability to perform. Making good choices and having robust genes isn't always enough. It' a delicate task to be aware of one's self and take the right actions. Those who take advantage of the expertise and multi-dimensional treatment approach that integrated physicians such as myself offer see a peak performance future for their lives.

You can be better, but what can you do? This decision is based on what you are facing. Is it from the top down (mind to body) or from the bottom up (body to mind)? We need to determine if you have a robust body, but not a robust mind. Maybe you're not as good at retaining material as you were just a few years ago. Or perhaps you're not as energized first thing in the morning as you once were, even if you are feeling good otherwise and your markers are "okay." Possibly, you may not be having a body issue, but a brain issue. You do not know if you do not find out, and cannot experience the rewards of having peak performance for the long-term without finding out.

Through performing a QEEG (Quantitative Electroencephalogram), we are able to determine where the "misfire" is taking place between our neurotransmitters and the brain's electrical activity. In addition, we learn what is functioning well, what is hyper-functioning, and what is underperforming. Through specific tests for immune markers we are able to detect the presence of a "leaky gut" and knowing this leads to solutions that may be simpler than one may think for their problems, and more importantly, they are non-invasive and natural.

Imagine...

- ...taking a supplement to find balance and achieve peak performance.
- ...being able to intervene so you can reduce or prevent any damage that can come from inflammation, leaky gut, or hormonal deficiencies.
- ...finding that your solution for peak performance exists within your mind and body—both which encompass your complete wellbeing.
- ...you are proactive and resilient because you are mindful of what is happening in your psyche and body alike—even 20 minutes a day of mindfulness meditations can positively transform the hippocampus and other areas of the brain.
- ...using neuro-feedback to better understand the activity happening within your brain and where it stems from.

For me, it's so exciting to be a pioneer in the bountiful ways that there are to integrate science and technology together to help those who are living busy lives, and really just wanting them to be the best they can be. They don't just assume that life is as good as it's going to get; they are willing to gain a better understanding of who they are in order to achieve that level of wellness—the Holy Grail of Peak Performance, if you will.

Through the continued efforts and international acclaim that the Mind & Body Treatment and Research Institute is receiving for our work with peak performance for life, we are vested in helping everyone, whether they come into our clinic or not, to find a better way to live their lives and recognize that they are using their full potential. Our beings, as a whole, are important, and that's why we focus on the biology, psychology, and spirit of the individual.

- We are near release of a line of targeted supplements that are of the highest grade and include Vitamin D, Fish Oil, Zinc, Flax, and Turmeric—all well-noted and documented for their positive impact for the body and mind's pursuit of balance and wellness.

- Downloadable Apps for guided meditations so everyone has the opportunity for self-care so they can achieve a higher level of mindfulness about their wellbeing.
- Health Coaching Courses that help people change the tides of their lives, going from average to peak performance.
- Continued one-on-one consultations and collaborations with people at our clinic, helping them to understand the connection between their biological, psychological, and spiritual selves.

Offering more than hope, I get so excited about the success that I am able to help others achieve. For me, it's through my patients climbing to extraordinary heights in their lives that I find the humbling marker of success. I want to make a difference and continue blazing the trail to better knowledge of how our body as a whole works and thrives across the life span.

Through a transformation of our mind and body, we are all able to achieve our peak performance, which will help us fill the void of what we sense is missing in our life and to experience abundant joy and happiness.

About Dr. Keerthy

With a driving passion for understanding how the entire body works together for better health, Dr. Keerthy Sunder, brings more than twenty years of experience to the Mind & Body Treatment and Research Institute, at which he is the Founder and Chief Medical Officer. Born in India, his idyllic early childhood in the beautiful Buddhist Kingdom of Bhutan had a profound influence on his philosophy and career path, including his deep desire to integrate the mind, body, and soul into all his professional and personal endeavors.

Dr. Sunder holds diplomates from the American Board of Psychiatry and Neurology, American Board of Addiction Medicine, and the Royal College of Obstetricians and Gynecologists, London. He is also a Distinguished Fellow of the American Psychiatric Association, a Member of the American Academy of Anti-Aging Medicine, a Board Member of the National Alliance on Mental Illness (NAMI), San Jacinto, and an Editorial Board Member for the Journal of Addiction Therapy and Research. He is also a Dream Builder Member of the Academy of Integrative Health and Medicine (AIHM), a member of the credentialing committee for the American Board of Addiction Medicine and a credentialed Menopause Practitioner. His integrative perspective to health lends great value to all these organizations.

Also serving as a speaker at many national and international conferences, Dr. Sunder has presented at the Marce Society of Psychiatric Disorders of Childbirth Conference in Oxford, England, the Mayo Clinic in Rochester, Minnesota, and the National Alliance on Mental Illness (NAMI) Annual Convention in Anaheim, California. His work has been published in the American Journal of Psychiatry, Journal of Clinical Psychiatry, and most recently, the Journal of Addiction Therapy and Research. His latest publication raises awareness of the importance of Mindfulness Meditation in building Resilience in the throes of Addictions and PTSD. His book, *Addictions: Face Your Addiction and Save Your Life*, an Amazon International Best Seller was published in 2014. He is also a co-author for the book *Success Blueprint* with renowned author Brian Tracy, adding Best Selling Author to his list of impressive accomplishments.

Through his life and work, Dr. Sunder continues to strive to help all individuals achieve their peak performance in their lives. To experience the best of the East and the West, visit the Mind & Body Treatment and Research Institute at:

- www.mindandbodytreatment.com
- www.doctorsunder.com

For further information, request contact with the Institute at:
- 951-300-4905
- contact@mbtrins.com

CHAPTER 6

SPEED, BALANCE AND AGING GRACEFULLY

BY LOUIS J. STACK

What is success to you?

To me it was skiing at 127.33 miles per hour. That was the speed I achieved in Les Arcs, France while on the Canadian National Speed Skiing Team training for the upcoming Olympic-qualifying World Cup Race. It was 1991, and I had just achieved my personal best speed of 127.33mph, or 205.57kph. My overwhelming feeling of success quickly vanished a few days later when FIS race officials threw out the results, due to slight irregularities with the timing system.

This event evolved into a set of circumstances that prevented me from racing for Canada in the 1992 Winter Olympic games in France. As an athlete, I set a personal best yet the outcome created a very unsuccessful feeling for me. An interesting dilemma - both a personal high and a personal low in the same event.

I feel fortunate that I skied for Canada until 1995. I was again very successful finishing 18th place in the first World Championships of Speed Skiing held in Yllas, Finland. Success is a personal experience. While many see skiing at 127mph as completely crazy, it was a character-building experience for me, one that shaped my future.

Stepping back to 1985, I felt a huge sensation of success when I, along with my brother, built our first working prototype of the Pro Fitter 3D

Cross Trainer. I was 25 years old, just off crutches and dreaming of getting back into my size 13 ski boots and on the slopes again. I borrowed $3,000 from my single-parent mother which my brother and I used to build our version of a ski training device. The goal was to help me regain my balance after knee and double foot surgeries. We successfully designed and built our first two units and I used them intensely to regain my former health.

In the process, I learned that other Canadian ski racers were interested in recovering from their injuries with our Pro Fitter 3D Cross Trainer - ski racing can be a pretty dangerous sport. As history would have it, the Pro Fitter was the first functional, closed-chain training device that integrated total body movement into a single training tool. Our product was often referred to in leading medical journals - the functional fitness revolution had begun! Everywhere I went, physical therapists loved the Pro Fitter and the results it gave their patients. Was I successful? I sure thought so. We had created a product that helped an industry see a new way to achieve successful outcomes for their patients.

In 1988, the Winter Olympics came to my home town of Calgary, and I placed Pro Fitters in all the training rooms - the world was watching. Media was everywhere, looking for great stories to fill the air time between events. To a cameraman, nothing in the gym was as eye catching as an Olympic athlete preparing for their gold medal performance zipping back and forth on this cutting edge balance-training device. We were very fortunate to get the amount of worldwide TV exposure we did - I made my luck and I ran with it!

More success followed with calls and letters from Olympic teams, suppliers and athletes who wanted to use and sell our 3D Cross Trainer. Team Denmark was first on board. It was the beginning of a very successful period for my new company, Fitter International Inc. (www. fitter1.com)

All this excitement and regaining my health lead me from the luge track, were I had been training (good feet were not required for luge racing), to Canada Olympic Park's ski jump in 1989. I was not jumping but instead doing speed runs on skis down the 90-meter jump outrun. I had swapped a Pro Fitter for racing skis with Canadian ski great Todd Brooker - those skis combined with my rubber luge suit had me ready to race. Speed skiing came to me very naturally as I loved speed, had the right body build and the nerve to point my skis straight down the hill. I was invited to join the National Speed Skiing Team the following year.

This began an amazing adventure of traveling around the world to race, representing Canada. I travelled with three pair of skis, two pairs of boots and all my racing gear, as well as a Pro Fitter, a pop-up display stand and brochures. I hauled over 200 pounds of gear with me to tradeshows on weekdays and competed in World Cup races on weekends. I remember the looks I got in Holland dragging my 8' long ski tubes, oversized boot bags and a Pro Fitter perched on top. I had wheels on one end of the ski tubes and shoulder straps on the other. I could pull or push the rig wherever I needed to. I would wear my backpack on whatever side of my body that the ski cart was not attached too. I really did not need to train as the load I was carrying was enough to get anybody into great shape. At tradeshows I would demonstrate the Pro Fitter for hours every day. When travelling, people asked me what was that thing I was carrying. I would pop the Pro Fitter off the top of the rig and demonstrate it right there. Crowds usually formed to see what all the action was. I made my own luck and success by presenting my product every time I could. Success followed me as I drove, trained, bused and flew around the World Cup circuit from 1991 to 1995.

My lovely wife, and now business partner Margaret, was 7 months pregnant when I arrived home from Europe after my last ski race. She was thrilled I was home safe. Together Margaret, myself and my new son Marquess (10 yrs. old) would soon welcome a new addition to our family. Tynan was born that June, and 21 months later his sister Teaghan was born. My goal was to be a great husband, dad and builder of my business.

Our slogan at Fitter is "leading the world to better balance!" This was very fitting as I am a Libra (balance is my sign) and my success in ski racing required immense focus and balance. I settled into my office working role and quickly realized how desperately I missed my prior work environment of mountains, travel and shows. The first ten years of business life was very active and now I positioned myself to be in an office ten hours a day. What had I done?

Fitter was expanded to offering a wide range of functional products including Exercise Ball Chairs, Bongo Boards and tubing products. Margaret had been ball sitting in our prenatal classes so I began to use one in my office. "Active Sitting" was the term we coined to describe the concept of movement in the trunk and pelvic girdle when sitting at a desk. The idea was simple. If you could shift your hips easily in 360 degrees when sitting, then it was natural to keep great posture with your head squarely on your shoulders working in harmony with gravity. The alternative was to sit in a fixed chair until you were so uncomfortable you would start to lean your head, slouch or stand up to give your body a break from the unnatural sitting position. I became a very active ball sitter, kneeling, straddling it like a horse and even rolling down on my back to stretch out my tight muscles. When I traveled I carried a sitting disc that physical therapists used to treat folks with injured backs from sitting all day.

Luckily I was still healthy and traveling extensively to tradeshows around the world, serving multiple different industries. I became a product expert who would find a unique new idea at an athletic trainers show and then cross pollinate it to physical therapists, fitness leaders, sports med doctors as well as the public. At an ergonomics show in the late 1990s, I purchased the power legs to build my own sit-stand desk. I remembered seeing these in Denmark years earlier, and the experience of being able to stand at my desk was game changing. I have ADHD and love to go, go, go until I crash and burn from exhaustion. As soon as I had the option to stand, I tried standing on a balance board. I loved it! I then kicked it up a notch with a Bongo Board - this was so dynamic that it was hard to focus on my work. The key point was that movement while standing at my desk was even better than the movement when sitting on the exercise ball. It became clear to me the goal was not just to sit or stand but in fact to move. The Active Office was born! The goal of the Active Office is to encourage subtle movement around good posture sitting, standing and on the journey in-between!

The time we spend hunched in front of a screen is a real health liability. The paradigm shift we face is how to turn that time into a healthy asset. We get 24 hours a day in life - it is best to use them all wisely. Incorporating functional movement into the work environment is so easy and the health gains are massive. Better core stability, balance, confidence and up to 46% increase in work place productivity. (Texas A&M). When you leave an Active Office your energy is higher, you feel more confident, rejuvenated and ready to take on the world.

As my friend Joan Vernikos, PhD and author of *Sitting Kills – Moving Heals* says, "Just be aware you are moving less than you used to. The best kind of movement to correct this condition is to stimulate your balance organs in your inner ear by changing your posture often. The key is to just keep moving."

My life journey lead to the four pillars that Fitterfirst is built upon. Each of these pillars were developed to help me succeed through the various chapters of my life:

I. Injury & Prevention – In my 20s I was injured. My goal was to regain my health.

II. Athletics & Training – In my 30s I pursued ski racing. The goal was to do my personal best as a national team athlete.

III. Family Fitness – In my 40s I wanted to help my kids to grow up healthy, active and make the most of their own skill sets.

IV. Active Office – In my 50s, I applied all I had learned to my work place that helps me stay active and enjoying a great quality of life.

Each of us have different wants, desires and goals in our lives. One thing we take for granted is the need to maintain balance in our daily lives. Not just between work and home life, or kids and personal time, but the innate balance that allows our body to function successfully within the gravity-based environment we live in. I encourage folks to "master the art of aging, gracefully!" - the alternative is to age ungracefully or to be dead; neither are very attractive options.

There are many important things we will learn in the future about the process of aging. I feel the simplest lesson we can all learn is to watch the movement of a mother with a baby. Hips shift from side to side and the head remains upright square on her shoulders. I call it the human way - maintaining a good relationship with gravity is like a golden rule of life. Stand up straight, move often - if you use it you will not lose it!

In closing, I will introduce my best friend, S.A.M.

Practice **Stability** in daily living
to improve **Agility** at play and
to enhance **Mobility** for life.

The fact is that time and gravity will have its way with us. To maximize your success, create a daily blueprint that incorporates as much movement as possible into your routine. With the benefits of a stronger core, better balance and more confidence, you will be better equipped to take on and enjoy more of life's wonderful opportunities now and in the future!

About Louis

Louis J. Stack, Founder and President of Fitter International Inc. has been "Leading the World to Better Balance" since 1985. His brand Fitterfirst is recognized worldwide for supplying premium professional and personal products that help people recover from and prevent injury, maintain balance and fitness, and keep moving at work. Throughout his 30-plus years' experience as a business owner, national athlete and father, he has built a foundation of integrity and quality in everything he does. Along his journey, Stack has been an advocate and industry expert, often leading the way in the physical rehabilitation world and setting precedents in the way we approach our office environment.

Stack's company stemmed from personal injuries, seeking a fix to his own discomfort. From there it has flourished into a worldwide, multimillion-dollar company that caters to families both young and old, high-performance athletes, injury and rehabilitation patients, and now includes the everyday office worker.

As with most aspects of Fitterfirst, the "Active Office" concept was born from Louis' own experience – after transitioning from being primarily an athlete to a full-time business owner, his body suffered the consequences of sitting, hunched over a computer day in and day out – he craved movement in his 9 to 5 routine. So rather than conform to the limitations of a sedentary office, he sought a solution to his problem, bringing in a ball chair and getting himself a sit-stand desk. Aided with his new productivity tools, Louis immediately felt an improvement in his quality of life and he knew it was the next track he would pursue with Fitterfirst. Fast forward to present day and the "Active Office" continues to be the fastest-growing component of the Fitterfirst lineup.

Grounded in his roots, Louis is very involved in Fitterfirst, helping out in almost every aspect of the company. On any given day, he may be assisting the production team build the next round of Pro Fitters, or chatting with the marketing group about new promotional ideas he has. Travelling near and far, he can often be found at tradeshows doing what he does best: showing off Fitterfirst and demonstrating the large collection of wellness products his company offers. Nothing makes him happier than improving someone's life with one of his products – a "win-win-win" as he likes to call it. Aided by his wife Margaret, who runs the day-to-day aspects of the company, Louis continues to be the visionary for Fitterfirst, developing new products, promoting his business, and continuing to learn everyday how to make his company the best it can be.

- Canadian National Speed Skiing Team, *1990 – 1995*
- Calgary's Small Business of the Year Award, *2002*
- Featured in INC. Magazine's "Business Case Study", *2003*
- Finalist of the Canadian EY Entrepreneur of the Year Award, *2015*
- Finalist of the EY Entrepreneur of the Year Award *2016*
- Volunteer, Alberta Alpine, City of Calgary - Rinks and Parks
- Husband and father of 3 happy kids

CHAPTER 7

CAREER PASSION: SIX SECRETS THAT WILL DOUBLE YOUR SALARY

BY BOB ROARK

Small towns and technology – not a popular combination back in the 80s! I grew up in a small farm community in Colorado, son of a TV repair guy, not a farmer. Dad also owned a Radio Shack, which is where I got my first real touch with technology; specifically, computers. Dad sold them and I was instantly drawn to them. Not many people had them and those that did usually preferred playing games, but not me. I wanted to learn how they worked and began writing basic programming. Yeah, I was the proverbial "computer geek" in the basement—before it became trendy.

Then in my sophomore year of high school, the economy took a bad turn and Dad lost his shop. The experience jarred me, forcing me to contemplate my own future. Things could happen that were beyond my control, and that didn't settle well with me. I decided to really apply myself and ended up graduating high school and then two weeks later, I also graduated with my Associates Degree in Electronics.

I hit the road, eager to make my mark. Taking advantage of the nice summer weather, I began working as a golf pro shop assistant and worked at a CompUSA store that opened up in the off-season. That job brought me back to what I was most passionate about—computers, and from there, some of life's biggest lessons were learned. It's within these lessons that the six secrets that will double your salary exist. And they may not be what you think! But I do know this; they have a proven record of success with me and with those I help.

1. Discover what you are passionate about.

I have watched scientists who worked for 30 years retire on a Friday, and then come to work on Monday as a volunteer doing the exact same work for free. Why do this? No answer other than passion makes sense.

Passion is everything when it comes to how we create a future that is one we are excited to participate in, day in and day out. If you get up in the morning to go do a job you hate, you're only going to make it so far. You'll get a paycheck, but little to no reward. We are all able to get tasks done that we may not particularly like, but repeating them over an extended period of time will wear us down. However, by bringing passion to our career, we'll also bring endless potential. Think about this… If someone woke you up at 3 a.m. to ask you a question about your work, would you come alive and be able to talk about it for hours? People who are living out their passions can.

Think about "pioneers" such as Steve Jobs. His passions lead to great innovations; technology was the vehicle he used to bring them into existence. We all have our own version of "Steve Jobs" inside us; we just need to bring it out.

2. Set goals that are designed to help you progress.

If you don't know where you want to end up, someone else will set a goal for you. You will always end up somewhere, so make sure it's a place you want to be.

By not having goals for your career, you're going to end up taking the path that others set for you. The path may not be bad, and may even be lucrative, but its purpose will be to best serve those who placed you there, not you. Why not set your own goals? Don't settle for what you "will get," create what you "want to get."

The term "goals" is overstated and underused, and mostly because people don't put their passions behind their goals or create logical steps to take. For everything that I have achieved, I needed goals to follow, because they were the milestones that helped me see the progress I was making. Life is busy, and without something to evaluate ourselves, we often forget to grow or get a false sense of growth through "busy work." For me, I have four levels of goals that are a part of taking daily steps forward with my ambitions. Some are big and some are small; some are short term and others long term. They include:

- Immediate goals—daily steps toward achievement
- 30 – 90-day goals
- 90-day – 6 month goals
- 6 months and over goals

Depending on what I'm working on, my goals vary. I have learned that writing them down makes a difference. It helps me understand how my actions in a given day are working toward achieving my goals. I will either reflect on this at the beginning of the day so I know just what I want to do that day, or else I will reflect on how my progress went at the day's end—maybe both. You have to know what you are doing to make progress.

The biggest failure that I've ever had with goals—that most of us have ever had—was waking up in the morning and thinking, *I want to be rich and make a ton of money.* Then our day goes on and we might have had a successful day selling or in meetings with new prospects. Things look good and feel good. Then a month goes by, and you're still no further ahead. You may be making a decent living but you're not ahead. This is because being rich and making a ton of money isn't a good goal; it's a wonderful outcome, but there's a whole lot that happens in-between.

Goals are not an end-all, either. You can go six months and realize your goal is wrong, and this is okay. Goals will change as you grow and learn, but never stop evaluating them so you know that you're working toward what you want to be, both as a contributor to this planet and to the best life possible.

3. Find great mentors.

Who you surround yourself with is who you become. Choose carefully.

Mentors are one of the most under-utilized resources when it comes to gaining financial success. There are people out there that have already taken the path you are on. They are usually glad to help a dedicated person learn more about what they can do to achieve their potential. And don't lock yourself into just one mentor. Choose many—make your own brain trust of people who have careers, philosophies, and passions that you admire. Being surrounded with great people such as this will help you gain wisdom, knowledge, and practical application.

My first mentorship experience happened quite by chance when I was working at CompUSA, but how it transformed me has impacted me my entire life. Through ten years of experiences with this mentor, he taught me how to look beyond the paycheck and at the customer, using a simple formula: *you need to figure out what people need and how to fix it without costing them a ton of money.* This is a golden formula for people in sales and in consulting, both arenas that I've spent a great many years in, and with great success. After that learning experience, which still impacts me to this day, I began looking at things differently. I'd change a job and seek out people who had what I wanted, whether it is a position, certification, etc. Anything. I would look to them and think, *if I build relationships with them and repeat what they do, I'll get similar results.* The way I found mentorship was more application-based than seeking out a formal mentor to have sit downs and interviews with. That was how I learned and worked best.

Today, I try to be this type of mentor to others; showing them through everything that I've done and the six principles in which I believe so firmly. It takes commitment, but that commitment does show results, which is exciting personally and professionally for me, and for the people who accomplish their goals.

4. Build connections with people.

People want to be around people they like. Therefore, becoming a master at working and communicating with others will take you far.

The best way to build connections is to take an interest in the person you are talking with. When you're around others, making them the spotlight is the easiest way to create a connection, and it works regardless of what type of personality you have. I am a huge introvert by nature, but by knowing my role and being comfortable in my expertise, I can still build connections—because it's not about talking about me, it's about me getting someone else to open up about their lives.

When you remember that making a connection is about others, not you, you are more likely to find someone who is willing to listen to your opinion and give it thoughtful consideration, because people listen to people who they like. Embrace the WIIFM (what's in it for me) approach. What does this do? It helps to sway others to see that you can help them and they can look at you as someone who will provide them the information that they want. From a sales perspective, this is huge. So, be friendly and find ways to connect on a personal level and in a way that people know what's in it for them. This will take you far!

5. Invest in your education.

Being committed to learning more to become better in any way you can, is a step that will make a difference in how your career plays out.

As my positions in the field of technology shifted, I recognized that opportunities that I was qualified for with experience, were not ones that I could actually earn because of one major factor—I did not have a bachelor's degree. While employed in a technical support position, I decided I wanted a job as a Technical Solutions Manager and my boss told me that I would only be hired if I got a degree. Well, I'd had a history of on-again/off-again with school my entire adult life. I'd go a half a year and then take time off. It was always hard and there was always something "more pressing" that came up. But I wanted success and this degree was a part of it, so I made it work, creating an arrangement in which I'd get that degree while working, and I even got tuition reimbursement for my efforts. I was on my way.

It wasn't easy, but I did it, and confidentially, enough that I wasn't opposed to getting my MBA, either. So I did that, too. And wow— suddenly my experience and my degrees were giving me "the opportunities" I'd been working toward through my entire career thus far. It was amazing. Long gone were the days of me being held back because I didn't have a piece of paper.

When you think about your career, what has held you back? If it's a degree and you know you are working in the area you want to be in, find ways to get that degree. It may not be easy, but the rewards that come after that piece of paper offer limitless personal fulfillment and endless professional potential. And furthermore, these steps also support an additional example of how those few years of work and commitment resulted in my salary nearly doubling.

Aside from the classroom—whether brick and mortar or virtual— there are other ways that you can continue to pursue education. Each one is worth considering.

- On the job: learn everything you can about your business. Be the one who has the knowledge of all positions and roles so you can find better solutions when they are needed. Be excited to show your value. Get certifications that will help lend to your value.
- Books and periodicals: read! Books, summaries, and industry periodicals will help you gain knowledge that is relevant today and beneficial to you, as well as your career and company.
- Events: attend as many symposiums and conferences as you can so you can learn what is currently happening and trending in your industry. Pick a few take-away ideas from these events and determine how you can utilize the information in your company, starting right away.

6. Create a "put it all together" action plan.

You will arrive. The question is, will you arrive in the same place you have been or will you arrive with the success you've designed?

When you claim your desire for something, how do you check your progress to make sure you're actually taking actions on your goals? You need to have a plan that helps you evaluate what you have actually done—not just theorized. Regardless of what you do, you can be assured that tomorrow will come, next week will come, next year, etc. What you get will be a result of what you have done.

Our goals are a general statement, and our action plan is what we are doing to achieve the goals. This mindset is the kick-off for all our actions in a given day. The old adage asks: how do you eat an elephant? The answer—one bite at a time. If you do not take the first step you'll never get there, so find out the immediate steps you can start taking and then go and meet that goal, step-by-step, day-by-day.

Start with your short term goals:
- Get the information
- Determine what makes sense
- Communicate and make it happen

I am a great example of this. For about twenty years I've said that I wanted to write a book. Yet, I still haven't. This chapter is a stepping stone to that goal. I've finally done it, and why? I took action. We all have an action we can take today to create a better opportunity for ourselves. We are the beginning and the end of our destinies.

As you go forward in life, always remember this: successful people don't have special knowledge that no one else has, they just started to do something. You've just learned six things you can do…starting today. By allowing these principles to be your guide, the career and the positive financial outcome will follow.

About Bob

Bob Roark is a results-driven Information Technology Operations and Service Management executive with an unwavering focus on delivering world-class satisfaction for internal and external customers. With a broad range of technical and business experience across multiple industries, he drives business value for all stakeholders through continuous process improvements.

Bob consistently achieves results by developing and retaining top talent, introducing best practices and standards, reengineering inefficient processes and systems, and building high-performance Information Technology infrastructure that supports multimillion-dollar profit growth, cost cuts, and operating efficiencies.

Bob is an MBA graduate of Western Governors University. He is the Vice President of Service Management for NuAxis Innovations, a solution-driven IT infrastructure support contractor for the U.S. Federal Government with offices in Washington, D.C. and Denver, Colorado, and more than 350 team members across 22 states. Bob was also selected as one of America's PremierExperts™ and holds numerous industry-leading certifications, including Project Management Institute - Project Management Professional (PMP), HDI Support Center Director (SCD), Microsoft Certified Systems Engineer (MSCE), ISACA - Certified Information Systems Auditor (CISA), and several ITIL certifications.

You can connect with Bob at:
- bob.roark@nuaxis.com
- www.linkedin.com/in/bobroark
- www.twitter.com/bobroarkdotcom
- www.facebook.com/NuAxis

CHAPTER 8

THE HEALTHY WOMAN: FINDING SUCCESS IN THE BEST PREGNANCY POSSIBLE

BY DR. MAHA SHALABI

As a consultant and Doctor of Obstetrics and Gynecology, an important part of my daily responsibilities to patients is to share the abundance of information I have about pregnancy and post-care with my clients. Reducing the risk of health issues, while offering necessary information that allow a mother to focus on the best pregnancy possible makes the difference. It's ten months of self-care to set a woman and her child up for their next stage in life; that of parent and child.

Planned pregnancies are best for both mother and child, allowing the woman to prepare her body for the pregnancy. In turn, this has great benefits for the developing child. The goal is to always have a term pregnancy, which is approximately forty weeks in length.

PRECONCEPTION CARE

Most pregnancies do result in good maternal and fetal outcomes, whether they are planned or not. However, making this assumption can be a mistake that leads to both physical and emotional duress. Not all problems can be alleviated, even with the best, preconception care. However, many can, and as a result, certain risks are reduced or eliminated.

Two of the most beneficial adjustments to be aware of and consider adapting to are:

1. <u>Begin a folic acid regimen:</u> this supplement has shown that it has a correlation to the reduction of potential neural tube defects such as Spina Bifida or Anancephaly.
2. <u>Make sure that you are exercising adequate glucose control:</u> women with diabetes are at particular risk of having maternal morbidity if glucose levels are not in check. The unborn child risks being spontaneously aborted, malformation, Macrosomnia, and neonatal morbidity.

Through my efforts as a consultant to educate women, I seek to offer them insight with a specific goal in mind of addressing what their health history is and linking that to the measures that can be taken to make the body better prepared to carry the fetus. It's a thorough process that addresses both the emotional and physical side of pregnancy, and includes:

- Known and unknown medical conditions, both untreated and/or poorly controlled
- High risk behaviors such as tobacco, alcohol, and narcotics use and history
- Social and mental health issues
- Immunization history
- Exposure and risks, including those from radiation, occupation, and environmental
- Family medical history to determine genetic risks
- Nutritional issues associated with diet

By working with women to create a Reproductive Health Plan, we can set up a standard of care based on their needs and the needs of the fetus that will be growing within them. They will know what steps are best for them to take, as well as what to expect throughout the process of pregnancy after conception. All of these transition the woman into a better place.

WHAT TO EXPECT IN YOUR FIRST TRIMESTER

The approximate time of your first trimester of pregnancy is three months. This stage is highly significant because the baby's most critical stages of development take place. A healthy first trimester means a lesser risk of miscarriage, as the highest risk for this happens during this time.

Each of the first three months of pregnancy brings about great change for both the mother and the child growing within her womb. Different stages of development take place, for both the mother and the developing child.

When you believe that you are pregnant you will want to schedule an appointment with your physician to:

1. **Verify your medical history**
   Preferably, this has been covered during a preconception care consultation. If it has not, it will be covered during the first visit with your physician.
2. **Determine a due date**
   With the studies and advancement of studies in pregnancy and fetal development, we are able to determine with a fair amount of accuracy the due dates for the unborn child.
3. **Perform a physical exam**
   This exam includes:
   - A height and weight check to calculate your Body Mass Index (BMI), which is used to determine what a healthy weight gain will be for the pregnancy
   - Blood pressure, heart rate, and breathing rate checks
   - A vaginal exam and an examination of the cervix and uterus to help determine the changes taking place as the pregnancy progresses
   - Possibly a Pap smear to check for cervical cancer risks
4. **Do lab tests**
   These tests are important, as they will determine:
   - Blood type and determination of Rhesus factor (Rh)—Rh is an inherited trait, referring to a specific protein that is found on the surface of red blood cells. If the woman is Rh negative and the father is RH positive, special care is required during the pregnancy.
   - Hemoglobin levels, which is a protein that allows cells to carry oxygen to all parts of the body, including the developing fetus
   - Immunity to certain infections, such as Rubella, as these can be significant health risks to both the mother and developing child
   - Exposure to other infections, including Syphilis
   - Checking for all types of Hepatitis

5. **Run fetal tests for abnormalities**

   Although this will not always be necessary, if there are determined risk factors or symptoms that your physician is concerned about, an ultrasound or other tests may be done to determine the fetal health.

6. **Expected discomforts for the first trimester**

   Swelling and tenderness of the breasts is common during this stage, as well as nausea, which is called morning sickness. Excessive nausea and vomiting may be problematic and you should consult your physician if it persists.

After this initial visit, you can plan on meeting with your physician approximately once per month to check in on the wellbeing of the expectant mother and the baby. You'll also want to put some thought into your birth plan, whether you want to deliver at home or at the hospital, with a midwife or with a doctor, with an epidural or medication free. These choices are especially important if the mother is found to have any medical conditions or specific concerns.

THE SECOND TRIMESTER OF PREGNANCY

The second trimester of pregnancy is the time between week 12 through the 28th week of pregnancy. During this time, the expectant mother will continue on with her monthly appointments with her doctor, and bringing your spouse or partner along is recommended, whenever possible.

Pregnant women often begin recognizing symptoms of pregnancy that are a bit more challenging during this time, both physical and emotionally. These symptoms include:

- Fatigue
- Heartburn
- Possible aches and pains in the back, joints, and abdomen
- Varicose veins

While unpleasant, these symptoms are not uncommon. If there are concerns about them, or any aspect of a pregnancy, an open dialogue with the physician is a must. They are there to help you have the best pregnancy possible.

During the second trimester visits, you can expect to be weighed and have your blood pressure checked. Occasionally, a urine sample may be taken to test for sugar or protein in the urine, as those are alerts to gestational diabetes or high blood pressure caused by pregnancy. Both of these conditions are temporary and with the proper care, they will not negatively impact the developing baby.

The abdomen will also be measured to see if the baby is growing as expected, as the slight bump will become noticeable during this time. And by week 20, it will be time for a low risk pregnancy to have the ultrasound that is telling for many things with the baby, including:

- The sex
- The developmental progress
- Fetal abnormalities or birth defects
- Growth of the heart, kidneys, and limbs

Some genetic testing can be done in the first trimester; however, there are other tests that are offered in the second trimester, which include:

- A quadruple screen test, which is a blood draw from the mother that takes place between the 15th and 22nd week to determine if additional genetic testing may need to be done. These tests are indicators, not conclusive determinations.
- Amniocentesis test, which is a test where the doctor inserts a needle through the belly and into the amniotic sac to extract a small amount of fluid, which is sent to a lab to test for chromosome abnormalities, such as Downs Syndrome or Trisomy 21. Genetic disorders such as Cystic Fibrosis can also be determined.

For women who are aged 35 and older (based on their estimated due date), they may have more extensive screening, as they are considered a high risk pregnancy. For all pregnancies, the symptoms to be aware of in your second trimester that may require additional care from your doctor include:

- Signs and symptoms that are not normal
- The addition of any new medications, vitamins, or herbs into your diet
- Bleeding
- Fevers and chills
- Discharges

- Severe cramping and abdominal pain

In both my practices as a doctor and a consultant, I highly encourage women to ask questions if they are uncertain. It is always wiser to find out from a professional that understands pregnancy than to make assumptions.

YOUR LAST TRIMESTER

By this trimester, the final stages of growth are going to be the main focus on the baby's development in the uterus. The time is nearing and things are growing more exciting as the body changes and you can see evidence of the baby's growth physically, through the mother's growth.

Much of the routine at the doctor's visits will continue through this trimester, including the weight gain checks, blood pressure monitoring, checking the baby's heartbeat and movements, and measuring the abdomen for growth. Urine samples may become more common, as well, as they are the most efficient and effective way to test for the presence of abnormal protein levels or infection.

The mother will want to pay attention to the changes in her body and how the baby is responding. They will be asked to participate in tracking the baby's movements. If the movement is noticeably less than it has been in the past, you'll want to alert the doctor to that. Sometimes the baby may be resting more, but other times there are indicators that it is not receiving vital needs, such as food or oxygen. These are triggers that there could be a concern with the umbilical cord.

When it comes to testing, the main test that may be performed on the mother is one for Group B Streptococcus (GBS). This is a common bacterium found in the intestines or lower genital track. It is seldom threatening to adults, but it can be to an unborn child who will be delivered via vaginal birth. Their exposure to this can make them seriously ill. If the mother has GBS present, she will be given intravenous antibiotics during the labor to protect the child.

With the closer it comes to the due date—weeks 36 and on—the expectant mother will find some changes in her doctor's appointments, which include:

- They will begin occurring weekly, if they have not been previously.
- The baby's position will be checked, which allows the doctor to estimate the weight and position. If the baby is a frank breech (rump first) or a complete breech (feet first), they may still be transitioning into the birth canal, but if they are not, the doctor may try and turn the baby around—especially if the estimated due date is within a week.
- A pelvic exam to determine if the cervix has dilated, which is an indicator that the body is preparing for birth. This is determined by centimeters and percentages. For example, a fully dilated cervix is approximately 10 centimeters and 100% effaced at the time of birth.
- Making the decision if you want to breastfeed or not. Professionally, if this is a feasible option, it is the most rewarding option for bonding with a newborn and for the newborn's health. If breastfeeding is not recommended for you, your doctor will have covered that with you by this time.

From here, you should allow for plenty of rest and prepare for the birth, whether it is at a hospital or at home. It will allow you to be focused on the birth when that time comes. Preparing ahead of time is recommended, as babies do not always come on their exact due date, as it is just an estimate.

POSTNATAL CARE: HAPPY MOTHERS AND HEALTHY BABIES

A new mother's life is transformed significantly after delivering a baby, whether she has other children or not. The body immediately goes into recovery mode, while the loving connection between the mother and child is also formed. Two ways to offer the best self care, which will help manage concerns about post-partum depression, as well as offering peace of mind that you are doing a wonderful job, are to:

1. **Get plenty of rest.**
   Mother's need rest and babies have different time clocks than they do. Ideally, there will be others around to help so the mom just has to be a mom, feeding and bonding with her baby, and making sure she's taking care of her body, which is recovering from the very giving process of growing a child inside of her. When the baby naps, consider napping too, not rushing around to do other tasks. The

more in sync you are, the more beautiful the experience will be, particularly if you are breastfeeding.

2. Focus on good nutrition.
Go an indulgent spree of healthy, nutritious foods after birth. They will help you produce better breast milk and also to rebound to a more energetic self more quickly. A diet that is rich in protein, grains, vegetables, fruits, and dairy is best. Avoid sugars and starches when you can, as those same things will be passed down to your baby through your milk.

With rest and nutrition comes better breastfeeding, if you have chosen to do this. As a breastfeeding parent, you will want to make sure you drink plenty of water and healthy, non-alcoholic beverages, as they will help with the nursing. With breastfeeding, your baby's chances of flourishing improve.

- Breastfed babies have healthier weight gain and don't risk weight loss the way they might with formulas.
- Babies have better immunity to infections and diseases such as Mellitus, Diabetes, and obesity.
- The baby is receiving raw nutrients, not processed ingredients, due to the milk coming right from the mother and the mother's attention to the diet during this time.

When a woman decides to have a child, she commits to offering it the best chances of success she can, from the time of conception on. Through paying attention to all the stages of pregnancy, as well as the best suggestions for proper preconception care and post-natal care, mothers and their babies are healthier and happier. This is definitely success!

About Dr. Maha

With eighteen plus years of experience in practicing Obstetrics, Gynecology, and working as a highly recommended and sought out consultant, Dr. Maha Shalabi is a passionate advocate of helping every female that she can, reach out to set themselves up for success by living their best, healthiest life possible. With a focus on care that goes from pre-childbearing through post-childbearing years, she helps women with all health related issues and concerns they may have as their bodies and lives transition. The goal is to always help women to be at their best. Through a nurturing and caring demeanor, she is able to give professional insight, proven wisdom, and the compassion that women need in their busy lives.

Dr. Shalabi is a graduate from King Saud University's College of Medicine. Her formal training took place in two of the best hospitals in Riyadh, Saudi Arabia—King Abdalaziz Medical City and King Saud Medical City. It was here that she gained her expertise in the fields of Obstetrics and Gynecology. In addition to her medical practice today, she is also Arab Board Certified, and is a highly-acclaimed consultant in OB/GYN at King Abdalaziz Medical City.

The opportunities to educate women on the processes their life may entail, pre-childrearing years through their golden years, is something that continuously inspires Dr. Shalabi to take action. She wants women to understand the full scope of every stage of their life and what they can expect, as well as what they can do to experience healthier, fulfilled lives. In addition to her outreach work, she has also co-authored a chapter for the book *Success Blueprint* with renowned author Brian Tracy. The more hands the valuable insight she has to offer can fall into, the better for her—the more she will know that she is making that impact she desires to have for women on a global level. Dr. Shalabi says, "I feel it is important to inform women about what they may be facing or are currently experiencing at all stages of their lives, regardless of which stage they are presently at."

Having been born and raised in Riyadh, Saudi Arabia, Dr. Shalabi enjoys the opportunities she has to meet women in her expansive community, as well as spending time with her family and friends. Any chance to travel is one she embraces. In addition to that, she enjoys exercising and reading—both wonderful ways to stay fit and be at her best for life. Much of her success she has today is credited to her parents, who were diligent in their support of her as she studied and worked hard to achieve her goals.

You can contact Dr. Shalabi about her services at:
- Shalabim@ngha.med.sa
- Or call 0096-656-632-2220

CHAPTER 9

ASKING THE RIGHT QUESTIONS

BY MARK SNEAD

Success comes when you learn to ask the RIGHT questions. Yes, asking the right questions! Many coaches and mentors will tell you, most people know the answers and solutions to their problems. The goal is to help them determine the questions they truly need to answer. For example, ask uneducated people what is hindering their career advancement. They will answer a lack of education. They know the answer to their problem but it doesn't help them. What should they be asking, "How do I obtain more education?" The answer to that question will move them on toward their desired career path.

Think of it this way. Most Americans have seen or heard of the television game show "Jeopardy." The game has a large video board with subject categories listed horizontally and predetermined answers, for those categories, listed vertically. The object of the game is to frame your responses, in the form of questions, to match the revealed answers in each category. These questions are simple, short and specific to the answers revealed. It makes for a fun and interesting game but it also illustrates how many people think. Relying on simple answers to simple questions will not help people overcome the obstacles to their success. Albert Einstein said, "The significant problems we have cannot be solved at the same level of thinking with which we created them." Success in life is not a simple game, it requires challenging and introspective questions.

After more than thirty years working with clients, employees and friends,

I have learned an important fact. All people face serious questions about life, career and business. I also learned that most people know the answers and have the ability to solve these serious issues. However, many have allowed their socio economic status, the culture of their businesses or companies, and their past experiences to shape their way of thinking into a narrow dialogue and perspective. Due to this narrowing perspective, *people predetermine the answers for the questions they think they know and believe they understand; therefore, they settle for much less than they deserve in life.* As coaches and mentors, our goal is to help people broaden their perspectives, investigate what the real questions are, so they can have confidence in their answers. In the next few paragraphs I will describe experiences which illustrate why a person needs to determine the right question instead of accepting a predetermined answer.

As a chemist many years ago, I was responsible for the training of our new laboratory technicians. It was a demanding environment requiring a high degree of accuracy. Early on I learned a valuable lesson, from my manager, about critical thinking and making assumptions when reporting my data. From that day forward, I made sure to look closely at all my results. Overseeing the work of one of the technicians, I noticed the results did not pass what we called "the laugh test." The technician had a set of numbers, ranging from fifty-eight to sixty-nine. He calculated the average of these numbers to be fifty-seven. It is impossible to calculate an average which is less than the lowest number used. When I asked the technician to review his results, he stated emphatically, "those were the results and the calculator was right." His premise was that the calculator could not make a mistake, but that was not the question. The question was could there have been a data entry error. This story shows how a person can believe in their answer so strongly they lose their perspective, because they are asking the wrong question.

This next story illustrates how a business culture can hinder growth and success within a company. In the past twenty years, I have had the opportunity to meet, work with, and converse with a number of credit union executives. Credit unions generally grow by increasing their membership, securing more deposits, and issuing more loans, to generate more revenue. Credit unions have specific membership requirements, so growth can be a challenge. Many of the executives said expanding their field of membership was the key. However, thinking through the challenges to membership growth, I remembered an experience I had at a credit union.

Standing in line at a credit union, I overheard this conversation. A college student wanted to open a savings account and cash a check. The teller asked the student to come back the next day, the credit union was too busy to open an account that afternoon. The teller believed that the student really didn't want to become a member, he just wanted to cash the check. The teller's attitude, he didn't want to waste his time for something the customer "really didn't want." This was the not first time I had encountered a similar attitude at credit unions. So these questions came to my mind, did credit union executives know they had employees who were discouraging people from becoming members? Could they do a better job signing up people who were already membership eligible?

In my corporate career, the largest and most lucrative contract the company was awarded illustrates how asking the right questions works much better than telling the client they are wrong. When my perspective changed, success was only a few questions away.

As a corporate manager for a NASDAQ traded company, one of my responsibilities was handling audits and inquiries from clients, government agencies, and potential customers. We were contacted by a government agency, which was overseeing a four-hundred-million-dollar project. Our potential revenue was as much as ten percent of the total project over a ten-year period. Obviously, my company was interested. The government engineers wanted to know our local division's capabilities and regulatory limits. After a short conversation, the engineer concluded we were not a qualified facility. As an expert in those particular regulations, I knew we had to be a qualifying facility. Not to be deterred, I asked for a bid package. The engineer informed me no bid packages would be sent to non-qualifying facilities. This just spurred me on. I made a number of phone calls and had several lengthy conversations, each ending with the same answer, "No, your local division is not a qualified facility."

It was then I realized the government engineers were answering "No" because I was asking the wrong questions. They already had a specific perspective of their needs and we didn't meet those needs. My approach had to change. I could not continue to tell them their perspective was wrong. Instead of telling them more about our company, I began to ask specific questions about the project. What was the project's history? What are the project's regulatory requirements? What were the agency's needs? What could they tell us about previous projects?

In the midst of these discussions, the engineers' perspectives changed. They realized they were applying facility and regulatory requirements from previous projects which were not required for this particular project. Our company was in fact a qualifying facility. Subsequently, we were sent a bid package which resulted in our company winning the portion of the contract for which we were bidding.

In retrospect, thinking we had all the answers was not helping us and it did not change the engineers' minds. Asking the right questions, clarifying questions, helped the engineers see the project from a different perspective. Seeing the project from a different perspective allowed them to see our company in a different perspective. So, asking the right questions lead to success.

What do you need for your success? *Learn to ask the right questions.* Why, because determining the right questions begins the process that leads to your overall success. Here are the five steps to follow:

1. **What are your needs?**
   These should be specific. As I discussed earlier, you can determine the answer to your need, but if it is not specific, the result may not be what you want. For example, **in your personal finances**, you need more money for living expenses. This is not specific. Why is this important? You could move in with relatives, have a yard sale, sell your car and get a bicycle. At this point, your current salary could support your lifestyle. However, what you really want is to maintain your present lifestyle which costs $85,000 per year. Well, that is specific. **In your career**, you want a better paying job in the banking industry but you aren't sure if you like retail banking, loans, mortgages, or financial services. It is hard to identify the right job if you are not sure of the career path you want to take. **In your business culture**, many of your customers complain the business needs better customer service. What is "better customer service?" You need to identify specific aspects of customer service which need improvement? Have you prepared a survey that identifies which areas of customer service are responsible for creating negative perspectives? After identifying your specific needs, you are ready for your next step.

2. Ask the right questions.

Write down, "What if ...? How could ...? Can we ...?" type of questions about your list of needs. Do not critique any ideas at the beginning. Negative thoughts and comments at this point will stifle your creativity and narrow your perspective. Remember, you want to broaden your perspective. **In your personal life**, you identified your need for $85,000 per year. You write down all the different ways you could get more money. What about a second job? What about overtime? What if you went back to school? Obviously some of these ideas could overlap **in your career**. Previously I mentioned banking. What areas of the banking industry pay the salary you are looking for? How would you crossover into these areas of banking? What if you were willing to relocate? What would that look like? **In your business culture**, a friendlier atmosphere has been determined to be a way to improve your customer service. How could the employees be more friendly? What if they greeted each customer with a smile? What if they answered all phone calls within three rings and with a pleasant greeting? What if you offered refreshments to any customer waiting for more than five minutes? Now that you've identified ways to meet your needs, it's time to take action.

3. Determine your course of action.

Review your questions and determine which are viable to implement. I need more money, so what if we won the lottery? This isn't worth consideration. What if you sold your car and purchased a less expensive one? Definitely worth considering if you need to cut costs. What amount of time and resources are needed to implement this course of action? I suggest starting with the easiest course of action to implement, then begin implementing the ones with greatest promise for results. Discard the ones with a low return on investment.

4. Make your plans with goals.

For example, you begin by working some overtime and going to school part-time. You make plans for a specific amount of overtime. You plan your course work. You set goals for the amount of money you need and the courses you need to complete. Monitor your goals to ensure your course of action is worth the investment. You may determine that discarding your overtime so you can graduate earlier may be more cost effective. Don't be afraid to make course corrections!

5. How will you celebrate your success?

I've asked those I've mentored, what are you going to do when you reach your goals? To business leaders, what are you going to do when your company or employees reach their goals? Why is this important? It is an opportunity for you to reinforce the changes in lifestyle and attitude which led to your personal success. It is an opportunity to reinforce employee behavior and productivity.

Above all remember this, asking the right questions can change everything on your road to success. It will invigorate you, change you, direct you, lift you, and most importantly, help you help others. To summarize:

- IDENTIFY YOUR NEEDS.
- ASK THE RIGHT QUESTIONS.
- DETERMINE YOUR COURSE OF ACTION.
- MAKE YOUR PLANS WITH GOALS.
- CELEBRATE YOUR SUCCESS!

About Mark

Mark Snead is a speaker, coach, mentor and best-selling author. Whether it's one-on-one coaching, facilitating a mastermind group, or speaking to thirty or three thousand people, Mark is able to motivate people to break out of their routine to the lifestyles and careers they've always wanted and deserve.

Mark was asked, "Why do you do what you do?" A mentor of his once said, "People don't need so much inspiration as information." If you give people the right information, they will generate all the inspiration they need. People tend to settle for mediocre relationships, low achieving careers, and unsatisfying lifestyles. They don't know or haven't been given the tools to break out of those conditions. Mark's desire is to inspire and help every person realize they have the knowledge and skills to achieve more in life.

Mark is a founding member, certified coach and speaker for the John Maxwell Team. He has a bachelor's degree in Microbiology and a minor in Chemistry from San Jose State University. He has a master's degree in Pastoral Studies from Faith Christian College. He has been trained in "Communication Skills for Healthy Families." He has several years training in Senior Pastor Coaching. He has also served as a board and committee member for two credit unions and is a regional director for a business leadership organization.

Mark has been married for over 34 years and has eight grandchildren. His wife has had her own successful career in business ranging from marketing director, branch manager, and corporate executive, while serving on the board of several community and state wide organizations. His three daughters and sons-in-law all have their own stories of achievement and success. He has helped numerous people with their relationships, careers and businesses.

In the business world, he helped start and obtain state certification for a multi-million-dollar environmental laboratory. He grew the testing capabilities of several other laboratories through the development of testing procedures, quality assurance policies, and training methods. As a corporate manager of a NASDAQ-traded company, he was involved in winning several multi-million dollar contracts, with the last being a four-hundred-million-dollar government contract. As a consultant, he helped companies streamline their processes and save hundreds of thousands of dollars a year. He helped start several churches and was the founding pastor of another. During this time, he oversaw the purchase, procurement, design and renovation of three commercial buildings for the church.

Mark is fond of saying, "Life is tremendous," a quote he personally heard from Charlie "Tremendous" Jones. His desire is for you to say the same thing about your life, business and career.

If you would like to learn more about Mark and how he can help you with your career or business, please contact him at:
- marksneadcompany@gmail.com

Or by calling:
- (208) 965-7526

CHAPTER 10

SELF-AWARENESS—THE FOUNDATION FOR ALL YOUR SUCCESS

BY MARK GYETVAY

I vividly remember the day that culminated the pinnacle of my work career. More than 25 years of perseverance was coming to a crescendo; it was a special day. It was in July 2005, as I stood at the podium ready to press the button that officially welcomed us to the London Stock Exchange. It was exhilarating and one of my dreams came true. We executed one of the most successful initial public offerings in the nascent days of Russia's ascent to the global capital markets, and I was standing at the epicenter of big finance. And, thus I began a new chapter in my own life story.

Humble Beginnings

It's said that we are a product of our environment and I was a long way from my humble beginnings. Born in Orange, New Jersey, an ethnically diverse city, located close to the world's financial capital – New York City – but a long way from Moscow where I would achieve my success. If you read Napoleon Hill's classic book "Think and Grow Rich" you'll recall Edwin Barnes quest to become Thomas Edison's future partner began when he exited the train station in Orange, New Jersey. You see, I grew up a stone throw away from Edison's Laboratory, the quintessential innovator of his time, and a source of inspiration as I freely visited his museum and experienced firsthand his marvelous inventions that changed mankind.

Raised in a lower-middle class family along with my siblings, my father unexpectedly died at 41, and his sudden heart attack left a significant void in my life. Losing someone special leads you to question many aspects of your existence. Luckily, my maternal grandparents helped with our upbringing and this bought us stability and love.

Living off governmental assistance and my mom's income was not easy. It was easy to quit and be a victim. I would not let my life's misfortune undermine my ultimate destiny. These difficult times galvanized my "burning desire" to succeed in life.

"Land of Opportunity"

My grandfather once told me, "they can take away your earthly possessions – your car, your house, your bank account, and even the clothes on your back but they can never take away your education." He encouraged me to be the first in my family to graduate from college. My grandparents immigrated to America from Italy around the First Great War. They came seeking a new life, to the land of opportunity. It was their dream to make a better life for themselves and their family, and America offered this opportunity to succeed.

We can create our own "land of opportunity" by following sound principles and focusing on our dreams, but our dreams are often derailed by our self-limiting beliefs. We all have our unique stories to tell – some good, some bad, some inspiring, some sad.

Self-Awareness is the Foundation to Succeed

As I look back on my life there were early warning signs that created my self-limiting belief system. Being told I was not good enough to date my first love because of my socio-economic background or hanging out with friends who were not the "school jocks." It was difficult accepting these realities because I worked hard to make something of myself but I understood these consequences.

Peer pressure at school can be difficult to escape. If you struggled in math, science or English, there was a stigma placed on you. You were branded a slow learner; someone who most likely will fail in life without a good education.

At my school, we had a "stupid box." If you misbehaved, you would sit inside the box until the teacher felt you were punished enough and it was time to rejoin your classmates. This isolation was an embarrassment but it also left you feeling self-doubt and your classmates often ridiculed you. I spent time in the box but I survived the ridicule with a renewed purpose. I was not going to let this experience define who I was as a person. These shocks changed my life and I set about life with a renewed determination to prove my worth. I now seriously focused on achieving my place in this "land of opportunity."

I spent the early part of my life with little confidence although I felt I could succeed if I applied myself. I thought it was impossible for me to learn as I struggled with my grades in school. This was my false, self-limiting belief. And, since I was told that I would never achieve success without a good education, I never expected to be successful. I eventually changed my thoughts about success in life. I was no longer going to live each day with these self-limiting beliefs that I was not good enough, rich enough or smart enough.

Anyone can change their life if they put their mind to action. Change requires a total commitment.

Everyone has a purpose in life beyond his or her current mindset. It is critical that you reach deep inside of you to understand your self-limiting beliefs.

Machiavelli said, "There are three kinds of brains: One understands of itself, another can be taught to understand, and the third can neither understand to itself nor be taught to understand." I believe the power of transformation begins when we understand ourselves through the process of self-awareness. Transformation begins when we deep dive into our hearts and minds to truly understand what we want in life and what is holding us back from achieving our dreams.

I learned during my soul-searching, self-awareness period that I saw the problem through distorted lenses, a false sense of purpose. I was harboring a set of false, self-limiting beliefs – an unfortunate child traumatized by the early death of his father, by the stigma of the "stupid box" or the comments that I was not good enough to be with someone I loved.

I never recognized the problem was facing me in the mirror. I was the problem. I had to move beyond my self-limiting beliefs.

Setbacks are to be expected

Unfortunately, we often revisit our past demons. One of my past self-limiting beliefs was awakened - I was not good enough for my college girlfriend because of my economic and social background. Her parents felt so strongly about this issue that they removed her from school. Again, I was deemed unacceptable, another debilitating setback.

After all I had done to improve myself I was still not good enough. The same self-limiting beliefs that haunted my life were now circling me like vultures ready to pounce on the decaying carcass. But this time the results were different.

I committed to myself I would never let self-limiting beliefs hinder my burning desire to succeed and achieve my life-long dreams. I'm convinced the understanding I received from these life lessons literally changed my life. And, when I say change, I mean change in every facet of my life.

When we hear stories of people changing their entire lives, we are skeptical. I understand this concern and have felt the same way too.

I went from an average student struggling to maintain good grades, to becoming a partner at large accounting firm, to earning the highest professional awards as a chief financial officer. My income skyrocketed through hard work and a relentless commitment to succeed. Today, I have achieved a significant net worth and I am debt free. I knew deep down inside I had the potential to be successful; I just lacked the awareness and belief in myself to truly commit to my dreams.

FUNDAMENTALLY, I LACKED THE AWARENESS OF MY POTENTIAL.

I know I don't have all of the answers in life. In fact, I'm still on my lifelong learning journey. But I hope through my own personal experiences, I can connect with you.

I'm confident if you take an honest assessment of yourself you will transform your method of achieving your goals and dreams, and shift your self-limiting beliefs. They've worked for me. They'll work for you.

If you overcome your self-limiting beliefs and incorporate success principles into your daily practices, I'm confident you can achieve anything in life. You must believe in yourself.

There is no magic formula to achieving success in life. It's not rocket science to learn and model these success principles. But it does require you to understand your self-limiting beliefs, the little doubters talking to your inner mind telling you it's impossible to be successful, that you are not smart enough or talented enough. You know what I'm talking about. You hear these internal doubts all the time.

Fear, Failure and Fortune

You have a dream, you get excited. . . then this doubting voice confronts you. Your dreams are shattered. Or, maybe fear enters the room. Doubt and fear are powerful buddies who do a lot of damage. I've heard them. Unfortunately, the people closest to you generally plant these seeds of doubt. I heard my inner voices of doubt and fear telling me that I would not be successful without an advanced degree from an Ivy League school or a membership to an upscale country club.

We all fail at one time or another, but failure is not bad. I read a story about Sara Blakely, Spanx's inspirational founder, and she said her father would ask her at dinner how many times did she fail that day. Failure was celebrated because failing meant she tried something new and expanded her knowledge base.

I truly believe that by taking an inventory of your self-limiting beliefs, you begin to move beyond your comfort zone. You've reached into that deep, dark place in your mind that has defined who you are as a person up to this point in your life. I know, I've been there too. I call this exercise "illuminating life" because it casts a new light on your perspective. It exposes areas of your life that were hidden deep inside your psyche, a new self-awareness of who you are as a person.

As I began to understand these important facts - why we do certain things we should do and why we don't do things we really want to do, I realized that my learning models were based on certain assumptions about myself. We're instinctively aware of things right in front of us, but we fail to look beyond our immediate circumstance.

Some people truly believe that success is achieved by being in the right place at the right time, but this belief is too simple an answer. *We are always in the right place at the right time. It's about being aware of your potential while you're in the right place to act upon this awareness.*

By overcoming your fears and doubts you begin to master the principles within a learning model of success and achievement, you'll find even if you're in the wrong place at the wrong time. You can win, because the potential for winning was always within you.

Everyone loves safety. It is a natural state of mind. Photographer Cecil Beaton once stated, "Be daring, be different, be impractical, be anything that will assert integrity of purpose and imaginative vision against those who play it safe, the creatures of the commonplace, and the slaves of the ordinary."

By expanding your self-awareness and conquering your self-limiting beliefs, you'll find that you can achieve your goals regardless of conditions and circumstances. You'll break free from a life of ordinary to reach your path of extraordinary.

What are you capable of achieving in your life? Are your desires for success tempered by past failures or self-limiting beliefs? Or, do you listen to your inner voice of doubt and fear, and the naysayers around you?

Changing your Narrative

What story are you telling yourself? Is it one of negativity and doubt, or is one of positivity and confidence? I surrounded myself with negative influence and the results I obtained were negative. It had nothing to do with the economy, or my work situation. I reached the level of my self-belief and never believed myself capable of outperforming that imagined in my mind. My internal belief system was creating an image of doubt.

Take a close look at your life. Examine areas where you've been really successful, where you felt that you achieved your goals. My aim is to change your learned behavior by changing your self-limiting beliefs. If you could make profound changes in your life, would you accept this challenge?

This challenge forces you to focus on a whole new learning process. Ask yourself, "Am I ready to make these profound changes in my life?" If your answer is a resounding yes, then you're on the path to reach your ultimate destination. *As a word of caution, you may never reach your final destination but the process of taking this journey is where rewards are found.* Once you imagine the success you want to achieve, you have taken the first step toward reaching your goal.

Look at your life through a new set of lenses, a new prism. You've mastered many individual challenges in your lifetime. Now is the time to master your life. There's never the perfect moment. Every day we procrastinate we let precious time pass. You can lose all of your money and regain it again, but once you lose time it is lost forever. So, act today.

The ancient Chinese philosopher, Lao Tzu wrote, "Knowing others is wisdom; knowing yourself is Enlightenment."

The truth is, in order for us to achieve success in life, we must take risks and move beyond our comfort zones. You must decide. Do you want to live an ordinary or extraordinary life?

Commitment to Change
When you honestly say to yourself, "I can no longer accept these conditions in my life," change begins. The moment you intentionally commit to change you begin to create your new life.

Perhaps you are skeptical. Your life has been unfulfilling and your self-limiting beliefs are well entrenched. Perhaps you tried to change but failed to see progress in your life. Maybe you gave up and are content to live an ordinary life without regrets.

It's easy to take the path of least resistance. In fact, if you don't know where you are going in life, any road will take you there. Don't let doubts and fears control your destiny. If you take the time to understand your self-limiting beliefs and conquer these fears and doubts and intentionally replace them with new empowering beliefs, you are on the pathway to success.

As President Franklin Delano Roosevelt once stated, "The only limit to our realization of tomorrow will be our doubts of today." It's time to change our inner beliefs. Embrace a positive mentality about yourself. Think boldly and creatively. Only then will we begin to achieve the breakthroughs we seek in life. Success is within our powers.

Your journey of a thousand miles begins with this first step – self-awareness.

About Mark

Mark A. Gyetvay is the Chief Financial Officer and Deputy Chairman of the Management Board of OAO NOVATEK based in Moscow. He has worked with NOVATEK since 2003, and prior to that time, was a partner at PricewaterhouseCoopers, or PwC, responsible for serving clients in the oil and gas sector. Mark was responsible for taking NOVATEK public at the London Stock Exchange in 2005, served on the Board of Directors from 2005 to 2014, and has frequently been recognized by *Investor Relations Magazine* as one of the best CFO's in Russia and the CIS, and by Institutional Magazine as one of the TOP Five CFO's in Europe's oil and gas sector. In 2015, Mark was recognized as the Best CFO in Russia by *Finance-Monthly* magazine.

Mark is a frequent keynote speaker at various global industry and investor events and a recognized expert in the oil and gas industry, and has published numerous articles on oil and gas topics. He has worked in the oil and gas industry in various financial and economic capacities since 1981 when he graduated from Arizona State University.

Mark is a Certified Public Accountant, a Member of the American Institute of CPAs, an associate member of the Society of Petroleum Engineers, and a former member of PwC's Petroleum Thought Leadership Council.

In addition to his professional career, Mark is also an entrepreneur with investments in various start-up businesses, as well as co-partner in Illuminum London, a niche fragrance company.

He is a lifelong learner, an avid reader, art collector and sports enthusiast. Mark is a strong believer in personal development and taking direct responsibility for your career development and advancement.

For more information, please contact Mark at:
- Email: markgyetvay@yahoo.com
- Twitter: @markgyetvay

CHAPTER 11

HOW TO FIND PASSION WITHOUT SPENDING ONE DOLLAR

BY PAUL P. CHENG, ESQ.

Stop listening to those that prey on your emptiness. Paying to find passion is a waste of money. Passion is a byproduct of feeling successful which occurs only when you put in 100%.

People talk about finding passion and think once they find it, everything will fall into place. It's a wonderful concept; however, it is unrealistic because of the one issue that assuredly stands in most peoples' way—money. We need money to sustain ourselves. And most, including me, cannot simply drop everything to find it.

Let's be frank. Any guru with a powerful voice and poignant message that tells us, "just let go and live your passion," has good intentions—they want you to be happier and more successful. Yet, upon further evaluation we find that the expert who can so eloquently state such a powerful message became successful only after they began reaching out to the average person and teaching them to...you guessed it, find their passion!

No matter where you are in life, you have worth.

Did you know that simply reading this book is a mathematical impossibility? The simple act of you, being a human, with the 37.2 trillion cells in your body in conjunction with you reading and synthesizing this article is already a miracle. Further, combine that with the seven billion people living in this world and you being here is not just an incredible feat, is it completely improbable.

What does all of this mean? It means that there is something special about you. No matter where you are in life, you have worth and meaning in this universe. And this value that you have is burning inside you. That loneliness tearing at you is your spirit telling you that you are worth more than what you currently feel. Regardless of which perspective you choose to look at, passion is consuming you and haunting you.

The real issue is not finding your passion—which many people are taught to believe. Instead, passion is a byproduct of feeling successful. And success occurs when you live each day 100%.

Think of your childhood. Think of one time where someone encouraged you or when you succeeded at something. Remember the result of what happened? You began spending much more time at it. Whether it was sports, reading, or a hobby, your passion began to develop when you felt that you succeeded at it.

Simply put, your passion coincided with the amount of success you felt. Success spurns the feeling of passion. And a higher chance of success only occurs when you give of yourself 100%.

This is the key. No matter the circumstance you are in, you must immerse yourself and embrace each day. Lackluster success is the reason why you feel unaccomplished at the end of the day. You may have done much, but still feel passionless.

Of course, there are no guarantees in life. I cannot guarantee that you will feel successful every single day you put in 100%. However, I can guarantee that if you refuse to squander the potential opportunities that come your way by living each day fully, the passion that eludes you will quickly find its way to you.

Passion is a beautiful, incredible, feeling that will overwhelm you when you live each day to its fullest. It is waiting for you.

Start with the "end goal" in mind.

After reading, you might start agreeing that passion is a byproduct of success. And you have every right to then ask, "How do I live each day 100%?"

To live each day 100% you must start with the end goal in mind, and then work backwards.

Let's use the simple concept of being successful (you can replace it with any goal you want). Then take that end goal and work backwards, using it as a roadmap to the decisions you make on a daily basis. For example, would a successful person procrastinate? Would he/she scream at others when they are stressed? Would a person of success be overweight?

Your life will quickly surround itself around the end goal you set.

Attorneys—a lonely profession.

I am a warrior. My time is bought to fight for others. And frankly, being an attorney is one of the loneliest professions out there.

During my second year as an attorney, I was told by a mentor: "Do not be discouraged, attorneys like prostitutes are paid by the hour. As long as you bill your clients, and keep your costs low, you will make it." How discouraging is that?!

This is unlike my big brother. My brother just retired from Loma Linda University Hospital as a Director of Spine Surgery. During his tenure at the hospital, if someone died (God forbid), the deceased's family would think it was the will of God. On the other hand, if I lose, no one ever thinks it is the will of God. Instead, they blame me.

No one ever realizes the number of tears we shed for our clients. And because of that, attorneys can easily convince themselves to become heartless, not giving 100% effort into their daily lives, and abusing whatever benefits they can get.

Xiao Wu: an example of how the "end goal" changed my life.

A lady came into my office, beautiful and statuesque. She was a Chinese woman with a recent Green Card obtained from marrying an American citizen. With her came her thirteen-year-old daughter, a carbon copy of her mother. When she came in, she fell onto her knees and refused to leave. She was desperate, pleading how she and her daughter had nowhere to go. Her husband was abusive and forceful, requiring her to have sex with groups of men while he watched and smoked drugs. Her daughter, similarly, only spoke in small whispers and refused to look anyone in the eye.

Like many new immigrants, she kept expressing her need for her Green Card. It was everything to her at that moment. She had contacted numerous lawyers before me that rejected her pleas and sent her away. And easily, I could have clammed up and done the same. However, the question I asked myself was the following: "Would a successful person turn her away?" The answer was clear, no.

A successful person would not turn this woman away. Instead, he/she would embrace the situation and help. Indeed, that is what I did. Less than thirty days later, this battered, crushed, human being, sent me pictures from a shelter we referred her to of her and her smiling daughter.

She is currently being processed under VAWA (Violence Against Woman Act), a statute that permits abused individuals to gain citizenship without their abusing spouse's support and living free from the abuse previously encountered.

The result of this event created a passion in me to continue being an attorney. The passion I felt occurred because I worked backwards, using my goal as a successful attorney to roadmap my actions.

I share this story of Xiao Wu, not because I'm proud to have helped her, but because I'm ashamed of the thirty to forty women I previously sent away. I'd suggested to them they had to "tough it out." Of course, I can rationalize by saying I hadn't known of the specific immigration statute applicable. Please, learn from my mistake.

36,000 Days. Yours are 1/3 to 1/2 gone.

With that said, I will say to you what no one else in this book will say. Your life is at least 1/3 to 1/2 over. You most likely only have approximately 18,000 days left (or less). You do not have time to reject the proposition of failing to engage each day. If you refuse to live your life fully you will likely never find the passion you so desperately seek.

By seeking integrity over dignity you will find both.

Passion is a feeling people desire because it is the child of Dignity. Ultimately, you are not seeking Passion. You are really seeking to feel dignity about your life. You want to close your eyes at night knowing and feeling that you are proud of who you are. You will never feel passionate about your life, unless you feel proud of it.

<u>CONCLUSION</u>

In summary, remember the following:
   (1). Gurus are steering you in the wrong direction because they are suggesting that passion is something outside of your current path.
   (2). You have worth, right where you are.
   (3). Passion is a byproduct of success.
   (4). Success occurs when you live 100% everyday.
   (5). Start with the "end goal" in mind and your life will change.
   (6). You do not have time to wait to change your mindset.
   (7). Integrity comes before dignity. You will never feel passion without living a life of integrity.

About Paul

Paul Cheng is a trial attorney and senior partner of a team of distinguished attorneys in Pasadena, California. He has extensive legal experience in small to large business operations and commercial realty transactions. Mr. Cheng has counseled individuals and businesses at all levels in a variety of transactional and litigation matters, including contract, land use, employment, franchise law, fraud, internet law, products liability, intellectual property, construction defect and general torts. He has also been featured on NBC, ABC, CBS, and Fox affiliates regarding legal issues.

Prior to entering private practice, Paul Cheng was a Deputy City Attorney with the City of Hesperia, California and a Mediator with the Los Angeles Superior Court.

Paul Cheng obtained a B.A. degree in Philosophy from the University of California, Los Angeles and a J.D. degree from Southwestern University School of Law.

He has traveled extensively through Asia and is a frequent lecturer at the universities there. He is fluent in Mandarin.

He can be reached at www.PPRCLAW.com or info@paulchenglaw.com

CHAPTER 12

GOING "BIG" WHEN YOU COME FROM "LITTLE"
— IMPROVING THE ENVIRONMENT WITH BIOPLASTICS

BY PAVINEE WAEWSEANGSANG

Finding ways to accomplish great things should never be hindered by a lack of resources; we are our own unstoppable resource, our desire to succeed is the fuel.

Drawn to doing my part and having the best practices I can to make a better earth, I have always researched the information and opportunities that would help me to make a real difference in this world. When I had the opportunity to co-author a publication in graduate school with well-known biotechnology researcher Dr. Jarunee Wonglimpiyarat, I became inspired. Through this paper about bioplastics, I instinctually knew that I'd found the fit I'd been searching for – my calling for an area of expertise in which I could do much good. Through bioplastics, some of the greatest experiences and learning lessons in business and the determination of my human spirit have taken place.

A bioplastic is a substance made from organic biomass sources, unlike conventional plastics which are made from petroleum and chemicals.

In Thailand, it is easy to start a small-to-medium sized enterprise

(SME), which is why there are many. It is substantially harder to make the business high-growth and high-profit. To do so, you need insight and must have a driving desire to pursue the right expertise, commitment, and resources. There is no resource harder to come by than a financial resource. To overcome that, I learned a great deal and discovered how it takes great personal effort to let nothing deter you from laying out the groundwork to build your dream upward – especially to the point where others can no longer ignore it. They want to become a part of it.

Today, I am on the cusp of this with my company, Bioform (Thailand), Ltd., and as its CEO, I connect the best talents in biotechnology, technology, and production with the resources I've gained to create innovative products for a better future. These products fall under the Pellena line, which is a part of my company, and they are healthy and environmentally friendly, while also being functional and useful for tableware and food packaging.

It hasn't always been easy...

REMOVING OBSTACLES AND CREATING OPPORTUNITIES

I knew my goal—to expand the use of biomaterial globally to preserve the environment for the next generation. What came next was creating a plan of action that would help to me succeed.

I have always been committed to smart and logical actions, but during graduate school I learned more about the use of best practices when it came to achieving business objectives. Why try to create something new, which takes considerably time, energy and resources, when you can adapt proven, existing methods to work for you in a more streamlined and efficient manner? To me, I see this as the difference between being the SME that is profitable and the one that exists and struggles without recognizing profitability.

Coming from a family of very meager means, I had only my dreams and ideas to drive me. There was no capital that I could get from family members to launch my business. In addition, I didn't even have any entrepreneurs at my disposal to learn business acumen from.

Everything I wanted to do had to start at the grassroots level—me, and my best efforts.

It would have been easy to think, *just go work for someone else, earn a nice check, and enjoy your life, Pavinee.* But easy bores me, and the ideas I had were ones that I felt strongly about, which meant that I wanted to navigate their outcome, not simply participate in it.

Knowing what was working against me, I began to focus on what would work for me. There were many things I could do. First, I had to leverage the playing field. And second, I had to move to the top of that field through innovation and my personal expectations. By focusing on this, I learned so much, and that is what I wish to share with you, as you seek out success and strengthen your entrepreneurial spirit.

1. **Learn in the areas where you are weak.**

   Since I started out not knowing much about being an entrepreneur, other than desiring to be one, I signed up for classes to increase my knowledge, learn about processes and systems that work, and began networking with people of affluence who could help to guide me in making Bioform (Thailand), Ltd. a solid business with excellent potential.

2. **Seek out mentors.**

   The importance of having a good mentor is expressed quite often in most any material you read that is designed for self-improvement and the development of skills necessary to conducting an elite level of business. For committed individuals who show they are serious about what they wish to achieve, a mentor is a wonderful sounding board to run ideas by and get reliable input from. They've been where you are going.

3. **Create a business plan.**

   By listing out what you need to do in order to begin the process of starting your business, you can create a business plan that is based on facts, solid information, and action steps that you are addressing proactively. Through this measure, the opportunity to gain an interested audience increases. The ultimate goal is to have people understand your product and your objective with it.

4. Seek out incubator groups.

In the business world, an incubator is an enterprise which provides office space, equipment, and occasionally mentoring assistance. In addition, it can give you an introduction to people with capital. Most often, business incubators are set up by universities, non-profit groups, and venture capitalists. This makes them an ideal source for entrepreneurs with sound ideas. With bioplastics, I have a sound idea that is also intricately linked to the wellbeing of our future generations. This draws interest and once I gain interest from someone, I strive to keep it.

5. Grow comfortable with developing partnerships for success.

One of the largest expenditures for a start-up company is hiring the resources that will help your vision come to fruition. By creating partnerships with qualified professionals who have expertise in the skills you need, you can still move forward, but in a more fiscally responsible manner. To this day, I have five partnerships that I have created, all of us creating value for the other and helping Pellena garner attention.

6. Continue to revisit and revamp your strategy, as necessary.

To be a visionary, you must see past what is just before your eyes, or in your mind, and look ahead of you and your current plan. Things happen and having the ability to be insightful as to how the tides of change may impact your plan and business development is necessary so you reduce the risk of being blindsided. Even something like a change in federal or local tax structure can impact your business. For me, using best practices to stay alert to the potential of change is how I manage it instead of allowing it to disrupt me and the business's plan for growth.

Behind every challenge and obstacle is an opportunity for expansion of the mind and strengthening of your business. Having resolve to give your set goals your best efforts takes you farther than you might imagine. While it may be stressful at times, it's also a joy, as you are investing in what you are passionate about—the business concept you've formulated.

The lessons that stem from opposition are what bring your passion out in your words and your message.

If anyone were to doubt my chances at taking Bioform (Thailand), Ltd. to its maximum potential, I would be able to list off the precise reasons why I can. I'm prepared, I'm researched, I have a product that is necessary, and I continue to gain access to the sources and resources that help in achieving my goal. For everyone who gets the chance to share their business's message, it is important to be able to relay it with passion and belief, not just through rehearsed words.

THE FUTURE STARTS TODAY

By taking action today, we may not see results tomorrow, but we are definitely building the platform up on which we can take our ideas to their maximum potential.

To me, every day has meaning, and there should be no day when an action that takes my goals forward is not achieved, whether it means I am learning something new or researching a new opportunity. I think of it like this...

I know that bioplastics is the technology of the future, but does everyone else? Do they know how bioplastics can positively impact their lives?

My mission will not be complete until everyone knows and understands this, and even when they do, there will be a new horizon based on this technology that is already being explored and by being ahead of the game, researched by my team so it can be implemented. Someone is going to do this, so why not Bioform (Thailand), Ltd.?

Insight and research have guided me toward innovative ideas that will help the goals that have been set forth for my business to take flight. These include:

1. **Participating in local and global expos.**
   There are endless opportunities for participating in expos for new business, green initiatives, and even the food industry, all of which are applicable to the business that I am growing. The two areas that I focus on at this time are:

i. Original equipment manufacturing (OEM) of pure-bio food packaging and other durable product that currently do not exist in our OBM product line.

ii. Owned brand manufacturing (OBM) of pure-bio tableware, which is marketed under the Pellena brand.

Also, a common question that I am asked at these events is, "What does Pellena mean?" This is an opportunity to start an interaction that allows me to share what it does mean, which is:

P—people
E—ecology
L—life
L—lifestyle
E—environmental
NA—natural

Through this focus, as well as using pure bio corn, natural color, no plastics or metamine's, being BPA free, and also being microwave and washing machine-safe make for a product that interests people, while also pioneering a way for a better eco-friendly future for everyone, based on the products we use.

Also, by interacting with people about *Pellena's* meaning, they leave with three important things. First, they leave with knowledge. Second, they walk away with information on Pellena and how to contact us. And third, they have a valuable piece of material that can be shared with others. The entire experience helps brand the product and establishes my leadership brand in the industry of bioplastics.

2. Engaging with exporters to gain a global market.
Thailand is the hub for my business at this point, but the benefits of bioplastics are something with global appeal. Through showing the research and feedback of the products that the business offers, the ability to use that data to show exporters that this is a product they want to be associated with increases exponentially.

3. Acquire government subsidies to assist with objectives.
With government subsidies, a global standard certification for biomaterials can be created, which will add to the credibility and viability of the product and the business innovator behind it.

Keeping in mind that results do not often show themselves for several years in businesses such as Bioform (Thailand), Ltd., it is important to always have growth initiatives in play and be implementing the steps that will make it a rising business—never stagnant and always highly relevant.

THE HUMAN SPIRIT: RENEWABLE ENERGY AT ITS BEST

The energy that surges through me whenever I create a new solution and take a step forward in my business motivates me, and sustains my drive to achieve what I've set out to do.

There is nothing more powerful than getting consumed by the type of exciting energy that is yielded as a result of your own actions and accomplishments. It feels great to know that you've started something— especially something that you are strongly committed to—and that it is taking off, drawing others in and growing. It's as much a part of you as your family is.

As I look to the future for my business and the goals that I have for it, I see endless potential to really impact the world in a positive way, by leaving less of an impact on the environment. To me, that is powerful, and I am fully committed to helping others see the benefits of bioplastics to their lives. As an entrepreneur, we cannot make our success just about us, because we will fail, but when we are inspired to help others through it, we truly become the game changers.

About Pavinee

Pavinee Waewseangsang is founder and Chairman of Bioform (Thailand) Ltd., a company that is dedicated to offering pure biopackaging for food packaging and containers, and bio-tableware under the brand name *Pellena*. Her inspiration to deliver safe products of the highest quality to people is inspired by a desire to help people live healthier lives and to treat our earth more kindly.

A firm believer in having an individual lifestyle to save the world, Pavinee has worked hard to gain the education and opportunities to promote her passion for bioplastics. She wants to spread a global message that will show how bioplastics can revolutionize the way packaging and household products are viewed. To cultivate this, she is a student of innovative thinking, dedicated to entrepreneur best practices and actions that will take her company from an incubator start-up to a global industry leader.

Pavinee has received her Master's Degree in Technology Management from The College of Innovation at Thammasat University. During this time, she worked on a joint publication with well-known biotechnology researcher, Dr. Jarunee Wonglimpiyarat. It was through this experience that she really connected with bioplastics as her platform to make positive environmental change and healthier lifestyle choices.

With a commitment to products that can save ten generations from the effects of chemically-made plastics, Pavinee has brought forth initiatives that have gained Bioform (Thailand) Ltd. many accolades, including: **Innovation Move #2** by the Thailand Institute of Scientific and Technological Research (TISTR); and **T.I.D.E. 2015.** In addition, she has had effective outreach with the Thailand government, obtaining subsidies from programs such as iTAP, and TISTR to promote and grow her business.

Although Pavinee enjoys her work and mission with bioplastics immensely, she also takes time to speak to others to help educate them, paying it forward from all the insight and time her mentors and instructors have given her, assisting in her rising success. As a co-author with Brian Tracy for the book *Success Blueprint*, she is grateful for the opportunity to be a Best Selling Author. She also cherishes those moments when she can sit down to a good book and get lost in its pages.

You can contact Pavinee at:
- Pavinee@Pellena.com

Or visit the website at:
- www.PellenaThai.com

CHAPTER 13

GLENN'S STORY

BY ROSE BAKER

My son's name is Glenn Miller. When he was eleven years old he came to me and said, "Mom, I don't want to be an only child anymore. Is there any way that I could get siblings?" I smiled at him and said, "I don't know how we would do that." When he was born we had been told there would be no more children. I told him I would give it some thought and ask around to see what others might think.

I went to work the next day, and shared that story with a friend. As we were talking, one of my customers at the furniture store where I worked overheard my conversation and said, "I have an answer to that! We are foster parents here in Humboldt County. They're always looking for more parents."

That was the beginning of a wonderful journey. Shortly thereafter, the process was started to license our home to become a foster family. Glenn was very excited and right away wanted to start deciding age, gender and how many children would come. We had great conversations and lots of laughter trying to decide how to make our choices.

After a short period of time we were licensed and ready to go. My friends who had shared with me about foster parenting had decided they were going to move away. That made me very sad because then I had no one to ask questions of, but they told us they had a 17-year-old developmentally delayed young man with whom we had connected. He wanted to come and stay with us because he couldn't leave with them. Glenn was very excited to hear this. A short time later Lyle moved in and life got to be very exciting.

Glenn and Lyle became good friends. It didn't take very long for our newly-enlarged family to get close and have lots of fun. A short time later I met a young man whose name was Pete and he and I started dating. Pete, Glenn and Lyle decided it would be fun to go fishing and camping. The guys became well connected in a short period of time.

As Pete and I got to know each other better, we found there were many things we had in common. We both loved to dance, laugh and share with others the joys of life. This made Glenn and Lyle extremely happy. It didn't take long for our lives to mesh. Pete asked me to marry him, so on June 16,1984 our lives were made perfect. WOW! This was a whirlwind and a very exciting time as we added him to our family. First there were two and now there were four!

It wasn't long before Lyle moved on after turning eighteen. He really wanted to be on his own, so in order to make that happen, the county moved Lyle back to his biological family and then on to Redding, California. He often would come to visit. We got to see him grow and be happy.

Pete decided that we needed a bigger home if our family was going to continue to grow, so we went in search of what we thought would be a wonderful place to raise children. As we looked around, we found a great four-acre parcel up in the middle of a hill called Humboldt Hill. There we built a four-bedroom, three bathroom, 2300 square foot, two-story log home.

By the time the house was built, we had acquired more children, so now it was Glenn, Pete, myself, and four children; three siblings and another young lady. We finished our home and worked very hard to help the children reunite with their families. The young lady that came alone went home to stay. That was our second success story. The three siblings also returned home but this one didn't go very well. After a short period of time, they ended up back in care. By the time they came back into care we had other children in our home and we didn't have enough room for all three of them. There were two girls and a boy so the boy came back to us and the two girls went elsewhere. This was very sad because we always want siblings to stay together.

Eventually, the little boy went into care to an adoptive home. The older girl stayed where she was and the younger one, being so young, came back to us, That's when our adoptions started. She was very cute but was often sad even though we did everything we could to try to cheer her up. The only thing that really seemed to cheer her up was her connection to Glenn. He was a wonderful big brother that always wanted to protect her, and found things to do that made her giggle so she always wanted to do more with him. A short time later other children went home and we got a call to take more children. With a home full of kids and so much laughter, it just never seemed to be a hardship.

We were learning more every day. There were some really tough times working with children that we didn't understand. Right away we began learning, going to seminars and talking to people in search of anything and everything we could use to prepare ourselves for each new set of children.

In September 1988, Glenn was diagnosed with osteogenic sarcoma, which is bone cancer. He had just turned seventeen. He had been playing basketball and looking forward to football season when this came about. It was a very sad time for all of us as we were constantly going back and forth to the hospital in San Francisco during his chemo treatments, working very hard at keeping him connected and excited about all things possible.

Glenn loved his family. He loved having the kids. When this was diagnosed I wanted to stop doing foster care and just keep the two we had adopted and let go of everything else. Glenn was very against that. He did everything he could humanly do to keep us going. This was his dream as well as mine. He taught me well. The children who came to our home while he was there would tell you to this day that everything he did has shown them what life was really all about. You can look at doom and gloom or you can take each day, turn it around and make memories. In February 1991, the doctors told Glenn that they needed to amputate his leg a second time. They had taken it off at the knee but now they needed to take it off at the hip so he said okay. It was worth it because they assured him that he would still live and have a prosthetic leg and possibly walk normally.

In April 1991 they did surgery and removed his leg at the hip. At that time, they told him there was no way it would spread to his other side, that everything looked normal. He was very excited. He just knew that the love of his life and he could get married. They could still have children. After his surgery he asked me if we could take a trip across the United States. My family set up a family reunion in Arkansas to celebrate him and all the good things that he had done. That was an exciting time for us! We went to the family reunion in Arkansas, went to New Orleans, Louisiana, then went to Mississippi for the Fourth of July and fun was had by all.

After our lengthy trip, we returned home. Upon our arrival Glenn had another scan done. The doctors who had told him it would never spread to his right side did not know what they were talking about. There it was in his right lymph glands. As Glenn became aware of the fact that things were probably going to happen soon, he assured me that he was OK, that I had been a good mom and had made him very happy over the years. He was more excited about the fact that he had lots of siblings and always wanted to make sure that I didn't give up my dream of having lots of children and that I hopefully would never forget him.

In July of 1991, I made a promise to my nineteen year-old son who was dying of cancer that I would continue doing the work that he and I started when he was eleven years old.

I can share with you that as of today there have been many children who have come through our home since that day, August 13, 1991, the day of his passing, who say they feel his presence in our home. After periods of time, some have come to believe that they know him. When people ask who is in that picture, they always say, "That's my brother. He passed but he always wanted us to be a part of his family."

The most wonderful part of Glenn's gift has been my staying connected to most of our foster children and their families, as well as getting to know all of those families that have come into doing foster care, sharing experiences and adding tools to everyone's toolboxes. With each new generation of children and families, Glenn's memory lives on. They will always be in my heart, as he is.

When you take children into your home don't give up. Keep learning.

Keep sharing. Help them to know there are answers. Even in a storm when things look dark, there will always be a light at the end of the tunnel.

About Rose

Rose E. Baker is the biological mother of one, adoptive mother of five, grandmother of many and a foster parent of over 440 children.

Dedicating her life to helping children, youth and families, Rose began foster parenting in 1982. In the ensuing decades, she has been tireless in finding the education, resources and energy to assist children, parents and social services in Humboldt County and throughout the state. The children, youth and families that Rose works with come from difficult circumstances. Rose specializes in children of abuse and neglect, foster children with multiple placements, failed adoptions, children with multiple diagnoses, and especially children whom others have not been able to help.

Rose works with educators, managers, mental health and healthcare providers, lawyers, probation officers, police, clergy, government officials, and individual families. Her life centers around getting the children and families what they need to grow, heal and prosper.

She has collaborated with such luminaries in parenting and child psychology as Dr. Charles Fay, Jim Fay, Dr. Foster Cline of the popular parenting system Love and Logic, Nancy Thomas, author of *When Love Is Not Enough*, and Dr. Bryan Post of the Post Institute with *Love-Based Family-Centered Parent Training*. Rose frequently travels to Foster and Adoptive Parent conferences and conventions, always advocating for youth and for the legislation that will provide much-needed funds and services.

Organizations and Positions

- YouthAbility, Inc., Founder and Executive Director.
  This nonprofit provides job training to at-risk youth. Started in 2006, the organization owns and operates Angels of Hope Thrift Store in Arcata as a training facility for youth and young adults emancipating from foster care, and from low or no-income lifestyles. Every year approximately 150 youth, young adults and others are referred to YouthAbility from Humboldt County programs such as Independent Living Skills, Welfare-to-Work, Step-Up, and Humboldt County courts.

- Parents in Training, Inc., Founder and Executive Director.
  Parents in Training provides parenting classes and consulting for parents raising difficult children. As a Certified Love and Logic Instructor since 1992, Rose has trained thousands of parents and professionals. Parents in Training receive referrals from the Humboldt County courts working to put families back together.

- Humboldt County Post Adoptions In-Home Behavioral Specialist
- Humboldt Juvenile Justice Commissioner, since 2007
- President of the New Directions of Humboldt Foster Parent Association, 2004 through 2014
- Alcohol and Other Drug Care Services, Inc., Board Member, 2007 through 2013
- Pacific View Charter School, Board Member since 2005

Awards and Credit

- Co-author of: *Advanced Parenting a Difficult Child*, with Nancy Thomas, nationally recognized parenting authority.
- An 'Elite Mom' one of seven in the U.S., highly specialized parent mentor/consultants for emotionally-disturbed children.
- California State Foster Parent of the Year, 2000.
- Humboldt County Peacemaker Award, 2002.
- Torch Award, 2010, honors community members who embody hearts, courage and inspiration in life and work.
- League of Women Voters, Humboldt County, Youth Advocate of the Year, 2010.

CHAPTER 14

MISTAKES, DETERMINATION, AND SUCCESS
— LESSONS FROM AN ENTREPRENEUR

BY DR. SAMUEL MUDAVANHU

*Our drive and determination is directly linked to the amount
of passion we have for what we wish to achieve.*

Hard work and doing the best I could, regardless of the job I had, has always been a part of who I am. Being committed to our choices is important, as they are gateways to information and an education that can take us far. And in a country like Zimbabwe, this is important, because it is a place that has as many struggles as it does heart and resilience, particularly when it comes to a volatile economy that never offers too much certainty.

As a young man, I started off as a casual worker, wanting to earn a living of some sort, but also having my sights set on a future that was better and brighter, for both me and my family. I continued my education and went to work as a civil servant, where I recognized the potential to help others through my position. This was a powerful lesson, one that guided me to becoming an entrepreneur in the distribution market, which I began in 2001. It was an ideal time, as the economy was in a sound place in Zimbabwe. Most people were not used to this and those who had entrepreneurial traits took advantage of these "golden years" and what the economy could offer.

The gains in Zimbabwe during this time were not lost on me, or the many others who were not afraid to work hard and take advantage of the thriving economy, one in which the currency's value was strong. The result was that many people could gain and earn money unlike many of us, who were not born into wealth, had ever seen before. Because of this, we were given the joys that come with the financial gains of hard work—the fruits of our efforts. Everything looked and felt like success, which was a lovely feeling. Then the feel of success left, which created pain and anxiety and uncertainty. With the return of a harsher economy, in 2007 everything spiraled downward rapidly—seemingly overnight.

The true heart of an entrepreneur comes to light when they realize they've lost it all. This is when we're faced with two choices—either to give up or to try again, keeping in mind the new knowledge that often comes with lessons hard learned.

Many of us are not strangers to adversity and struggle in achieving our goals. Imagine you're me. You've just went from a place where you felt like you were on top of the world, everything was going your way and there was nothing that you could predict that would indicate that it was going to change. My distribution company had grown so much that many offshoot companies had been created from it, each profitable in some way, whether I sold them or maintained their interest. Then my years of hard work were gone, just like that. It was tough to grasp, really, because it felt like I'd just begun. Now, it was gone.

The thing with money is that our obligations we owe those monies to don't just dissipate with the loss of money. That's a pretty stressful feeling, one that can challenge someone of even the greatest faith. However, this is the lesson in the experience, the mark of excellence. Do you run and hide or stand up and start again, rebuilding or starting something new? I chose to pursue something new.

Looking at the chaos that was all around me, I saw one thing that was so important missing from the lives of many people; especially young people. This was a high quality education. Then I knew. Education was where I was meant to give my all now. That was my future, just as much as it was the future of the children. A way to help develop young minds that would grow into positive, achievement-based adults in Zimbabwe was the starting point for a process that would bring the country more prosperity, stability and opportunities for all, certainly more than what it currently offered. It just felt right, but there was one huge problem I had to deal with—I had lost everything. Even the best dreams on a big visionary scale require money, and nothing changes that.

Without any financial resources recovered from the hyper inflationary environment of 2007 we had to sacrifice the family properties to raise financial resources to start a school. Back into a rental environment we went, and anything that we had left of value that could be sold had to be sold—and that was not much. Many people may think, why not a bank? It was not a feasible option for us, because getting a business loan from a Zimbabwean bank is not easy, particularly in a bad economy. If, by chance, you're fortunate enough to get one, the interest rate is highly unfavorable—20% and upward, typically.

*The process of making the most meaningful change that
I could think of for the lives of young people began.*

Knowing that money was tight meant that there was no room for costly do-overs. This plan had to be organized, efficient, and be effective in guiding us to the goal of opening up our first school. This was 2008. We'd decided on a primary school first, and set an aggressive goal of opening it up in 2009. And through a lot of sacrificing, commitment, and belief in what we were doing, we made that goal. When we opened up our first school, we had thirty-five students enrolled and six teachers, all wanting to be a part of this unique curriculum, one based in the lessons of God and the Bible in relationship to all areas of education, helping to cultivate a culture where faith was directly associated with the education that builds a stronger foundation for life.

Today, we have over one thousand students and have two primary schools, two secondary schools, and now, much to our excitement, a university, as well. This growth has happened so fast and in many ways, it's the message based in taking the right actions, propelled by the powerful word of God that has really guided us there. It wasn't always easy, but our path has always been tried and true.

There is seldom one specific thing that guides us toward success, but rather a series of lessons and understanding about one's self, combined with the integrity of the mission. For us, this was all based on wanting to be of service to man, and our Creator.

The success principles that took me from casual worker in a restaurant all the way to the ranks of a Group Chief Executive Officer who is fully committed to the education of students in a new, nourishing curriculum has come to be from the many lessons that I've learned and practiced in my life, also earning me wonderful accolades such as: first runner-up for Entrepreneur of the Year in 2010; one of ten outstanding young Zimbabweans in 2011; and Businessman of the Year Award for 2015.

Everything that has lead to the kind acknowledgements from others come from me understanding the place where I've come from and where I want to be and want others to be, as well—that spot where we recognize our dreams and goals, and also participate in their achievement. Here are the success principles I espouse:

1. Refuse to be poor.

Africa is a rich continent with the majority of the populace poor. Through encouraging people to cease the day and look at the potential of the world around them, I always hope to show them that there is always a pathway to opportunity. It may be hidden and overgrown with clutter, but it is there. By gaining knowledge and believing in yourself this pathway can reveal itself—regardless of how negative the environment you may be in is. There are opportunities to make a difference everywhere. It just takes the initiative to not join the others in complaining and remaining stagnant. Choose to be a game changer who takes advantage of positive opportunities around you and your story will be different.

2. Never hesitate to invest in your dreams.

Our investment is our commitment to make our dreams become tangible goals that we are working to achieve. It was not easy to sell my house and belongings and invest the little bit I had just to start a new opportunity, one that seemed farfetched on the surface. After all, the sudden decline in my life from 2007 was tough on me. But my dream was one worth investing in, and by selling everything that I could to get the capital for starting the school, I showed how vested I was in giving it my fullest efforts. The plan for the school was a driving force that demanded my best. In turn, I would settle for no less than giving students the best education possible, with the most gifted and highly qualified teachers available.

3. Pursue your dream with all your heart and soul.

When you feel the fires of passion intensifying within you for a worthy pursuit, you should not be dissuaded by anything. If someone says "no", keep seeking out that "yes" or learn what it will take to overcome the "no". There is a lesson and an answer in everything that we encounter while trying to achieve something. For me, the negative environment of Zimbabwe could have been a hindrance, leaving me with a "why bother" attitude, but it was the needs of my country that helped fuel my desire to pursue the dream of educational options. Our perspective, when not optimistic, is often the largest obstacle we have in finding success.

4. Be innovative.

Innovation goes hand in hand with the entrepreneurial spirit. Those who seek to make a difference and fulfill their life's aspirations need to have the innovation that it takes to find solutions and look at ways to approach business that will work—both proven existing ideas, and new methods.

5. Add value to your community.

True success cannot come when you are greedy with the opportunity that you've been given. Our successes should be inspirations to give back to our communities and the environments that helped make us who we are. For me, I can think of no greater gift than offering scholarships to underprivileged students in my community as a way of giving back. By choosing actions such as this, we also feel a sense of satisfaction from helping someone else—someone whose destiny may have been scattered—to connect with their potential for something greater. Knowing that you've taken an action that helps someone else turn a dream into their reality is a powerful visual to have; good for the heart and soul and a true tribute to our God-given purpose.

When you look at what inspires you to action, do you feel this determination to succeed and truly make an impact? This feeling is easy to pinpoint, because you sense it in your every action. It's a joy to put in the hard work and give your goals your "all", because the potential outcome is so incredibly inspiring and the work becomes more than a job, it's an act of love. This is exactly how I've felt as I began working toward changing education in Zimbabwe one school at a time.

I had accomplished things in the past that I was proud of and definitely enjoyed, but what came alive in me when I began using my gifts toward bettering educational opportunities for children left no doubts in my mind that I'd found the place I was meant to be.

When I look at my country, a place I love greatly and want great things for, I see the most precious, untapped resource of all—children. These are children who can grow up toward the light and learn the ways in which they can be the catalysts for change in their world, giving back to both their communities and the world as they grow older. This is a beautiful thing for me and when someone asks me what success looks like, I can easily point to a child near me or visualize it by thinking of that look of promise and hope in a child's eyes as they are experiencing learning in an environment that makes them feel safe and welcomed.

About Dr. Samuel

Always driven by the pursuit of personal excellence and service to his country of Zimbabwe, Samuel Mudavanhu is a proven leader in his community, always moving forward despite an unusually tumultuous economy. To some, his accomplishments may be viewed as "fairytale-esque", but they are the result of a tireless commitment, a spirit of perseverance, and a no-excuse attitude.

In 1988, upon completing his primary education, Samuel enrolled for Form 1 at a school in Harare. This was significant, as it was at this time that Samuel answered the Lord's calling and took the teachings of the Bible to heart in everything he did, including as a casual worker in the private sector, and then as a government worker.

While working toward an ICT Diploma through Africa Virtual University, the University of Zimbabwe, the opportunity to become an entrepreneur presented itself when a crisis arose from a lack of the required books for taking certain classes. The ones that were available were costly and not easily obtained. Samuel didn't hesitate to act, offering the University photocopying services for a more affordable, nominal fee, and they accepted. Upon receipt of the order Samuel initiated the steps to raise capital by taking small loans from family to fulfill the order. This was an exciting adventure for Samuel. Two intensive weeks later, the order was fulfilled, and the University became one of his biggest clients. He delivered what he promised, efficiently and affordably. It was the birth of his stationary company.

By 2005, the stationary company diversified into a land development company. The company entered into triple PPPs with government to provide affordable housing while reducing the housing backlog in the capital city of Harare. With this initiative, the company acquired land, developed it, and sold stands for people to build their own houses and conduct commerce at. They succeeded with 500+ residential stands.

The necessity to focus on better educational opportunities for children spurred on Samuel's interest in 2009, and he became so passionate about it that he and his wife invested all they had into raising the funds to open up Maranatha Junior School, a private school with elite teachers and a curriculum based on the principles of the Bible. Today, there are five centers of education, including a university.

In 2014, Samuel became Dr. Samuel Mudavanhu when he was awarded an Honorary Doctorate degree for his achievements. Other accolades include: 1) First Runner Up for ZNCC in 2010; 2) Nominee for the ZNCC Businessman of the Year Award 2011; 3) JCI's ten outstanding persons in Zimbabwe 2011; 4) Award of Excellence Nominee in 2014; 5) Businessman of the Year in Zimbabwe 2015; and, 6) Academic Leadership Award.

Aside from the love of his wife Barbra, a woman he attributes much of his success to, Samuel has three children, Merrilyn Tadiwanashe, Ashley Isheanopa, and Samuel Larry Tinotenda, who all bring him great joy. In his free time, Samuel enjoys nature conservation photography, and is an avid collector of cameras.

CHAPTER 15

RISING UP: GOING FROM POOR VILLAGE BOY TO THE MILLION DOLLAR ROUNDTABLE

BY THOMAS NTUK, LTCP

We can all rise up and do great things, regardless of what the world perceives as our "odds." It all starts with how we see ourselves when we look in the mirror.

Growing up poor in a small Nigerian village meant that my mirror was blurry, but when I looked through the haze I saw that there was more for me than what my environment indicated. It all began with one word, given to me by one influential woman, my mother, a hard working widow who did her best in every situation. She told me about a word that she taught through example: honesty!

These lessons have taken me from a small village in Nigeria, West Africa, to my current home and life in the United States. At times, large successes would have been easier to achieve with a bit of dishonesty. The question is: would that single "easier" moment in time ever guide me to the type of life that I truly wanted to live? No! But, I certainly never dreamed that it would take me to where I am now, lesson by lesson.

Measuring Cups with False Bottoms

In Nigeria, small towns have open markets where people go to purchase their staple needs, but not all vendors in these markets are the same. This is a universal truth, as not all businesses operate with the same ethos.

The open market—a place where you can go for the staples you need. That's how commerce is conducted in the village where I grew up. My mom usually tended to the shopping, but when she was busy, she would give me the money and the instructions I needed in order to help her out. If it was market day, she would say, "Go to John in the middle of the market." I would assure her that that's exactly what I would do, and then I was on my way.

One day, however, I decided to play soccer with my friends before going to the market. Well, not able to leave the game, which was a great one, I ran behind schedule. Knowing I still had to go to the market, I hustled over and then had to make a choice. Get home late or on time. I chose to get home on time. When I got to the market I chose to go to a vendor on the edge instead of going to John in the middle. I got my cups of rice and beans, paid the guy, and then hurried home.

Handing over the goods, I didn't think much about it, until Mom looked at me...and then the bags. "They cheated you," she said. I thought, *how would she know that just by looking at the bag?* I kept silent, knowing that was a wise decision. Very soon my mom proved her point.

Marching back down to the market with Mom, she walked right up to the man I had done business with, gave him a piece of her mind, and returned what I had purchased. Then she showed me the bottom of that measuring cup. It was filled with wax, so what appeared to be a full cup was actually not. If you were to buy ten cups of rice, you were actually only getting about eight.

I was shocked! That is precisely when I learned the value of honest business. John may have been over in the center of the market, but by doing business honestly, people returned to him and sent their children to him. They could trust him. As for the vendors with those false bottoms, well, they never remained in business long. As a young person, I processed this in my head and took it to heart. You could still succeed in business being honest like John.

We can all make money and still do the right thing.

Shortly after this experience, I began to study the Bible. The teachings of honesty and accountability to God reaffirmed what I'd learned and reinforced what my mother always shared with me. It led to a strong sense of purpose, one rooted in my spirituality and relationship with God. This has formed the foundation for everything I do.

Customs and Cash

What may seem like a gift at first can never end up being a blessing if it is not based on honesty and integrity.

Upon finishing high school, I got a job working as a customs officer in Lagos, the former capital of Nigeria. This customs department is laden with corruption and those who followed the rules were truly the exception to the rule. That was very stressful for a guy like me. I approached each work day honestly, not with aspirations of bribing my way to the top or of collecting bribes to gain wealth.

One time, when asked to help a gentleman with a customs concern, I began helping him, going through all the proper channels to take care of his needs. Throughout the process he kept asking me, "How much do I owe you for this?" My response was always the same, "Nothing. This is just part of my job." He couldn't believe it, because my colleagues always asked for bribes, and to be honest, I couldn't believe his reaction either. I could help him without cutting corners and taking bribes. It was just part of my job.

After some months, we finally had success with this particular gentleman's customs request. I was able to help him save on extra port and storage fees and lost or stolen goods. Again, he asked, "What can I offer you?" Again I answered, "Nothing. What I want, you cannot give me." Then he asked what that was. I told him, "I want to go to the United States to study. I can't get there because my family does not have the money to sign as a guarantor on my visa application." This man took it upon himself to write a letter of recommendation to the embassy, suggesting they should give me a visa to study abroad, and that he would be my guarantor. It worked! That was how I ended up in the United States.

Every stage of my life has provided me with great benefits and pathways to the opportunities I wanted. Each and every one of them happened because I was not afraid to follow my faith and remain honest.

By being patient, what I need always presents itself at the right time. I did not always expect things to turn out the way that they did, but when they did, I saw it as a reward for my honesty.

Green Card Love versus Genuine, Sustainable Love

When we cut corners with our heart, we sell ourselves short.

Not long after I began studying in the United States, I knew that I loved living here. Some of my friends, other students on visas, also thought the same, and thus began searching for the easiest ways to ensure they could stay. Their solution—green card marriages. Find a US citizen to marry you, and you can stay. Frankly, the thought horrified me and I refused to even entertain it. They thought I was stupid, but I was at peace. My faith and moral compass could not fathom doing such a thing. Scripturally, marriage is a serious commitment and I would never marry for the wrong reasons.

My friends "carried on" getting married to US citizens, and they seemed happy with their new opportunities. They were also able to get better paying jobs than I was able to get. Still, it didn't make me second guess my decision. I waited patiently for the one I truly loved and no one could have been more joyful than I was when Sarah finally said "yes" after eight years of saying "no"! It was well worth the wait, and I am just as happy now as I was then, thirty-seven years ago.

My relationship with God is the foundation that strengthens my honesty for everything that I do in life; through this foundation I receive the strength I need to be a good person.

My wife and I have experienced many great gifts, including four amazing children, Sonia, Lloyd, Gershom and Jonathan, and one beautiful granddaughter, Haylie. I joke about how my wife is the one who taught me all about persistence and determination. By saying "no" for eight years she made me keep going until I got a "yes". This has been the foundation of a successful sales career.

Honesty and Rooted Beliefs: The Best Business Practices

Treating every person you meet with dignity will open up opportunities for you to grow in business, and as a person.

I began working in the insurance industry while living in Fayetteville, North Carolina. This was an economically poor area of the US, a place with many economic hardships and struggles. Some professionals may think that there is not much opportunity in a place with this demographic, but I am not that type of professional. I choose to look at every person and see the potential for something greater which can be met by what I can provide. People sensed this and I was able to build my business rapidly in a most unexpected place, through honesty and a strong work ethic.

Out of the first 1,400 customers I earned, 720 lived in mobile homes and not a single one of them ever owned a brand new car. These were the types of people many agents avoided, but I wanted to treat them with dignity, helping to educate them about insurance and how to protect their families and the few assets they did have. They grew to love me. They referred others to me, and this was a great help to my agency's growth.

Through dignity, sincerity, and honesty, a winning business blend is created. It is also one in which you can make a difference while remaining rooted in your guiding principles.

The Attributes of Success

Spirituality is a foundation and guide to self-discipline so you can work hard and be persistent.

The Golden Rule, as stated by Jesus in the Bible says: "All things, therefore, that you want men to do to you, you also must do to them." For me this was simple, I wanted for others what I wanted for myself.

We are all amazing individuals, capable of great things that will help us to be of service to others in this world through our chosen careers. Within all of us, we have a few core attributes on which we should build our life's foundation. These things are tried, steady, and true—seldom failing us, if ever. These core attributes are what I wish you to embrace in your life, as my experiences have proven that they make all the difference. May they touch your heart and tantalize your mind as they illuminate a better way to conduct your business and life in this world.

1. **Be guided by what you stand for.**

   My faith in God serves as a perfect guide. Stay rooted in the belief that honesty and dignity help to form a foundation that makes all things possible.

2. **Be an ambitious learner.**

   I made a resolution many years ago that I would make sure to spend more "in my head" than I do "on my head". What I mean by this is that whatever I spend monthly on my head—haircuts, shampoo, hair care, etc. will be matched or surpassed by what I spend in my head. It's important to grasp opportunities to learn using things such as books and seminars.

3. **Practice simplicity.**

   I may have left the small, simple life of a village boy, but simplicity is still an intricate part of everything I do. I highly recommend it for you, as well, because breaking things down to their simplest terms makes things easier. It helps make the picture clearer. For example, do you choose to be honest or dishonest? It's pretty simple. Do you choose to give someone your best efforts or not? Another simple choice.

Today, my life consists of outreach to others, helping them to tap into what is in both their hearts and minds, specifically in two areas:

- Active involvement in Bible education work
  By reaching out to people at their homes, places of business, and even in prison, I am giving people the same scriptural knowledge that helped me and has helped millions of people to discern right from wrong.

- Promoting education in my field of sales
  Through helping thousands of sales professionals in the insurance industry and hospitality sales industry (resort, vacation, and time

share sales) to simplify their sales presentation in order to educate and help the public make the best choices. By doing this, these sales professionals can see the wisdom in allowing honesty and hard work to be their path to success.

Into the Future

Through focusing on and promoting education in my field, I am able to create connections with others that help to redefine the way we approach better business.

With coaching, webinars, and public speaking, I am able to help guide others to the wonderful transformations that will help their lives evolve into amazing journeys that serve incredible purposes. Knowledge will always be power, but when people struggle against it, they cannot build the solid foundations they need to achieve their full potential. It has been an awesome ride from the village all the way to multiple Million Dollar Round Table qualifications, along with consistent sales ranking among the top 50 out of more than 17,000 peers with my company! Wow! A *million dollar roundtable* with our nameplate on it is waiting for each and every one of us. We just have to take action based on honesty and integrity, successfully earning the key to get in and take our rightful seat.

About Thomas

Thomas Ntuk, LTCP has been involved in the insurance and financial services industry since 1979, and is committed to providing the highest quality of service and sound advice based on client's needs. He has built an impressive sales record with his insurance company. In fact, he has set numerous production records, and remains one of the leading agents nationally in terms of sales.

He understands the special needs of professionals and business owners. He has also traveled to many parts of the country doing public speaking, conducting seminars, and teaching numerous classes to fellow agents, professionals and civic groups. Among his honors and awards, Thomas is a member of the prestigious international Million Dollar Round Table and a member of his company's President's Club.

Thomas helps educate his clients to make the right decisions in life and business. For example, with his insurance clients he simplifies the insurance concepts to help them choose the best way to protect what is important to them: family, paycheck and assets. On the other hand, he educates sales professionals to simplify all sales processes to help their clients to make the right choices. He has just launched online training webinars on a subscription basis to properly train sales professionals.

Thomas is very devoted to his family, worship, and community.

You can connect with Thomas at:
- Email: ntukspeaking@gmail.com
- Web: ntukspeaking.com
- Facebook: Thomas Ntuk
- LinkedIn

CHAPTER 16

CHELSIE ANTOS' BLUEPRINT FOR SUCCESS: THE POWER OF SISTERHOOD

BY JW DICKS & NICK NANTON

You won't find many entrepreneurs who started at a younger age than Chelsie Antos.

It's rare that someone on the verge of turning seventeen is involved with getting a mission-based business off the ground. And it's rarer still to see that business flourish and thrive through an extensive worldwide network that provides women in developing countries with a path out of poverty – and women in America with an entrepreneurial opportunity.

In this excerpt from our forthcoming book, *Mission-Driven Business*, Chelsie reveals her unique Blueprint for Success, which began when she was schooled in mission-based entrepreneurism at a very early age – you might say, from birth.

I had a background in business, my parents were pastors, but they were also entrepreneurs. They loved the model of business, they were passionate about how business could be used to change lives through pastoring.

That background came about because my Dad owned a very successful company that had been in my family for more than 50 years. And we developed our own soap line, water-processing cleaning systems, things

151

like that. He owned that business for most of our lives and, since I was home-schooled, I was able to go on field trips with him on his business trips once a week.

During these trips, we would spend time together and he would explain things to me, like how to deal with clients. I might be doing my math lessons while I was with him - and he would teach me how to relate that math in the real world, when you're doing business. My Mom was always starting different ministries, counseling-related, where she would work with women to find their potential and empower them to become world-changers. When I was 14, we took a business class that my Mom taught, and her first assignment was, we had to start our own business. So I started my own fitness training business. I had five different clients, that were probably doing me a favor too, but I helped them get to their goal weight and the way they wanted to look. They were happy at the end of it, and it was a cool process. And I ended up making enough money to buy a plane ticket to Italy.

Because of my homeschooling, I was able to enroll in college early. That's when I began to see that my parents had ingrained this sense of entrepreneurship in me – and that business can empower you, give you choices, give you freedom, and make you really believe in yourself. So I was passionate about helping other women do that too.

That led her to join her mother, Holly Wehde, as well as another mother-daughter team, Gretchen and Elisabeth Huijskens, in founding a new company that would, in fact, provide a measure of hope to women all across the globe who face incredibly difficult economic circumstances on a day-to-day basis.

One of our partners had started an orphanage in Haiti – which, of course, is a very important effort in that country. But she began to not only look at the babies that were being brought into the orphanage – but the mothers who were bringing them in. These were women who had to give up their children because they simply didn't have the resources to take care of them. And she could see that the orphanage, while necessary, wasn't really getting to the root of the problem. If these moms could be empowered and given an opportunity to make an income, they could support themselves and their children, instead of being at the mercy of whatever charitable endeavors might be available.

That was the seed of Trades of Hope. We were passionate about it, but you never know how you're going to get a dream to reality. So we used our own resources, we didn't take any income and did almost everything ourselves in the beginning. We built our own website, kind of figured it all out ourselves, which is awesome, because I had gone through the same process when I started my fitness business when I was 14 - so it prepared me to do all of this.

We began reaching out to artisans all over the world who could create and design products for us to sell. The idea was that these women in developing countries could make a steady income and we could import these products to the U.S. – and sell them through home parties – kind of like the Mary Kay process of selling beauty products in neighborhoods. Our idea was to reach out to American women who wanted to be entrepreneurs themselves. They would take these products and become our army of marketers. Basically, they bring our products to the American people, they speak for these women in developing countries and share their stores, and also make a percentage of whatever they sell.

Meanwhile, we would make sure that our artisans were paid fairly. They now make approximately 6 times more than they would normally earn in their countries. They make 100% of the asking price for their products – and it isn't until after we have paid the artisans that our entrepreneurs add on shipping costs, business expenses and their percentage for being a voice for women in need.

As Trades of Hope progressed, the founders had to forge viable connections with women artisans in undeveloped countries who could deliver marketable products to sell. They tapped into networks that would help them identify potential candidates.

At the beginning, we didn't have a ton of connections. We would research through missionary groups and other organizations that were doing very reputable things all over the world. We worked with missionaries who were ministering to women both mentally and emotionally, but maybe weren't quite able to meet their economic needs – we were hoping to fill in that gap. And that's how we did it, working through all kinds of groups that could help us identify women to work with us. They helped point the way for us. They knew the need, they were living in the same country, and they could say, "Work with these women here."

There were also some artisan groups already up and running that didn't have an American marketplace to sell through. They might be trying to sell in their own country, online, but, outside of those borders, no one had ever heard of them before. They were selling to the poor in their own country and didn't have access to a wider market. We would be able to bridge that gap for them.

That's how it worked in the beginning. Now that we're bigger, most of the artisan groups contact us and then go through our application process. We look at it as an awesome opportunity to help them grow and to work with us and our entrepreneurs – and, in turn, support themselves and their loved ones.

With the artisans in place, the next challenge for the Trades of Hope company was to find their circle of American entrepreneurs who would be willing to help sell their products, which include jewelry, handbags, scarves, home furnishings and more.

Our name for our American sellers was "passionate entrepreneurs." Our passionate entrepreneurs began as our friends and family, and the selling parties began in our home. Our friends thought we were a little crazy, but we showed them our first sample kit and shared the compelling stories of these women all over the world.

As the people we knew became compassionate entrepreneurs, their friends also wanted to participate. We did do some marketing to attract other consultants, but most of our recruiting was just done through word of mouth. We were very intent on reaching stay-at-home moms who wanted to do something on the side that gives them purpose as well as extra income. Our excitement for Trades of Hope was contagious and that's how we signed on many of our compassionate entrepreneurs.

At this time, we have a website and marketing campaigns – just, in general, more of a process in place - to find new consultants. Still, a lot of it is through word of mouth, which keeps us growing. We're currently up to about 1500 passionate entrepreneurs right now, located all over the United States.

To get them started, they purchase a starter kit online at our website at www.tradesofhope.com. We have various kits, running from $69 *(designed for college kids who want to sell out of their dorm) all the way to $399 (a kit that includes a wider selection of samples from our products and even a 30-day personalized website to use for marketing). Each kit contains some business supplies to get you started, as well as access to our online training resources.*

Chelsie has been gratified to see Trades of Hope succeed to such an amazing extent in such a short period of time. But she's also careful to make sure that she and the other founders don't lose touch with the enormous network they've created. To that end, she travels all across America to visit with their entrepreneurs and see first-hand how they follow through with their roles.

We're at this awesome point of growth and really feel like we're a sisterhood. That helps fuel the idea that their sisters are overseas as well and we're helping all of them. As we grow, we want to maintain that personal connection, that closeness that we're a sisterhood.

That's why I frequently travel the country to meet or catch up with our compassionate entrepreneurs. On the last trip, we had 31 different stops. We had meet-ups with all our compassionate entrepreneurs and I shared my personal story. I've been overseas lots of different times and met many of the artisan women who provide us with great products. Telling their stories to our U.S. consultants helps fuel their passion and makes them even more motivated to sell for these women.

I love our compassionate entrepreneurs - it's cool to have 1500 people that are all united in the same purpose of ending poverty. Many of these women, like I said, are stay-at-home moms – some also have other careers but they want to do something to change the world and end poverty, but they can't necessarily fly to Cambodia and live on the ground there. This is a way for them to actively make a difference in another woman's life and have a purpose that feeds their soul – all while making an income to help put food on their own table, send their kids to college, whatever financial need they might need to meet. They're passionate about Trades of Hope and that makes it exciting for us all to work together.

The artisans who provide products to Trades of Hope have overcome some incredibly traumatic incidents in their home countries – thanks to the company's outreach. One of the most powerful stories centers around one woman who felt completely hopeless about her future – to the extent that she felt unable to even go out her front door any longer.

A woman in Cambodia named Ya was the victim of what's called an acid attack. In Cambodia, in Pakistan, in a few countries in the developing world, the way to shame someone is by throwing acid on them and disfiguring their face – and often the victim is simply a woman who decided to speak out for herself. The attack can even happen at the hand of someone's father or brother.

Ya wrote to us about three years ago and told us, "I can't leave my home anymore. Every time I leave my home, I'm spit on, there's physical abuse, people call me horrible names because they believe I'm an animal." She went on to say that, in her community, they believe in reincarnation – and they also believe that Ya did something very evil in her past life, so she deserved this kind of humiliating treatment. It got to the point where even Ya believed it. What went through her mind like a drumbeat was, "I'm worthless, I'm an animal, I deserve this." She couldn't work her old job or ride on the bus to get to the marketplace, so she stayed in the house and grew completely depressed.

She thought we could help. She said, "I need something to do from my home, because I can't leave my house. I need to sell things I can make from my home so I can make money and take care of myself - would you be willing to work with me?" We were excited to help, so we sent her suggestions for things we thought she could make. As she started sending us products, she would ask "Is this a good idea? Do you like these colors?" We began to see her bloom. And she began to see herself as an artist.

Now, two years later, she's the head of an artisan group. She's excited she can help other women now; she doesn't just have to help herself. She flies to Thailand and Vietnam to get different products and the resources to get more. She views herself as a business woman, an artist and a designer and she feels wonderful about the fact that she can help other women like her.

It's the kind of movement that will change the face of poverty, because it's happening at the grassroots level right in these artisans' communities.

Currently, Trades of Hope employs artisans in the countries of Bangladesh, Cambodia, Colombia, Costa Rica, Guatemala, Haiti, India, Jordan, Kenya, Nepal, Peru, Philippines, Thailand, Uganda, United States and Vietnam – with, no doubt, more locations on the way.

To further its mission, Trades of Hope also has in place a program it calls "Gifts of Hope," where, throughout the year, the business gives donations to programs that promote long-term business or education. The money for these donations comes right out of the profits from their product sales.

The future looks great for Trades of Hope – and for the women it employs in this country and others all over the world. By using a business model to accomplish its mission, it has gone beyond the limited impact of one-time charitable contributions, which are obviously important. But it's more important to give these women an ongoing and viable way of making a living, so they are empowered to not only take care of themselves, but others in need in their communities.

We've doubled in size every year. We're estimating a tripling of growth this year, allowing us to make an even bigger dent in worldwide poverty. Last year alone, we employed almost 7,000 artisans all over the world.

Four years ago, this was just a dream. We were hoping we could accomplish something, but we didn't know how effective we could really be. But today, to reach the heights we're at is incredible.

We've been told that, when you help one woman out of poverty, she brings four other people with her. Our artisans are helping their children, aunts and uncles, parents, others in the community in need. And if that 1 to 4 formula holds up, that means we're impacting over 26,000 people. To think we might triple that this year is amazing.

Trades of Hope provides a unique and powerful template for others who want to create a Mission-Driven business that delivers these kinds of wide-reaching results – and Chelsie has some valuable advice for those who'd like to duplicate this Blueprint for Success?

Think of it as a partnership. None of us can do it by ourselves. We needed to learn from other people, we needed to find mentors, not just in business, but also in nonprofits and in home party companies.

You need to be bold and call them or email them and say, "Will you mentor me?" And just ask them to pour into your life, because none of us started off knowing much about any of this.

When you have something you're passionate about, you can change the world - but you do need those people who have walked before you. And you can't be afraid to ask them for help, because the only way you're going to get success is by asking for that help and seeking out those resources.

Trades of Hope is unique in our portraits of Mission-Driven organizations because of its innovative blend of business and altruism. The former feeds the latter, which is why Trades of Hope was not founded as a nonprofit. That very fact, in the founders' minds, strengthens their capabilities to do more and help more people. It motivates their entrepreneurs in America to sell as many products as possible – which, in turn, provides their artisans with a consistent and fair income that helps them pay for food, shelter and clothing.

Chelsie sums up the mission, as well as the company's method of fulfilling it, thusly:

We set up Trades of Hope as a business because we believe that model can be the mechanism of change. We love nonprofits, have friends that have nonprofits, but they serve different purposes. In the case of our artisans, charity will only get these women so far. We'd like to think compassion doesn't run out, but unfortunately it does. Here in the U.S., if you have trouble feeding your own kids, your compassion is going to run out. You're going to have to get a job. So why not allow the woman in the U.S. to make that income, while also helping her sister in a developing country to support herself?

About JW

JW Dicks, Esq., is a Wall Street Journal Best-Selling Author®, Emmy Award-Winning Producer, publisher, board member, and co-founder to organizations such as The National Academy of Best-Selling Authors®, and The National Association of Experts, Writers and Speakers®.

JW is the CEO of DNAgency and is a strategic business development consultant to both domestic and international clients. He has been quoted on business and financial topics in national media such as *USA Today, The Wall Street Journal, Newsweek, Forbes, CNBC.com*, and *Fortune Magazine Small Business*.

Considered a thought leader and curator of information, JW has more than forty-three published business and legal books to his credit and has co-authored with legends like Brian Tracy, Jack Canfield, Tom Hopkins, Dr. Nido Qubein, Dr. Ivan Misner, Dan Kennedy, and Mari Smith. He is the editor and publisher of the *Celebrity Expert Insider,* a monthly newsletter sent to experts worldwide as well as the quarterly magazine, *Global Impact Quarterly.*

JW is called the "Expert to the Experts" and has appeared on business television shows airing on ABC, NBC, CBS, and FOX affiliates around the country and co-produces and syndicates a line of franchised business television show such as, *Success Today, Wall Street Today, Hollywood Live*, and *Profiles of Success*. He has received an Emmy® Award as Executive Producer of the film, *Mi Casa Hogar.*

JW and his wife of forty-three years, Linda, have two daughters, three granddaughters, and two Yorkies. He is a sixth generation Floridian and splits his time between his home in Orlando and his beach house on Florida's west coast.

About Nick

An Emmy Award-Winning Director and Producer, Nick Nanton, Esq., is known as the Top Agent to Celebrity Experts around the world for his role in developing and marketing business and professional experts, through personal branding, media, marketing and PR. Nick is recognized as the nation's leading expert on personal branding as *Fast Company Magazine's* Expert Blogger on the subject and lectures regularly on the topic at major universities around the world. His book *Celebrity Branding You®*, while an easy and informative read, has also been used as a text book at the University level.

The CEO and Chief StoryTeller at The Dicks + Nanton Celebrity Branding Agency, an international agency with more than 1800 clients in 33 countries, Nick is an award-winning director, producer and songwriter who has worked on everything from large scale events to television shows with the likes of Steve Forbes, Brian Tracy, Jack Canfield (*The Secret*, creator of the *Chicken Soup for the Soul* Series), Michael E. Gerber, Tom Hopkins, Dan Kennedy and many more.

Nick is recognized as one of the top thought-leaders in the business world and has co-authored 30 best-selling books alongside Brian Tracy, Jack Canfield, Dan Kennedy, Dr. Ivan Misner (Founder of BNI), Jay Conrad Levinson (Author of the Guerrilla Marketing Series), SuperAgent Leigh Steinberg and many others, including the breakthrough hit *Celebrity Branding You!®*

Nick has led the marketing and PR campaigns that have driven more than 1000 authors to Best-Seller status. Nick has been seen in *USA Today, The Wall Street Journal, Newsweek, BusinessWeek, Inc. Magazine, The New York Times, Entrepreneur® Magazine, Forbes, FastCompany.com* and has appeared on ABC, NBC, CBS, and FOX television affiliates around the country, as well as on CNN, FOX News, CNBC, and MSNBC from coast to coast.

Nick is a member of the Florida Bar, holds a JD from the University of Florida Levin College Of Law, as well as a BSBA in Finance from the University of Florida's Warrington College of Business. Nick is a voting member of The National Academy of Recording Arts & Sciences (NARAS, Home to The GRAMMYs), a member of The National Academy of Television Arts & Sciences (Home to the Emmy Awards), co-founder of the National Academy of Best-Selling Authors, a 16-time Telly Award winner, and spends his spare time working with Young Life, Downtown Credo Orlando, Entrepreneurs International and rooting for the Florida Gators with his wife Kristina and their three children, Brock, Bowen and Addison.

Learn more at:

- www.NickNanton.com
- www.CelebrityBrandingAgency.com

CHAPTER 17

THE POWER OF POSITIVE THOUGHT

BY EDWARD FITZGERALD

It was a red rag to a bull.

About a year after my head injury, I expressed my frustration to my counsellor.

"I am working with a firm that is stuck in little league; I always used to consult with clients who were in the premier league."

"You are going through a period of bereavement for your memory loss," she said. "You won't be able to perform at the same professional level as you did before."

I got very angry. I snorted. I huffed and puffed. I actually became that bull for a moment. I remember saying a few things that I later regretted. But the other half of my reaction – the flipside of my anger – was that I promised myself, there and then, that I would become 100% more successful than I was prior to my injury!

I had total belief that the human brain is an amazing organ and that I would recover. I'd already discovered that I was able to learn and recall new information. I had social proof that others who had been told they would never walk again, had indeed walked unaided. And if they could do it, then so could I!

* *

Since my early teens, one of my passions has been yacht racing. In adulthood, racing yachts became a way of switching off the multiple threads of thought in my head, and just being "in the moment," just trying to make the crew work as a team, the yacht go as fast as possible and in the right direction tactically. And, obviously, win the race!

It was during a particularly windy (Force 7) Round The Island Race (50 nautical miles, Isle of Wight, UK) on 30th June 2012, that I was hit on the right side of my forehead by a stainless steel ring travelling at about 30 mph (48 km/h), and with the extra weight of the rope and the foresail to which it was attached.

The blow knocked me backwards, but not unconscious.

As we were leading our class at the time, I didn't want the nausea, the chronic headache, the floaters in my vision and my inability to focus beyond the mast to prevent us finishing. So, for the next 8 hours I raced on, sometimes conscious and sometimes drifting off to sleep on the side deck. At one point my friend and the owner of the 32-foot yacht, thought it would help with my 'sea sickness' if I took the helm which I did.

We completed the race 3rd in class, having lost the spinnaker over the side shortly after rounding the Needles lighthouse.

* *

Initially, I wasn't correctly diagnosed at Accident & Emergency (ER). It was only in the weeks and months that followed, with agonisingly intense headaches, vertigo and my slow and slurred speech (slow due to constantly searching for the right words), that I was referred to a consultant neurologist.

Among my other symptoms were hypersensitive hearing, smell and taste. I had a 'fog' that would descend, dulling my vision, and I would feel detached from the outside world. I was unable to hold onto a thought from one room to the next, and my family described me as wandering around in my own little bubble.

Whole sections of my memory were absent – it was as though someone had erased the index file that allowed me to access acquired knowledge and experiences.

I also discovered that I had become sensitive to abnormalities in the earth's magnetic field. This was as a consequence of being asked to investigate why a friends ME had become worse following installation of Solar (photovoltaic) panels at her home. After much research and investigation, I discovered the issue was actually abnormalities in the earth's magnetic fields. As I conducted measurements in both my own home and my friend's house, I found my own head injury symptoms were intensified in the stronger fields resulting in me needing several hours to recover.

I borrowed measuring instruments from my contacts in the scientific community, and thus was able to avoid spending time in the worst areas, which also involved moving my bedroom around so that I wasn't sleeping in the strong magnetic fields.

My neurologist attempted to explain my condition and my ability to carry on racing that day, including retrieving the sail from the water. He likened it to the injured service personnel he'd treated, explaining that, because I was extremely competitive, my brain was essentially stuck in a heightened state, the adrenalin acting as a physical and mental stimulant and a pain suppressant.

Whilst under the consultant neurologist, I was referred to several support organisations dealing specifically with head injuries. I found that I was unable to articulate my difficulties to them. I took it upon myself to learn about the brain, to understand the parts of its functioning that I was struggling with. From this exercise, I discovered that I was able to gradually learn new things and eventually recall them from memory.

After eight months, with only a relatively small residual income, and almost being made bankrupt because I was unable to manage my business affairs, I had to return to work. My neurologist advised me to forget international consultancy and take a contract closer to home.

This I did, and it was in reflecting on this 'demotion' that I expressed my frustration to the counsellor, who then unwittingly triggered my determination to improve – a bull's eye!

* *

On this new path, I started to realise that I was not conscious of why I was so successful prior to my head injury. I had not acknowledged all the great things I had done naturally; I didn't see their significance and the role they played in my life.

Whilst growing up, I was extremely fortunate to have loving parents who supported me, and largely allowed me to make my own decisions. This included the areas of study I wanted to follow and the schools I wanted to attend, for example. So, when I became stifled and disenchanted with corporate life at the age of 23, I decided that I wanted to set up my own specialist consultancy practice. The biggest single factor was that it enabled me to make my own choices.

I've never struggled with a lack of ideas: if anything, I had too many and the issue was identifying what to focus on. Interestingly, during my recovery, I discovered that the source for the abundance of ideas was my brain dwelling for extended periods in the theta wave state.[1] Previously I struggled to get good quality restful sleep, I would often enter a trance-like state whilst awake and at other times appear to fall asleep mid-conversation. I am now able to control this through meditation, and I find that my creative imagination is less detrimental to my health and mental state than it was previously.

As a consequence of my flexible mind-set and creative free thinking, I developed a rather eclectic consultancy practice mainly centred on technology (Electronics, Telecommunications and IT), advising clients how to overcome the technical and regulatory barriers in order to trade in over 80 countries. Whilst I was probably amongst the best at what I did, I also recognised early in my professional life that there were many things I didn't know or lacked the necessary skills to do.

I have essentially worked in the knowledge-based economy for the better part of my life and my acquired specific knowledge was (and still is) a currency. I believe it is the original currency. For me, knowledge is a legacy that transcends both time and the monetary systems devised by man, e.g., the bartering of goods and services, precious metals and gem stones, coinage and electronic cash.

---

1. For more information about brain wave activity and Theta state, you can download a resource on brain wave activity at: www.thesuccessblueprintbook.com/bonus.

Knowledge is your RICH inheritance from which you can learn and earn, applying your specific knowledge for money, whether that is in a job or in your own enterprise. General knowledge doesn't pay nearly as well!

In most instances, there is a time element associated with the exchange of your specific knowledge: the more value associated with your expertise, the more you are paid for your 'time'. My loss of memory, and of that specific knowledge I had previously been able to recall instantly, had a devastating impact upon my income potential.

It would be correct to say that my specific knowledge was securely locked away with all neural access disconnected!

The goal I had therefore set myself, was to assist my brain in reconnecting those broken neural paths.

But I had been actively engaged in personal development for around four years prior to my head injury. And that quest, coupled with the personality traits that were buried in my subconscious, must have been working for me. Various words spring to mind to describe those traits, words such as driven, stubborn, never give in, keep on keeping on.

* *

Sincerely, therefore, I thank the counsellor who told me I would have to accept my situation, as that moment was the key to activating those base survival instincts in my subconscious – the same ones that kept me racing that day. She ignited my new-found passion and commitment to achieving a full recovery.

Wealth and freedom does not come to those who tiptoe through life, they come to those with passion and a commitment to take action.

I can truthfully say that I am not the person I was before my head injury. I am now consciously aware of the character traits and skills that made me successful in the past and the skills and capabilities that will enable me to reach even greater success in the future.

I am now fully conscious of *the power of positive thought* and the amazing capabilities of the human mind, especially when those are coupled with emotion, desire and faith!

I therefore want to share with you the ten things I did to aid and ultimately achieve a successful recovery. You can apply these same steps to your own life to achieve all that you desire:

1. No alcohol *(I've never smoked or taken drugs – but those should be included)*. The one time I had a single celebratory drink at New Year, I was scared by the almost immediate regression that followed. Now that I am fully recovered, I do have the occasional social drink.

2. I started meditating twice a day, initially to relax, but in the process discovered the power of pure thought. I used these periods of tranquillity to explore and experiment with the power of my own mind and have since learnt to control both mind and body, using self-auto-suggestion to create the results I desired, thinking only of the things I wanted.

On this topic I'm truly thankful to my cousin Kellie for her spiritual and practical guidance, especially early on in my recovery.

3. I turned off all negative information streams from the media (I became, and still operate in, a *zero news zone*). If something was that serious that I needed to know about it, then I'd be told about it by family, friends or colleagues.

4. I immersed myself in personal development, my car became a mobile university stacked with audio books.

5. I exercised my mental muscles (against the recommendation of my neurologist) from around nine months after the injury. I attempted crosswords, quizzes and read mainly personal development books.

6. I learned many new things, researching different subjects including brain wave functionality and NLP.

7. I created a safe environment for a positive mental attitude: I had to erect a firewall to keep out the constant negativity I found myself subjected to, both in work and in social environments.

8. I have always operated in a *zero blame culture* and therefore refused to be drawn into an unhealthy blame culture atmosphere whenever

I came across it. I openly express to people the simple fact that everyone needs to take ownership of their actions, their tasks and ultimately their life.

9. I started working on my own positive action plan, partly to rediscover my core values and beliefs, and thereby to define a path for my new 'life plan.'

10. During my recovery, I followed the steps that felt natural to me. When I had no reference point in my conscious mind, I trusted my gut instinct.

Brian Tracy talks about the seven ingredients for success;[2] looking back on that painful period of my life I can identify that I unconsciously applied each of these elements to my life.

As my recovery progressed, I actively sought out others with a positive mind-set. I helped them to own their lives, using the positive action plan that I'd created. I now use this with my mentees to assist them in achieving their life goals.

*There is ultimately only one success, to live your life by your own choices and thereby **own your life**. If you don't own and take control of your life – someone else will!*

Science now acknowledges the existence of neuroplasticity, the brain's ability to reorganize itself by forming new neural connections *throughout life*, not just up until early adulthood. Through mental exercise and learning something new, you can stimulate new cell growth to overcome memory-related issues as I have proven.

That's why you should, in the words of Zig Ziglar, *'always be learning something new,'* regardless of your age.

* *

Once you accept that you can keep on learning, changing and growing, you can set yourself any challenge that you like.

---

2. Brian Tracy Seminar, "The Power of Personal Achievement." : Lesson 1 - The Psychology Of Achievement.

I believe that your strength of character – perhaps even the quality of your life as a whole – can be measured by the scale of the challenges that you set yourself and the adversities that you face along the way. And then, it's about how you react to those challenges and adversities:

- Do you step up to the challenge, or do you shy away?
- When you face a crisis, are you the only one that keeps your head whilst all around you are losing theirs?
- Do you have a stubborn streak that enables you to be focused, to persevere and be determined to reach your end goal in life?
- Do you have 100% belief in yourself?

If, for whatever reason, you currently lack any of these qualities, I invite you now to harness the power of positive thought, as I did, to bridge the gap between where you are now and where you want to be. After all . . .

The power of thought is the only thing over which you have
complete unchallenged and unchallengeable control.
~ Napoleon Hill

About Edward

Edward Fitzgerald has an eclectic business background having started, owned and operated businesses on three continents, the first at the age of 23 in 1992. Edward has been a trusted advisor to start-ups, multi-national organisations, NGOs and Governments. He has provided hands-on support, coaching and advice to almost 100 start-ups ranging from entrepreneurs in the making to VC-funded Silicon Valley success stories.

He has been privileged to have worked in 80 countries around the world and is actively looking to double this to 160 countries!

Edward is both a Mentor and Coach to University Graduates and Undergraduates as well as business clients. As a consequence of these engagements and running entrepreneurial boot camps, he firmly believes that it is essential that a number of key skills need to be taught at a far younger age in schools and high schools. Skills that foster a positive mental attitude, self-awareness, self-worth, true value, leadership, entrepreneurial endeavour and of course the power of positive thought!

Whilst Edward has a passion for technology and sailing, it is on those rare occasions when both are co-joined in a project that he loves most. His own yacht racing endeavours have taken him to South Africa, the Mediterranean Sea, North Atlantic, the Caribbean Sea, Australia, non-stop Round Britain and Ireland, plus countless Offshore and Fastnet Races. As with any sport, Edward has seen success in its many forms from trophies to pure survival – just thankful that he got both crew and boat home intact. As skipper and helm of the smallest yacht in the fleet (*J-Fever.com*, a J-92 at just 30 feet/9.2m long), the yachts were battered by high seas and violent storm Force 11 winds in the Royal Ocean Racing Club's Inaugural GPS Yacht Race. RORC organised the race to commemorate the 75th anniversary of the first Fastnet Race held in 1925. Edward and his crew took home the Talisker Trophy winning the race overall, despite minor damage to the boat his philosophy of 'never give in' resulted in them being the only yacht to finish.

However, it is the journey he undertook utilising the power of positive thought, which has had the most profound impact on his life and that of his family. A journey that ultimately led him to a full recovery from his head injury and made him conscious of the secrets of achieving success.

Subsequently therefore, Edward has become passionate about equipping people with the necessary tools to enable them to make a positive impact on both their lives and those around them. He wants to provide them with the choices, to own their life and enable them to think and grow rich in the process.

Edward, an international speaker, has spoken to audiences of around 200 on a variety of regulatory, trade, technology and entrepreneurship topics since 1994. Edward's focus since fully recovering from his head injury, has been to continue speaking internationally on the power of personal development and entrepreneurship.

Edward was also the Producer on the documentary film *Maximum Achievement* about Brian Tracy's life story.

You can connect with Edward at:
- successblueprint@edward-fitzgerald.com
- www.edward-fitzgerald.com
- www.linkedin.com/in/edwardfitzgerald
- www.twitter.com/edfitzgeralduk
- fb.me/edfitzgeralduk
- Instagram: edfitzgeralduk

CHAPTER 18

FOUR SECRETS TO BUILDING A SUCCESSFUL, SELLABLE BUSINESS

BY ANNE MARIE GRAHAM

INTRODUCTION

There are very simple reasons why some entrepreneurs are more successful than others, and why some go on to be multi-millionaires while others don't. In this chapter I will share with you the Four Secrets of my success that led to me building and selling a profitable business.

Like many business owners, I was very "technically competent" at what I do, devising and implementing Health Strategies in Organisations. Four years in, I realised that it wasn't growing any further and I realised that I had to start doing something differently if I wanted better results.

I learned that Brian Tracy was delivering a seminar in Dublin and having read some of his books, I took myself off to learn more about how I could get myself to the next level. I came away newly-focused with simple, practical principles of peak performance, a new mind-set and a clear plan of attack. Although simple in theory, their execution persistently was by no means easy. I needed steadfast discipline to put them into action to ensure that success unfolded. And success did unfold, which is why I want to share those four principles with you now.

The four (4) main principles that became an absolute part of my daily, weekly and monthly routine were:

I. Laser Focus
II. Action
III. Managing YOURSELF as opposed to your "Time Management"
IV. Persistence

I. LASER FOCUS: KNOWING WHAT IT IS YOU WANT, KNOWING YOUR GOAL

The indispensable first step to getting the things you want in life is this: decide what you want.
~ Ben Stein

The Oxford English Dictionary defines focus as "an act of concentrating interest or activity on something." That something is your goal.
• What do you want to achieve, by when?
• What do you need to do (and give up) to achieve it?
• Why do you want to achieve it?

These are all the essential elements of Laser Focus!

It is not the person with the highest qualifications in their field or the person with the best product or service on the market that necessarily achieves the most success. It is the person with Laser Focus as to what their goal is, that knows what they want, what they have to do to achieve it, and has a <u>written</u> targeted plan of action for achieving that goal, that will most likely achieve greater success more quickly. You also have to take responsibility for reviewing that goal and be 100% accountable so that you can ensure you are on track.

As a nurse by profession, the one thing the profession taught me is, "What gets measured gets done." You can have the most elaborate business plan in the world, but if you don't have a measurable goal of what you want to achieve and in what timeframe, it is unlikely to bring you the success you desire.

Goals need to be specific, measurable and they must stretch you out of your comfort zone in order to achieve them. Your goals should be constantly changing and moving you to the next level, but this only happens if you set goals, set deadlines and you measure your success in achieving them. For me, I set the goal of building a successful business with a ten-year exit strategy. I aimed to become a leading Workplace Health Service provider, working with National and International companies, employing highly-trained nurses and to achieve financial growth and profitability year on year. Through weekly and monthly review of my goals, I was able to achieve this and annually I reviewed my plan and set about planning new, bigger goals for the year ahead.

One of the fears we have when starting out in business is how are we going to achieve our goal, how will we get there? In my experience it is essential to do two things.

1. Set your ultimate goal and then break down the steps required to achieve it. What daily tasks do you need to do? Have you prioritised the top five steps of your goal? What weekly tasks and monthly tasks do you need to do? Again have a top five or at the very least a top three.

2. Identify why you want your goal, know why you have set this goal, that way, the "what you need to do" becomes clearer.

II. ACTION: THE ART OF MAKING IT HAPPEN

Inaction breeds doubt and fear, action breeds confidence and courage.
~ Dale Carnegie

Our actions are dictated by our behaviour and behaviour is largely controlled by our habits. If you want success, you must assess your habits. Once you are conscious of your habits, you can take action to replace poor habits with good ones and good habits with better ones.

Your entrepreneurial success starts with taking concentrated action, TODAY. What is it that you need to do TODAY to achieve your goals? This is what will lead you to achieving your weekly, monthly and annual goals and this will ensure you achieve your ultimate goal successfully.

Whilst having a vison for the future of your business is vital, if your action is planned for the future, for example next month, then it will always be in the future. This type of procrastination will not lead you to success; in fact it will likely demotivate and frustrate you as you are not moving forward. You are standing still which really means you are going backwards. In my opinion, my success has been ultimately due to doing these simple actions consistently.

- Firstly, I set daily goals and writing them down in order of priority. I have always used a "Top 5" and looked at the five most important tasks for me to do today that will move me forward. Having worked my way through my list, I then ticked them off when they were achieved. The feeling of ticking all the boxes and knowing I was moving forward is hugely gratifying and this becomes addictive.

- Secondly, you must get into the habit of practising discipline. As a nurse I was no stranger to having to practice discipline, having had it instilled in me in my training, but there were still times when I had to give myself a reality check and say, Anne Marie, just get on with it, just do it. This is ShowTime! It is only through doing the difficult, unpleasant, least enjoyable tasks, that you come out of your comfort zone and it is here where you will achieve your greatest success.

As I have already stated, what gets measured gets done! It doesn't really matter how you choose to measure, as long as you have some measurement for the actions you are taking to achieve your goal.

Let me share a sample of the targeted plan I had for my goals on an ongoing basis.

Daily Goals: My Rule of 5

1. Make Sales Calls.
2. Send follow up proposals/promotional material to prospects spoken to and met with.
3. Update Prospects and Progress Spreadsheet.
4. Call one current client to set up "Quality Control Meeting" this month (designed to review level of service, but also keeps me in front of our customers and try and get more business and/or referrals).
5. Read for 30 mins per day.

Weekly Goals: My Rule of 5

1. Call 20 prospects per week (*and speak to someone* rather than leaving a voice mail).
2. Meetings - I measured that this led to two meetings per week and a 50% conversion rate meant one new client per week.
3. Quality Control Review and follow up with five current clients.
4. Review Debtors and Creditors list.
5. Complete and review Weekly Progress Diary.

Monthly Goals: My Rule of 5

1. Achieve a minimum turnover of $41,666 per month with a Profit of $20,000 per month and review monthly management accounts to assess target.
2. Review Time Management Schedule: Daily Plan, Weekly Plan, Actual Time Spent, document monthly score.
3. Develop and update Prospects Listing.
4. Document five things you have learned and applied from this month's reading
5. Review this month's goals achieved.

III. MANAGE YOURSELF RATHER THAN "TIME MANAGEMENT"

Either You Run the Day or the Day Runs You.
~ Jim Rohn

The Pareto Principal states that 20% of your activity will account for 80% of your business growth and success. To that end it is vital that you spend your time doing the highest value, highest productivity and highest revenue generating tasks as a matter of priority on a daily basis.

Let's look at my goals above and apply the 80/20 rule. In relation to My Rule of 5, let's say we take 10 tasks and apply the 80/20 rule, 2 of these tasks contributed most to my success. The two highest value tasks for me were calls to prospects/customers, and arranging meetings to get in front of them to win business thus generating revenue and sales growth. My second highest value task was to send proposals relevant to their needs and follow up on these until a decision had been made.

Planning your tasks is essential to maximise your effectiveness in carrying out high value tasks in a timely manner. Plan tomorrow today, plan next week this week, plan next month this month and PRIORITISE!

One of the most powerful tools you can use to assess how effectively you use your time is to keep a time diary, even just for one week. This is one of the biggest 'eye opening' things I have ever done. For one week, I kept a diary that assessed for every 30 minute period exactly how I had used my time. I quickly realised on review of that one week that there were many parts of my day where I was not performing my highest value and highest productivity tasks, and I had total clarity on where I was using my time most and least effectively.

IV. PERSISTENCE

Persistence is Self-Discipline in Action.
~ Brian Tracy

One of the single biggest reasons why some entrepreneurs succeed and others fail is their ability to persist. You need to persist through fear, failure, disappointments and challenges. Persistent people usually view these as opportunities to learn, grow and do things differently.

Six years into my business, Ireland went through the worst recession in its history, something that was documented globally. With the Irish State almost bankrupt, organisations turned their attention towards spending only on the essentials, and in many organisations Proactive Health Strategy wasn't one of them.

Suddenly Health and Wellness Activities were discontinued overnight as they were seen as an "unnecessary spend" – particularly as many organisations were making people redundant. These activities represented 70% of my business and revenue! In Ireland it is estimated that 1-in-5 businesses went out of business in the recession.

Persisting Through a Recession

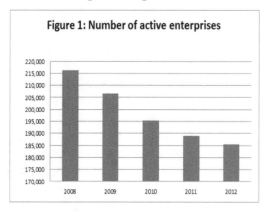

CSO, Ireland 2012

Determined not to be one of the causalities after six years of hard work, I looked at what I could do differently, what other services I could offer and how I could use clients' current needs to offer services that met them.

I realised that Occupational Health, obligations under Statutory Health and Safety legislation were now pivotal to an organisation's survival as well as to my own, and so I offered more of these services. I networked in networks where there would be Human Resource Personnel, the buyers of this service. I built up a team of associate trainers who worked under my company's brand. I did compliance review meetings with all clients with the purpose of ensuring they had all statutory obligations covered, whilst helping me gain and retain business. For employees who went on a 12-month contract and retainer, I offered them some additional incentives.

One of my competitors approached me in 2012 as their business had gone into decline, and I acquired that business. My persistence and discipline had paid off and ensured my survival and not only did I survive, I thrived!

CONCLUSION

You can hire the best business coach who'll help you set your goals, the best accountant to keep your finances on track, the best PR agent to help you sell, but the one thing you cannot hire...is someone to reach your goals for you. The only person who can reach your goals...is you!

About Anne Marie

An inspirational leader in her field, Anne Marie Graham successfully sold The Healthforce Group in 2015, following a bid between an Irish Provider and a U.S Provider, which led to the acquisition of her company with Healthcare Screening Ireland, where she now works on the Senior Management Team.

Anne Marie, who is also an experienced trainer, has worked with a number of Corporates across a wide variety of sectors both nationally and internationally, helping them to develop a Health Strategy that maximises the benefits and values of best practice for Employee Health and Wellbeing. She has also worked as an Advisor in relation to Occupational Health Statutory Obligations for Corporate National and International clients including successful defence of medical legal cases for over 15 years.

An experienced speaker on radio, she has presented to a number of businesses and Business Networks for almost 15 years. She has served as National Chairperson for the Irish Nurses & Midwifery Organisation Occupational Health Branch – which saw her innovate in areas such as Lobbying, Policy Development and speaking to organisations on Best Practice. She has also lectured in Nursing Studies with Dublin City University, a University that has forged its reputation as Ireland's University of Enterprise.

Anne Marie has served on a number of Boards as a Non-Executive Director, bringing the value of her Business Experience and Expertise to these organisations.

Trained in Nursing at Beaumont Hospital Dublin, Ireland's Centre of Excellence for Neuroscience, she further achieved an Honours Degree in Health Studies from London's Royal College of Nursing, one of the United Kingdom's leading Colleges in the field, as well as a Master's in Occupational Health.

Her strength, focus and determination led her from this to setting up The Healthforce Group in 2004, acquiring the company Employee Health in 2012 and selling The Healthforce Group in 2015.

CHAPTER 19

THE MAGIC OF PERFORMING CEO DUTIES

BY ARTIE MCFERRIN

Have you ever read a self-improvement book, and after reading the last page, said to yourself, "I didn't learn anything new!" Success is difficult to attain for so many people because, in many aspects, the steps to be successful are just as elusive and intangible as success itself. I am a firm believer in emulating successful people. For example, I often ask myself, "Would Warren Buffet do this?" If I can't picture him doing it, I don't do it. Napoleon Hill went a step further. When he wrote *Think and Grow Rich*, he sat down and extensively interviewed 500 of the most successful people of his time to compile a book of success principles. Many of the names of those he interviewed might ring a bell – Ford, Rockefeller, Edison, Roosevelt, Wright, Taft, Carnegie, Gillette. He wanted to know how they did it. He wanted to deconstruct excellence to create a blueprint for success.

As an entrepreneur since 1975, I wanted to develop a better way to blueprint my own success. One of the first things I advise is to find a mastermind group, or peer advisory board, such as I did after nearly 24 years as an entrepreneur at the age of 55. As a new-member gift for joining my local mastermind group, Vistage, in 1998, I received an audio tape by Walt Sutton called "The Duties of a CEO." The instant I listened to it, I knew it was the missing link for me. I had studied countless business and motivational books, listened to every audio program on success principles, and attended every seminar I could for over 30 years. But after listening to Sutton, I discovered my biggest weakness: I thought

181

I was responsible for everything in my business. Was I successful? Yes. At that time, I had turned a dilapidated research facility that should have been condemned into a thriving multimillion-dollar chemical plant, along with some other plants, and had achieved a personal net worth of over $100 million. But I was enslaved by crises, constant problems and a slowed growth rate. By focusing on Sutton's duties of a CEO, I immediately got my business steaming ahead much more smoothly.

In the process, I also learned to utilize the 80/20 principle, in which the CEO focuses on only 20 percent of the effort, which produces 80 percent of the results. Few people understand that *all* CEO duties should encompass the 20 percent that allows the business to achieve 80 percent of its productivity. In this chapter I will touch on how focusing on CEO duties helped me to progress so much more than the success principles or other techniques of many great business books. Acting on the CEO duties listed will also teach you how to practice the intangible 80/20 principle.

CEO Duty #1 – Separate CEO duties from manager duties.

Manager duties should be for managers, not CEOs! They are toxic for a CEO. In the beginning I helped manage and direct every department of my businesses, as most had major problems. But after listening to Sutton's theory, I started to separate the CEO duties that matter most from the manager duties. I homed in on the duties that only I could perform. Vistage helped me learn where I should focus my attention by combining my knowledge with other CEOs' years of experience. Those monthly meetings allowed me to better understand not only my duties, but also how to grow my business.

Being a CEO became so much more productive and fun than being enslaved by manager duties. I found that narrowing my responsibilities was infinitely more effective than limiting myself to the success principles. Plus, it is so much *easier* to focus on CEO duties than all the other approaches. It is magic, in fact. It took me a long time to learn what even most CEOs never understand.

CEO Duty #2 – Keep a true positive mental attitude.

Having a "can-do" attitude is paramount to your business' success.

According to Malcolm Gladwell in *Outliers*, it takes a minimum of 10,000 hours of the "right stuff" over a minimum of 10 years in the job alone to develop this mastery of successful thinking. Most entrepreneurs possess that "can-do" spirit, but to successfully grow your business beyond a certain point, you must develop a stronger positive mental attitude without the fear of failure.

CEO Duty #3 – Develop the right survival mindset.

In addition to positive thinking, you also must develop the "boot-camp tough" survival mindset when it comes to your business and finances. While few of us begin with good financial habits, the people who never learn will be undone by financial irresponsibility no matter their talent. Heed the old saying to "hope for the best and prepare for the worst."

CEO Duty #4 – Build a team of the right people on your bus.

This can be one of the hardest things to accomplish, but the people you hire have to be compatible with the desired culture of your business. Obtaining, training and retaining the right-minded people in all positions was a long time in the making for me. Even though it is an ongoing effort, it is one that cannot be overlooked. Only the CEO has the insight to do this well. Managers tend to want people now to do chores, while CEOs want the right people to build their future dreams.

CEO Duty #5 - Identify and maximize your secret, unfair advantage.

Success is heavily determined by the fact that each of us has unique, genius talent in an area that surpasses that of others. To discover my secret, unfair advantage, all I had to do was see where most of my profitable business was coming from and why. I began to maximize it by pushing our sales where we had an advantage. Conversely, I also learned not to compete where our competitors had an unfair advantage, even though we could have done the work.

As a result of identifying my secret advantage and building our sales and prices around it, nearly every aspect of my business became more profitable over the following year or two. Perceiving this progress, I continued to develop my unfair advantage to grow my profits even more. What is your secret, unfair advantage? What do you do better than your competitors? It's nearly always the few CEOs with the most profit who know what drives their business best.

CEO Duty #6 – Navigate your ship.

Think of your business as a ship. As a CEO, it is your duty as captain to navigate your ship into deep rivers of profit to solidify your business' future. The CEO is the only person who has the right insight to make the major decisions regarding which course to chart. And as a CEO, you know that these decisions often can have massive repercussions. Turn your ship down the wrong canal and you could find yourself in shallow waters that aren't deep enough to sustain your business! These navigational (directional) decisions must be guided and controlled by the captain (CEO).

CEO Duty #7 – Create a great culture.

I have always used personality profiles to determine which applicants would fit best in our existing culture. Hiring the people with the right mindset makes training much easier. You can always train for skill – you can't train for culture. A great culture solves many problems – the least of which is attrition. I have numerous people I hired in the '70s who are still working for me! When you hire the right people and set the tone of your business, you create a culture that leads to success. That harmonious day-to-day interaction breeds achievement.

A large part of culture is making sure that not only do you have the right people on your ship, but that they're in the right seats! For an entrepreneurial business, you have to hire differently than you would if you were running a corporate bureaucracy. Huge corporations want static, linear thinkers with Type A personalities. After 40 years in business, I have found that these don't work well in my environment. I need more of a semi-disorganized, freethinking, work-motivated, competitive and positive person. Some of the best hires I've made were employees who previously worked for other small businesses where they had a wide range of duties.

CEO Duty #8 – Build your business' process excellence.

This dynamic CEO duty develops the excellence that will help you build a highly valuable and sustainable business. This is a process that encompasses all of the CEO's duties. The whole business should be striving for excellence by following the CEO's leadership. The vast number of inexperienced and unsuccessful CEOs are trying to make profits without first building excellence. It's not very effective. I learned the hard way that good people and hard work alone cannot make up for average processes, which enslave your employees with problems, double work, crises, delays, rework and a slew of other production issues. All business is essentially organizing chaos with the right level of flexibility, leadership, teamwork and processes to make it productive and profitable.

Think differently than everyone else – go for smooth and simple, not perfect and complex. In smooth operations, a business maintains fast, simple, efficient and economical processes, with the employees possessing the flexibility and autonomy to fix problems and make decisions on the spot. This requires a good performance-based culture of working in harmony with good CEO leadership to pull it off. Pause here for a moment to think about that. If the autonomy and culture are in place, the many daily flaws are handled easily without delay and are rarely passed on to the customers or management.

CEO Duty #9 – Develop your goals.

As stated in a Brian Tracy audio program, "Success is goal setting, and all else is commentary." Effective long-term goal setting is paramount to achieving great success. Ever wonder why it's so difficult to set goals and meet them? It's because of your mindset and lack of mastering the goal-setting process. The first step is to possess a positive mental attitude and set aside any self-doubt. No matter what your goal is, begin here. This first step allows you to have the insight, understanding and confidence to achieve your goals.

Here's a Tracy trick I use when I set my goals: List 20 different approaches to achieve your goal. The next day, without looking at the list from the day before, do it again and try to list another 20 approaches. After the first few approaches it becomes quite difficult, but don't quit. This is the point at which your creativity will emerge and you will birth your best ideas! In the meantime, you may fulfill your life's purpose through accomplishing your overarching goals. Your plans will always be in the process of change. Be ready. When I began my goal setting, it took me three years and many rewrites to start getting results! You will experience failure along the way – it is inevitable. But, make the choice to build on it. Use that experience to strengthen your success muscles.

CEO Duty #10 – Focus on entrepreneurial action.

None of the learning, experience and progression happens without entrepreneur action, which creates the sales, orders, manufacturing, delivery and serving of customers. The CEO has to lay the groundwork for others so that he or she can pull back and have a birds-eye view of the business. Here is where you can practice the 20 percent of effort that leads to 80 percent of results.

Action will remove the doubts that theory cannot solve.
~Tehhi Hsieh

All the effort in the world will not guarantee success. But when you work smarter by developing your proven CEO duties that matter most and that only you can do, your path becomes much clearer. You become less enslaved by linear manager duties, vague success principles and millions of pages of information. You can, in turn, more effectively develop yourself, your team and your business culture by focusing on these duties. The roadmap to success is filled with curves, detours and potholes, and there's more than one way to get there. Use your internal compass and your magical CEO duties to guide you toward your life's purpose. Take the first step with me on this path to success.

About Artie

Artie McFerrin is a successful entrepreneur, author, public speaker and chemical engineer, owning as many as nine chemical plants around the world. In 1975 he turned a dilapidated research facility into a multimillion-dollar profitable chemical plant. After over 40 years as a bootstrap entrepreneur, Artie attained a level of expert knowledge in chemical specialty products. Serving hundreds of clients every year, Artie certainly has discovered his niche in the chemical world. He has founded, bought, built, expanded and sold other businesses, amassing a fortune along his road to success.

Regarded as a thought leader in the chemical world, Artie still holds his professional engineering license, remains an active chemical engineer and is continually looking for ways to grow his businesses. Not one to rest on his laurels, in 2015 Artie authored his first book, *The Executioner – Implementing Intangible, Elusive Success Principles.* It is a comprehensive, modernized update of Napoleon Hill's 1937 success classic, *Think and Grow Rich.*

Artie graduated in 1965 from Texas A&M University with his bachelor's degree in Chemical Engineering, and remained for his master's degree. He spent two years in the Corps of Cadets at Texas A&M, where he learned the importance of discipline and culture. His love for A&M is transparent, as he is the largest contributor to A&M Athletics and one of the top contributors to the university overall. Artie was inducted into the Hall of Honor for the Corps and Athletics, and received the Distinguished Alumni of Chemical Engineering honor from the university. He has served as chairman of the Chemical Engineering Advisory Board, President's Corps of Cadets Board of Visitors, Chairman of the 12th Man Foundation Board of Trustees, Texas A&M Research Foundation and the Engineering School Advisory Council.

Artie and his wife, Dorothy, established an endowment in 2005 to support Texas A&M's Department of Chemical Engineering, which now bears his name. Many of Artie's other contributions are visible throughout the campus in ten other facilities. As a true industry leader, Artie wants to give students more opportunities to be entrepreneurs and follow in his footsteps. Artie was recognized as the chemical industry recipient of the Chemical Education Foundation Vanguard Award in 2009.

An advocate for helping others, Artie is a member of Vistage, a mastermind group of CEOs that provides peer advisement, leadership training and business coaching. Artie uses his positive mental attitude to better his quality of life. After beating cancer, Artie looks at each day as one more chance to leverage his wisdom and learn even more.

Artie and his wife of 50 years, Dorothy, proudly own one of the world's largest private collections of Fabergé. Much of their collection is shown at the Houston Museum of Natural Science. His son Jeff and daughter Jennifer have blessed him with four granddaughters, Sydney, Karsen, Allie and Lexi – all of whom he enjoys immensely.

Learn more at:
- www.ArtieMcFerrin.com

CHAPTER 20

INSPIRE FOR BETTER LIVING

BY IMRAN Y. MUHAMMAD, Ph.D.

A bright, intelligent child with an insatiable thirst for knowledge was born into a business family in the late 60's where education was not a priority. Yet he got admission into the best school because he was on scholarship – where no expense was required to be paid by his family. In Grade 3 he was tutoring students of Grade 5, and at Grade 6 he was tutoring Mathematics and English to Grade 9 students. He was always curious, open, enthusiastic and adventurous to explore, know and learn new things.

In particular, he was always inquisitive about how things manifest themselves in life; all his income earned through tuitions was spent on books in the field of intuition, magic, parapsychology, pseudo sciences. The child started experimenting on mental and spiritual dimension manifestation already when he was in Grade 5. The thirst was on until he finished high school and the demand came from his family to stop his education and join the family business because of the ideology: "Why do an MBA, when you can hire an MBA?" By that time he had already made up his mind to get a university education. His strong will clashed with his parents' expectations.

Due to the ideological difference with his family, this rebellious teenager of 16 decided to leave the country on his own with a strong driving purpose, i.e., to fulfill his thirst for knowledge, to identify himself, and finding out who he really was, what would be his own identity? The decision was a tough one, but his sheer determination, hard work, and optimistic attitude got him through it. His faith remained a driving force throughout his journey to success:

Sheer Determination, Hard work, and an Optimistic attitude are the Keys to Success.

Luckily he found a scholarship for his B.S. program in Computer Science. He had to maintain high grades in academics to retain this scholarship and his student-visa status. He embraced all suffering, pain, and obstacles with patience and courage because of his strongly-held belief:

Precious metal like gold has to melt in fire, and a diamond has to be cut, polished and go through a certain process before it is converted into fine-crafted jewelry.

His keen interest was always in the subjects of Psychology, Sociology, and Morality Ethics since he was captivated by the idea of how the human mind works to shape our intricate personalities and diverse behaviors, the role it plays in our everyday life and why people are so disparate from each other. As business was in his blood, he decided to take additional business subjects such as accounting, marketing and management to pursue his Master's in Business Administration. His constant struggle, efforts and hard work paid off well, and he finished his Master's degree with pleasing results. He then stepped into the arena of his professional life with great confidence regarding his future, and great confidence in his ultimate success. His thirst for knowledge, however, was not quenched, but continued to be present.

Without inheriting a single penny from his family, at the age of twenty-five he started his clothing business, and he was met with failures and roadblocks and ultimately had to close down his business within one year without making any money. He had strong convictions like: *don't fall in love with your business* and *when some business is not working, then it is the right time to close the business*. Hence, his early failure did not deter him from leaping forward.

He did not lose hope and enthusiasm while struggling through periods of failure. He pushed through these limitations and had a breakthrough because of his underlying operative principles:

There is no failure, always feedback.
and
As today is better than yesterday, therefore
tomorrow will be even better than today.

His strongly held adaptive principles and visionary characteristics of openness, imagination, creativity and persistence preserved him and helped him to start his new venture of setting up a business from scratch. Now, endowed with true entrepreneurial skills as well as with guts, he decided to purchase a bankrupt fast food chain store on a 100% loan and turned it around into the food chain store with the highest sales in the territory. The strategy was ***to search for businesses closing down and turn them around into profitable ventures***. Confidence was at its peak and the underlying conviction was:

Risks pave the way for brand new and exciting opportunities.

He was allegedly wise; his willingness to take risks and his dedication, wealth of knowledge and self-confidence unwrapped the way for a future that was incredibly bright. Money started pouring in, his hands were turning everything into gold – whichever business he acquired. He developed multiple businesses, ranging from *high-tech construction, renewable energy and luxury automobiles to premium jewelry, food distribution, and premium textiles, etc.*, on three continents in the world. The secret of success in his businesses was a combination of genetically-inherited business information from his father (who had never been to school), the wisdom of the East and higher education of the West.

The principles at the root of his incredible success in business were:

- *A Product/Service should be of the highest quality in its category* – as quality creates feelings and emotions in its users. That principle eventually generates product or service preferences, influencing users' purchase preferences.
- *The product must be backed up by warranty/guarantee* – as it gives a sense of protection and security to the customer, ultimately building their loyalty.
- *Only compete with your own product, the next one should be better than the previous one.* He found out that customers are not interested in knowing that your product or service is better than

191

any other product: they are more interested in how your product or service is different.

- **Be proud to use your own product/service** – if you can't or aren't willing to use your own product or service with pride, then no else will.

He knew that customers don't always understand the value of a product, thus his strategy was: *to use the best means to communicate the value of the product/service to your customers to revolutionize their experience and make the venture worthwhile.*

In addition, in business, he always ensured his customers have an outstanding experience and receive value. His philosophies driving his success were:

1. **The customer should receive more value than what he is paying for when purchasing your product/service,**

2. **Always take the product back if the customer is not satisfied.**

During his journey of success into multiple businesses, he attended a stage hypnosis show by chance and all of a sudden, the suppressed child's curiosity of hidden unseen power popped up. Once again a search started for knowledge. It started with the misconception that through hypnosis, one can control anyone without his will. Application of Power is the basic instinct of a human being. He believed that learning never stops and there is always something more to learn and do. He excelled in the field of mind sciences and attained personal and professional training in every possible field of the mind sciences, i.e., Hypnosis, Neuro Linguistic Programming (NLP), ESP, etc.

This young man one fine day was thinking what more he could ask from nature. And all of a sudden he realized that he already had achieved/ received what any person in the world could possibly ask from nature, and this even in abundance: *health, wealth, popularity, status, family (a perfect wife with two kids, a son and a daughter), and education (Gold medalist throughout his academics – from primary school to PhD).*

So the big question arose: "What is the purpose of life?" Why was he sent to this world and why were there so many blessings on him? And with a "search within" on a journey inside, the reply came: '**You are the "chosen one"** for other fellow beings. Your job is to make this world better for others.'

'You are blessed, so that you can *"Inspire People for Better Living"* and here comes the foundation of the registered forum – Transformation International Society (TIS). The TIS has a vision *"to aspire to inspire optimism in everyone we come in contact with, by infusing their hearts, minds and souls with enthusiasm, hope and positive thinking."'*

The TIS operates on the ideology that *you are always on the cause side of the situation*; it means through proper steps you can solve any problem. Your remote control is in your hand. When you are willing to take control and you refuse to be a victim of your external circumstances and your luck, you are willing to take charge of your life and circumstances. Some other ideological principles of TIS are: **solutions are created before the problem, one just has to search for them and the solution lies in people.**

The TIS believes that people have all the resources, yet they are not producing the best results in any field because of their constant negative state of mind. Their unlimited, untapped resources need to be drawn, channeled and trained to produce positive results in their lives.

The TIS mission and objectives are to inspire and motivate people to positively change their lives by making positive changes within; to change hopelessness, misery and melancholy in society into hope, determination and motivation; to teach skills that will create positive life changes; to help identify and remove personal barriers, and replace them with effective and powerful tools to change lives; to help members achieve the right mental, emotional, spiritual and physical states to achieve their goals and perform at their fullest potential, achieving excellence in whatever they do.

The TIS is achieving its objectives via regular Free Consultation and Therapeutic Services, monthly Free Seminars and via TV programs, of which almost 700 programs are already broadcasted on all leading channels. Moreover, TIS arranges experiential-based and educational seminars, training workshops and awareness programs of international repute with well-known self-made people and internationally-known experts and trainers.

Yesterday's little bright and intelligent child and today's Dr. Imran Y. Muhammad, attained a Master Trainer status in every possible field. He is a Silva Ultramind ESP Trainer; Board Certified International Master Instructor of Hypnotherapy for the National Guild of Hypnotists (NGH™, USA) (the first in Pakistan and the third in Asia) and the only NLP Master Trainer in Pakistan trained by all the Co-Creators and Developers of NLP – John Grinder, Richard Bandler, Frank Pucelik, and Robert Dilts. He is the Developer of the Abraq® Healing System. He is also a certified Intuitive Counselor, Motivational Public Speaker, Facilitator, Trainer and Coach based in USA, Canada, Europe, UK, Australia and Pakistan.

In recognition of Dr. Imran's outstanding performance in the field of public service and education, the President of Pakistan has conferred on him the highest civil award, the Sitara-I-Imtiaz (Star of Excellence). Furthermore, upon noticing his enthusiasm and never-ending efforts in the field of education and social service, recognition awards were given to Dr. Imran by the governments of The Netherlands, Canada and the USA.

He is blessed with all that a man can ask from nature: **Health** (he looks younger than his 22-year-old son), **Wealth** (earns more than he can spend), **Popularity** (with 700 TV programs and half-a-million social media fans, he is already a celebrity), **Status** (achieving the highest civil award and awards from the governments of The Netherlands, Canada and the USA), **Family** (a perfect loving home maker with the most obedient son and daughter, who are achieving the highest recognition in academics and for good moral conduct) and **Education** (Gold medalist throughout his academics, from primary school to PhD).

His journey doesn't stop here, as he believes that our lives have more meaning when we serve others. He is determined to make each life he touches a little better in every possible way. When you make people happy, nature will give you more than what you can expect.

The value of a man should be seen in what he gives and not in what he is able to receive. Only a life lived for others is a life worth living.
~ Albert Einstein

Being a smart business person, he has a firm belief in the investment plan given in the holy book by the Almighty Creator promising a rate of return of up to 700% for those who spent their wealth for fellow beings.

The example of those who spend their wealth in the way of Allah is like a seed [of grain] which grows seven spikes; in each spike is a hundred grains. And Allah multiplies [His reward] for whom He wills. And Allah is all-Encompassing and Knowing.
~ Holy Quran Chapter 2:261

About Imran

Dr. Imran Y. Muhammad is a self-driven person and the Almighty Creator has bestowed on him a marvelous character, a gorgeous personality and exceptional qualities regarding practical initiative, courage and perseverance. Above all, he has the determination to bring positive change into the lives of the people of our society and is devotedly working for this noble cause.

Dr. Imran is a Pakistani and Canadian citizen. He is a reputable and highly-qualified personality both nationally and internationally. He is the Managing Director of a Multinational Group of Companies involved in various businesses (High-tech Construction, Renewable Energy, Luxury Automobiles, Premium Jewelry, Food Distribution, Premium Textiles, etc.).

Dr. Imran is a Board Certified International Master Instructor of Hypnotherapy for the National Guild of Hypnotists (USA) – the first in Pakistan and the third in Asia – and the only NLP Master Trainer in Pakistan trained by all the Co-Creators and Developers of NLP: John Grinder, Richard Bandler, Frank Pucelik and Robert Dilts. He is a certified Intuitive Counselor, Motivational Public Speaker, Facilitator, Trainer and Coach working in the USA, Canada, Europe, UK, Australia and Pakistan.

Dr. Imran is a distinguished social campaigner. He is the developer of the Abraq® Healing System and Founder of the TRANSFORMATION® International Society (TIS). The TIS has a vision *"to aspire to inspire optimism in everyone who it comes in contact with, by infusing their hearts, minds and souls with enthusiasm, hope and positive thinking."* The TIS helps both young and old people, irrespective of their age, sex, ethnic background, religion, etc., to make the most of their life by teaching them to optimize their performance, boost their motivation, achieve excellence and live their life to its fullest – using the latest human development technologies and wisdom of the ages via regular Free Consultation and Therapeutic Services, monthly Free Seminars and TV programs, of which almost 700 programs are already recorded on all leading channels. Moreover, TRANSFORMATION® arranges experiential-based and educational seminars, training workshops and awareness programs of international repute with well-known, self-made people, and internationally-known experts and trainers.

Dr. Imran has the honor of introducing Mind Sciences Transformation Technologies to Universities in Pakistan, and in this regard he is providing free teaching services at Universities.

In recognition of Dr. Imran's outstanding performance in the fields of public service and education, the President of Pakistan has conferred on him the highest civil award of *Sitara-I-Imtiaz* (The Star of Excellence).

Furthermore, upon noticing his enthusiasm and never-ending efforts in the fields of education and social service, Recognition awards have been given to Dr. Imran by the Governments of Canada and the USA.

You can contact Dr. Imran at:
- info@transformation.com.pk
- www.transformation.com.pk
- https://www.facebook.com/TransformationInspireForBetterLiving

CHAPTER 21

LEVERAGE YOUR SELF-ENTERPRISE

BY MOENIQUE PHILLIPS

My definition of self-enterprise is one's perspective of one's self as the equivalent of a profitable business. You provide goods and services to an employer (or client) in exchange for wages. As the physical owner of yourself, you need to learn to best manage yourself in order to create the most beneficial situation possible. Mind your business by adding value to yourself.

The self-enterprise blueprint I've created provides four characteristics that make the enterprise more valuable. I began this journey, and started to develop my blueprint about 12 years ago when I was introduced to my first network marketing organization. To be honest, I had the same perspective that most people do who are not familiar with multi-level marketing. That is to say, I was apprehensive about participating and joining as a member. I actually remember my very first thought being, "I can't sell and I'm not a good salesperson." Yet I am a very ambitious person and I was surrounded with great people (I still am!), therefore I was well supported when making the decision to join as a representative.

What came as a surprise after becoming a member is the large amount of professional training, regular meetings where training is provided, as well as quarterly or annual meetings where people from all over the country meet together for additional training, encouragement, and recognition. I couldn't believe the wealth of information I was surrounded by and decided to use it to my full advantage.

After all, as iron sharpens iron, one man sharpens another. I began to collect many pieces of personal development material; which is how I began to grow my library. As I was introduced to books and collections of CDs with the best nuggets of information on encouragement, self-development and self-improvement, I became more self-aware of my speech and my appearance. I made sure that I was speaking using correct grammar and that my physical appearance showed how I truly wanted to present myself. The environment I'd found myself a part of became a big inspiration in my life. These people who were not born with wealth nor did they acquire it by means of an inheritance, were still able to live a lifestyle of abundance and wealth. Needless to say, my thoughts and feelings about my activities with the organization began to change.

What changed, you ask? I had altered my perspective about the fee I was paying each month for the membership. Instead of looking at it as just a purchase I was making, I came to see it as a monthly investment. I came to realize that I wasn't necessarily investing in the products and services I received, but instead in my own personal development by using the tools they were making so readily available to me. I became disciplined to listening to the audio CDs and reading material that was mentally stimulating without becoming drowsy. You can bet that as a professional my skills improved, but I was also able to refer good books to those around me.

Being able to help others in such a way boosts confidence and provides reassurance among your peers. It is a really great feeling to have someone come to you for your recommendation, and being able to suggest a book to help them solve their problem. Which is why I wanted to not only continue to make excellent book recommendations to people, but provide them with some of my own nuggets of wisdom that I feel will enhance their lives as much as they've enhanced mine.

So, with no further ado, here are the four characteristics that will make your enterprise more valuable:

BE SELF-RELIANT

To be self-reliant is to believe in yourself and to trust in your own abilities. You do not need validation. You don't have to have someone to support your dreams or goals if you believe in them. You don't need motivation from someone else in order for you to be encouraged to take action. I once heard Jim Rohn say, "If someone does not believe in your dreams it is probably because you have not demonstrated..." Take a moment to reflect on that. The more momentum you get and the harder you work toward your dreams the more believers you will acquire. Guess what, the naysayers may criticize you. They may judge you. But, they won't be able to doubt your determination in achieving your goal.

BE RESPONSIBLE

According to Webster's dictionary, one definition of responsible is "being the cause or explanation." This is a way of saying that in order to be responsible for something, you must take action. Be the reason that a specific outcome came into existence, or that a success was achieved. Because you took action, you are responsible for this outcome, for this reward, for the success, for this personal growth. Seek ways to allow your personal responsibility to positively impact your community.

One of the saddest things that I have seen is a person with the mindset that being responsible is of no value. When in the workplace, responsibility adds value to an employer. The person that is able to assume responsibility for tasks that others shy away from make themselves valuable. It is as if the majority of people confuse the term responsible with accountable; since perception of the latter is sometimes negative. Change your attitude toward responsibility. Doing so increases the value of the enterprise— YOU.

BE PERSISTENT

Success is a derivative of persistence
~ The Circle Maker

Be persistent in your willingness to use your tools creatively. Understanding the function of our resources, and how to use them to the best of our ability, can sometimes be difficult. This can be especially challenging when we see that the same tools or resources are working for others. Continue to pursue a better understanding of how to use your resources. There is nothing but success as a result for your persistence. Your enterprise gains value and cultivates collaboration with these other characteristics when you actively persist against rejections and limitations. Persistence is a necessity for any undertaking that requires resources outside of yourself. So, how does that apply to the self-enterprise? If you have ever read *The Battlefield of the Mind* (if you haven't, I highly recommend it), you will have become more aware of the opposing thoughts that we, ourselves, face regularly. Don't listen to those voices telling you not to continue on, whether they come from others or from your own mind. We have to persist beyond those self-limiting thoughts.

LOVE

Self-enterprising is loving yourself first. True success will materialize when you allow the abundance of love that you have for yourself to flow into the relationships that you have with others. From experience, love is a characteristic that makes your efforts grow. Therefore, I say to you that love may be the most important of all characteristics when adding value to yourself. 1 John 4.8 of the Bible tells us "God is love." Love is a language that we all speak and understand. Success will present itself to you if you walk toward it with love and passion for your goal in each step.

What is listed here are but a fraction of what characteristics could be used to enhance the self-enterprise. Yet, transforming the thoughts from leaser to owner, from job to career, from buying to investing, just to name a few, can significantly impact your efforts and growth of passion. It also expands your vision for yourself and strengthens your belief in yourself.

If you ever think of your dreams and question, "How?" Start practicing these characteristics. Create good habits. Add value to yourself!

About Moenique

If you were to ask, "Who is Moenique?" In reply she would say, "I am Mother, student, and teacher." She places a high priority on her role as a parent. She and her son support community ventures by participating in 5k and 10k walk or run events. She enjoys daily exercise, reading and keeping company with loved ones. Moenique likes to try new things and does not like to repeat herself when speaking. A softer side to Moenique is that she loves the rain and gardening.

Moenique Phillips is a change agent. She helps her clients apply force to the potential of their mental attitudes (mindset). This activity allows them to create motion and build momentum throughout their goal achievement process. Moenique helps her clients to build the enterprise of self; therefore activating their vision and creativity and add value to their brand.

Moenique is a University of South Alabama graduate. She has built her enterprise in the field of human resources. As a change agent, Moenique has supported many professionals during the developmental stages of their careers by motivating, teaching and offering resources that aided their growth and added value to their enterprise.

Moenique started MyFunClub, which is an exclusive travel club that draws learning from traveling experiences that builds the confidence of members. Administering this program has given her an expanded network of self-enterprising professionals and impeccable personal development. Moenique agrees with Oprah who stated that, "Education is the way to freedom." Therefore, she makes reading a part of her everyday living.

Moenique is a selfless and intentional giver. Moenique is passionate about inspiring others to become their best and to develop a mindset needed to prepare one's self to maintain a sound mind while in pursuit of a goal. Moenique uses her personal experiences to help the reader to relate and deduce that her life's philosophies are viable. Moenique refers to this work as a ministry which bears good and favorable fruit. What you may have in common with Moenique is a flint foundation of faith.

You can connect with Moenique at:
- myfunclub@worldventures.com
- www.facebook.com/moenique.phillips
- www.twitter.com/WillChangeLater

CHAPTER 22

COMMITMENT TO SERVICE: VISION, INNOVATION, AND STRATEGIES

BY PAUL M. LAWLESS, ChFC®

COMMITTED TO SERVE

At 23 years of age, I began in the financial planning and advisory business of counseling successful entrepreneurs, families, and executives. Through a very rigorous training program that was offered from a large company with a small division of highly-educated and well-trained advisors, I received one of the greatest educations and on-the-job, in-the-trenches training experiences for dispensing financial advice in the United States. Today, this training is a lost art. Unfortunately, financial corporations and insurance companies presently fail to extend the necessary capital and time investment in their people through this meticulous training process. It is an expensive and arduous task to train people in the financial disciplines. Therefore, most large companies no longer involve themselves in extensive training in investment and financial advice/planning programs. I was very lucky to receive this training at this inflection point of my age, career, and timing in the cycle of business that would come in the years ahead.

My studies were in International Business and Finance with a Bachelor's degree earned from the Florida Atlantic University. My graduate level studies continued in the subsequent years with The American College of Financial Services, whereupon I earned the Chartered Financial

Consultant® designation (ChFC®). This highly-specialized curriculum required mastering over 100 topics through 27 semester credit hours and nine courses on integrated advanced financial planning such as:

- Investment Planning
- Insurance Planning
- Employee Benefits Planning
- Income Tax Planning
- Estate Tax, Gift Tax, and Transfer Tax Planning
- Asset Protection Planning
- Retirement Planning
- Estate Planning
- Comprehensive Financial Planning and Consulting

The company's training that I received over the next three years of my life was designed to make me an expert in Business and Estate Underwriting. We were taught to counsel privately-held business owners in wealth accumulation, fringe benefits, business and corporate continuity, and generational wealth/federal estate tax reduction planning.

My target market at age 23 were business owners making over $100,000 per year of income, with a net worth of more than $1 million. We saved people substantial income taxes and estate taxes on a regular basis. We began investment programs for college, retirement, and charitable planning purposes. We insured executive and owners for key-person benefits and family income to keep survivors in their homes, schools, and lifestyles. We worked to keep family businesses intact and protected from a confiscatory 55% federal estate tax bracket. These clients in their 40-, 50- and 60-year-old age zones chose to work with me at my young age because of my enthusiastic, educated, and trained approach to solving their problems. Counseling clients through changes: life, technology and the internet, economic upheaval, Bull and Bear markets, recessions and financial crises as well as current events like Brexit, are all impact events that must be managed from a personal and financial planning, tax, and investment market perspective.

Today more than ever, the world is full of information and access to data that has never been better. Investments, Funds, expenses and rates of return, direct investment opportunities, life insurance and Internet term quoting proliferate the air and Internet waves. Direct legal documents, as well as accounting programs, are ubiquitous. How things work has never been more accessible and transparent for anyone with a smart phone or a computer. However, information without context, techniques without experience and wisdom, will always prove to be worthless for most consumers. Successful people and their families require a team leader with distinct skills to guide, negotiate, and manage forward and positive action in their situation and planning transitions. A client advocate to advance a family's planning agenda in using experienced judgment to "make things happen" and "stop things from happening" cannot be purchased over the internet.

We have found that success today demands an experienced and creative perspective which is applied in a client-driven custom application. This focus allows you to keep more of the money that you make, and make worthwhile the money that you keep for yourself and family.

The focus of our business today has evolved from all of the training, experiences, and interaction gained with other advisors, unique client work, and personal family and business experiences. Our firm has saved close to one billion dollars in income and estate taxes and currently manages several hundred million dollars of client funds for education, retirement, and philanthropic purposes. We have learned over the last 30 years from our clients who have taught us a great deal. Specifically, that quality financial advice needs to be much more than just managing their investments. Therefore, Wealth Management for our clients is a fully integrated and comprehensive system to managing all of their financial affairs. Our clients appreciate a global perspective and completion-oriented focus. A plan's success demands deliverability in thought and action. It is not enough to tell what must be done; we champion the plan's implementation.

Our clients are unique and their outlooks, needs, and requirements are distinct. We limit our practice to work with a select number of Business Owners, Executives, and Successful Families with whom we can make a significant impact. We are not for everyone, but those with whom we work benefit substantially.

Our clients seek assistance in the following areas:
- Capital Preservation Strategies
- Protection from Unintended Creditors
- Increased Liquidity
- Reduced Income and Estate Tax Exposures
- Distinctive Strategies for Charitable, Community, and long-term Philanthropic Goals
- A Collaborative Approach to Strategies and Implementation

A Special Focus for Execution:

Clients appreciate our systematic five-step consultative process because they know what to expect. Clients benefit in strategic and tactical planning that takes into consideration current, as well as future, factors and variables. Their plan is executed and kept current.

Your circumstances are unique. A tailor-made plan will be crafted for you. Your values, your judgments and your perspective are integral for building a successful foundation. We will help you attain the goals that define you – passing your estate, reducing taxes, maintaining a family legacy business or endowing your favorite charities . . .

We seek to help you fulfill and Achieve Your Ambitions.

Investment Consulting:

Your assets and Investment Consulting are core components of our Wealth Management Process and the facet with which you may be most familiar. Our process recognizes that Investment Consulting is often a key aspect of client relationships. Portfolio performance over the long term is essential to help meet your financial goals. Your identified objectives become our focus in allocations of assets, risks, cash flows, growth, and tax requirements. We take a carefully structured, diversified and disciplined approach to portfolio management, with the ultimate target of balancing your family's needs and goals.

Since many of our clients own privately-held business entities, we navigate the complex world of qualified and non-qualified retirement structures. We help you assess your objectives, whether you are driven for self-accumulation, key executive needs, or general employee retirement issues. You'll gain a plan and strategy to help meet your needs and work within your corporate situation.

At times, different techniques and strategic efforts are appropriate. These may include assets and structures that offer deferral, generate income or growth, and allow diversification over concentration.

Advanced Planning:

Business Owners, Executives, and Successful Families have financial needs that go beyond Investment Consulting. Your needs will likely include Advanced Planning.

One of the most distinguishing features of our Wealth Management Consultative Process is the use of Advanced Planning Strategies. You and your family can look to us as your Personal Chief Financial Officer, guiding you through a specific process to create results. During the Discovery Meeting phase, we identify your complex financial issues, many of which you may have never realized existed. Next, we work with a professional team of advisors (i.e., Attorneys, Tax advisors, Property & Casualty Brokers, etc.) to generate strategies for your consideration that will help meet your near and long-term goals. Equipped with this knowledge, you gain the confidence to make sound long-term decisions in your family's best interests, and we work together on attainment. This may involve the utilization of Wealth Enhancement, Wealth Transfer, Wealth Protection and Charitable Giving Strategies.

Wealth Enhancement:

Wealth enhancement comprises the balancing of your ideal income level compared to expense levels and the ongoing monitoring of your tax situation. You want to maintain a comfortable lifestyle and be prudent about risks, inflation, and escalating costs. Your tax issues today and well into the future, can better be managed with a monitored and anticipatory approach that considers your holdings and portfolio allocations.

Wealth Transfer:

Your transference of significant assets from one generation to another is a complicated process. Deciding how to divide your estate and doing so in a tax-efficient manner requires planning and action. Discounts, liquidity, and estate equalization become factors. Your family structure and dynamics may evolve and even a well-designed plan can become obsolete. Your estate planning will be regularly reviewed, then updated and adjusted accordingly to keep up with your changing circumstances.

Wealth Protection:

Your assets are hard-earned and are of great importance to you and your family. You want to protect your lifestyle and legacy from Unintended Creditors. Today's world of litigation and identity theft issues can invade your privacy and alter your financial existence. Your customized plan will factor these risks, in keeping with your needs, goals, and objectives.

Charitable Giving:

You seek to give back to your community, charity, or cause. Structures that benefit you and your family legacy today and for generations to come will be considered. Income benefits, estate tax reduction, and connection to philanthropy for your family can be realized with good planning and a clear understanding of your objectives.

RELATIONSHIP MANAGEMENT FOREVER . . .

Your long term relationship with our firm is of utmost importance. Staying in contact with you, in a manner you deem worthwhile, keeps us up-to-date. Whether regular in-person, email, teleconference or video conferencing, we work to be in-touch. We host regular client events of special interest to you and seek interaction as you like. Our Relationship management will likely go beyond you and your spouse and may extend to your family and successive executives in your business and professional network as well.

You may want to involve us in key business, personal and financial decisions as they evolve. Circumstances will change, such as when you bring a new member into the family, or exit an in-law, when you hire or fire a key executive, or want to assist children as they expand their families and business footprints; these activities will often require consultative business and professional advice and we will help. You can be assured that our Professional Network Relationship Management means working effectively with your other professional advisors, such as attorneys and accountants, to ensure the entire team is operating to achieve the same goals you define.

THE IMPORTANCE OF CONFIDENTIALITY

You can be assured that your personal and corporate information is safe with us. All that we do for you and your family is to be held in confidence as you would expect. All of our associates are trained in computer security protocols to safeguard your data. All associates have confidentiality agreements as well. Additionally, non-disclosure agreements can be executed as necessary, if you prefer.

About Paul

Paul M. Lawless is a Chartered Financial Consultant® and a founding partner of Lawless, Edwards and Warren – Wealth Management. For over 30 years, his clients have been owners of large, privately-held businesses, executives of public companies, and successful families.

Mr. Lawless was honored by *Inc.* magazine as a nominee for their prestigious Entrepreneur of the Year Award. He has been recognized in the "Who's Who Worldwide Registry for Financial Services," "Who's Who in Executives and Professionals" and recently included in Manchester "Who's Who Among Executives & Professionals." In 2014, he was recognized as one of America's Select Financial Advisors.

Mr. Lawless earned a Bachelor of Arts degree in International Business from Florida Atlantic University. He continued his post-graduate professional studies earning the Chartered Financial Consultant® (ChFC®) designation from The American College of Financial Services, Bryn Mawr, Pennsylvania.

Mr. Lawless is an active community member in South Florida and has served on various community, not-for-profit, and corporate boards. Currently, he is President of The 100 Club of South Palm Beach County, a chartered organization which supports families of fallen police officers and firefighters. Also, Mr. Lawless is an active member of the Florida Highway Patrol Advisory Council and a Trustee of the Boca Raton Police and Fire Pension Fund. In addition, Mr. Lawless is a Board Member of Royal Palm Improvement Association; a member of Legatus, a Catholic CEO and Business Leaders Organization; and a Board Member of The Pelican Group, an investment bank specializing in capital formation, management, and consulting to the Catholic Church. He is also a Board Member of the Spitzer Center for Ethical Leadership and an Advisory Board Member of Catholic Charities Birthline/Lifeline Pregnancy Care Centers. Mr. Lawless is a Knight of Magistral Grace in The Sovereign Military Hospitaller Order of St. John of Jerusalem of Rhodes and of Malta, and a Steward of St. Peter, and member of The Papal Foundation.

Paul makes his home in Boca Raton with his wife, Lynn; their daughters, Kathleen and Emily; and sons, Paul Jr. and Mark Christopher.

CHAPTER 23

PLANT. CULTIVATE. HARVEST.

BY REBECCA CROWNOVER

Sometimes we find our callings from the most unexpected experiences.

I grew up a farm girl, but always had this driving desire to become an entrepreneur. The exact way that I would go about achieving that worthy title was never really clear. I just knew that I wanted to create something for the world that had my mark on it, and helped in some way. So despite being the "small town" farm girl from Sunray, Texas, I thought big. I went to college and set my sights on graduating and finding a job where I could explore the world.

And I did. For several years I was a technology consultant and traveled the world, seeing many things and enjoying the success that my goal had brought me. But I wanted more.

My more came with a combination of falling in love and going back to the farming life that I'd left. The timing was amazing, as I'd begun to get burnt out on traveling fifty weeks a year, seldom having time to feel grounded because my roots were never planted in one place for too long. And finding the guy of my dreams and getting married made it all that much better. A winning team had been created, and together we worked to achieve our big entrepreneur-minded goals. Since we were both hard workers, we embraced the land for the life it could provide us. It was wonderful and when our daughter was born, it was even better.

Too early, most unexpectedly, tragedy struck. A husband, business partner and father was lost in an ATV accident at the prime age of thirty-one. I was shocked and devastated. We were only six years into our marriage and still building a life together. Then, looking into those big blue eyes of our small two-and-a-half-year-old daughter, I knew I had to be strong for her, and to do that, I didn't have time to be swallowed up in grief. She needed me, and wow, did I need her.

The big question that remained: what came next?

I. Plant the Seed.

With every seed that is planted, we will face both failures and successes. When those failures come, we can use them as a learning lesson to walk away stronger and smarter than we were before.

We laid my husband to rest on a Monday and a week later I began counseling. I knew that I needed help and a sounding board to talk out all these overwhelming feelings and emotions that were taking place so they didn't fester inside of me. I couldn't remain stagnant despite my aching heart; I needed to grow, even if I didn't understand the "why" of it. Thinking I could do it alone would have been a foolish mistake. And I didn't have any time to play the fool. In the end, counseling was a smart suggestion, and its benefits set me up for success in coping with what I had faced, and would be facing in my new life as a single mom and only parent. I was also fortunate to have amazing family support from my family, my friends and my in-laws, with whom I was a business partner in a growing family-farming operation (Lone Star Family Farms).

Through my healing, I was better able to help my daughter put things into perspective. She was two and a half during the time of the accident, but as she grew older, she had so many questions. I tried to explain to her, but it wasn't always easy. Never short on determination, I began seeking out solutions for the problem. Like many people, I went to books first and was disappointed to find that there was nothing appropriate for a child her age, or easy for her to understand. That's when the seed was planted.

If what I was looking for to help young children cope with the grief, and gain understanding about losing a parent, wasn't out there, I would create something to help.

One night after reading a book to my daughter and putting her to bed, I had an epiphany to write my own children's story. Words flowed out onto paper along with my tears. The result was the book, *My Daddy is in Heaven with Jesus*. This story helped in my daughter's healing, and my continued healing, as well. It was an unexpected opportunity that would launch me into great things I didn't know existed at the time.

My daughter learned how to handle the loss of her daddy better.

Other people, young and old alike, expressed how the book had helped them in dealing with the loss of a parent, whether from a long time ago or recently.

However, despite the goodness of the book, I was shocked to see how many media outlets were resistant to it, because of one word—Jesus. It took a long time for me to get to the right avenues that embraced Jesus and the book's faith-filled message. But eventually, I did, and the book became known widely, earning some wonderful awards and media attention. As all this unfolded, this energy began to grow inside of me and slowly made its way out. I saw the power that words and faith have when combined. Knowing that this lesson stemmed from one of the greatest personal tragedies of my life was hard to believe. Aside from being a mother and a farmer, it guided me to a new identity, that of a children's author.

With a sense of purpose about writing meaningful children's books, I was so excited. Since I'd never been afraid of hard work I did not hesitate to commit to doing what it took to realize this dream—lessons, bumps, and bruises along the way. Because being an author is being a small business owner. It takes work and promotion. You've got to cultivate it!

II. Cultivate.

With perseverance, hard work, and determination to succeed you can have all of the meaningful things in your life you wish to pursue. If you choose the sidelines, you are nothing more than an idle dreamer.

You don't have to be the smartest kid in the class or go to a fancy college to learn how to create something and become successful. I've never been the top student in my class, not even the top 10% of a high school graduating class of 30 people, but that never stopped me from knowing that my results were the outcome of my actions. You see, the process of achievement is a state of mind that spurs on action, if it's the right goal. Personal determination, motivation, and embracing hard work can take you a long way.

When my husband and I started our farm, we started it from nothing. The only assets we had were our personal vehicles and both with a car loan. He worked the land all day, taking care of the endless to-do list that comes with farming. I had to work a full-time job during the day so we'd have enough money to live, because we knew that the farm's success depended on reinvesting in it, not taking out the profits for us to live on. Then at night, I'd do the farm's books, and on weekends, I was a farmer, too. We both worked many seven day weeks.

Taking steps and thinking of the future, not just "the moment" is something that all people in business have to do in order to build success, regardless of the type of business they are operating.

When we cultivate our lives we are willing to give ourselves the nourishment we need through understanding that what we harvest is a direct effort of what we grow, and how we go about it. Laziness was not a part of any success formula that I'd created for myself, or ever read about in my endless love of learning and growing to move forward and upward—like the sunflower facing the sunny sky as it opens up to reveal its full potential.

After I realized that I wanted to be a children's author, I had to think long and hard about what I was good at. What was my brand and my expertise? I didn't want to have my first book be my sole identity, because it wasn't healthy for me or a part of life's plan to keep reliving the tragedy of my loss repeatedly. If I would have done that, I wouldn't have been cultivating anything, just plowing the same bit of land over and over again. This gets you nowhere!

It was time to think about what I wanted and what I had to offer.

- What was I an expert at? Farming.
- What did I want to do? Be a farmer, a good business partner, a good mother, and be a children's author.

216

How could I achieve this additional title? By writing about what I knew best.

This process of evaluating what I wanted was easier because I had always made deliberate decisions to not veer too far away from the heart of who I was. The result of this self-evaluation was a concept for a new book series that instantly excited me then, just as it still does today—*Texas Farm Girl*. This series has the heart and soul of good life experiences in it, mixed with the type of integrity and ethics that often come with that "country girl attitude."

Texas Farm Girl is a book series that teaches and inspires through words and includes these vivid, wonderful images that draw in even the youngest, curious minds into its story. There's something magical about a person's connection with the land and all the lessons that can be learned by using a Texas farm girl for an example.

Through tapping into the magic of that, my efforts to cultivate the success that I wanted as a children's author really came into play, becoming an Amazon Best Seller and gaining national media attention. The hard work continued, of course, and I found out how much I loved thinking outside of the box, marketing and promoting these stories, and bringing attention to the parents of kids who could really benefit from these types of stories—they are for girls and boys from all walks of life! Yes, boys too!

When all these accolades for the book series began to come my way, I was thrilled, not because they were a notch in my cap, but because they helped to solidify what I'd been striving to achieve with the series. Nothing is more wonderful to experience and feel than seeing the onset of a wonderful harvest, which cannot happen without hard work, dedication, and faith in the end result.

III. Harvest Your Yields.

We yield great things when we refuse to be a victim to life's circumstances, or focus on the negative aspects of what we see in ourselves or in the pursuit of our goals.

Accentuating the positive is how we get to that point where we can harvest all of the hard work we've put into succeeding at something. There's a reason that farmers have always celebrated a bountiful harvest, because they know that it was hard earned and is a direct result of their efforts to make that happen. You have to have solutions and innovative thinking for everything—when it's too hot, too cold, too stormy, not enough rain, etc.

I've always been a strong person and find ways to create my own ways. By doing that, people have never doubted my seriousness in achieving what I want to or the authenticity of my smile and happiness when things come together and begin to deliver results.

Today, so much is happening that is all a bountiful harvest that couldn't take place if I'd never sown the seeds or cultivated their growth. I never assumed anything, other than that I have always given my best efforts.

A true entrepreneur never stops working on their own growth, or the growth of what they have created. Today, wonderful things continue to happen, including a movie about *My Daddy is in Heaven with Jesus! Texas Farm Girl* even has its own song and country music video, performed by award winning country artist, Billy Dawson, and produced by Grammy award winning producer, Skidd Mills. As all of these things happen, they offer me daily reminders of who I am and where I come from. It's a great place, and where I'm going looks pretty great, too. Success feels pretty good, but it will always be a work in progress.

PLANT THE SEED. CULTIVATE. HARVEST YOUR YIELDS.

When we do what we need to do every day to keep our dreams alive and growing, we are taking steps toward achieving goals. Right when you wake up in the morning you should know what you want to do for the day and go start doing it. Sure, small hiccups to big tragedies may come up that throw you off track, but if you're committed to your success and always being better today than you were yesterday, you can never really get too far off-track from it, because it's a part of you. And by pursuing it in a manner that's authentic to the person you are, you'll find those blessings that lead to the abundance that you seek in life.

- Be abundant in love.
- Be abundant in accomplishment.
- Be abundant in your thanks and praise.
- Just be you and find what you do best, and you'll be great!

Plant. Cultivate. Harvest. Choose the seeds you would like to plant in life and focus on them wholeheartedly. Remember, success does not come from skipping the cultivation process. A successful harvest derives from your commitment to cultivating the paths you have sowed. You cannot reap the benefits if you aren't willing to put forth the effort.
~Rebecca Crownover, *Forbes Magazine*, November 2015

About Rebecca

Always willing to work hard and make the necessary commitment to achieve her dreams, Rebecca Crownover is a shining example to anyone with an entrepreneurial spirit. Through example, she shows how anyone can achieve their dreams with some determination and ingenuity. With a strong understanding of business and as a partner in a family owned and operated farming operation, Lone Star Family Farms, she has been diligent in finding success. But it wasn't until an unexpected personal tragedy in 2009, that Rebecca found an even greater purpose. Rebecca lost her husband, leaving her a solo parent and minus her business partner.

Challenges on how to best help her young daughter cope, Rebecca sought out books and resources that could help a small child understand and deal with grief. When she didn't find what she was looking for, her entrepreneur mindset lead to her to a bigger calling, a pouring out of her heart and soul in the form of a children's book—*My Daddy is in Heaven with Jesus*. With hard work and persistent marketing, the book gained international attention, earning several awards, including the 2013 Award Winning Finalist in USA Best Books Awards in the Children's Religious Category, and 2013 Christian Literary Awards: Henri Award and Reader's Choice Award in the Children's Book Category. It was through this process that Rebecca really connected with the idea of being a children's author who offered teachable moments to young people through captivating and interesting stories.

Today, *Texas Farm Girl* is the book series that has continued to establish Rebecca Crownover as an elite children's author, having earned accolades which include: 2014 Christian Literary Awards Nominee – Children's Book Category; 2014 Mascot Books Author of the Year for *Texas Farm Girl* series; and the 2014 "Moving America Forward" Award, presented by retired Rear Admiral Kevin F. Delaney for being an innovative entrepreneur in helping America move forward through the *Texas Farm Girl* series (an award that was presented on William Shatner's *Moving America Forward* television show).

Rebecca has been featured in publications about farming, business, and her book series, including *Forbes* magazine, *Yahoo! Finance*, CNBC, Reuters, the December 2014 cover of *Progressive Farmer* magazine, and numerous other farming and business publications. She is an actively sought out speaker for her inspirational personal and professional message. Today, Rebecca is also excited to be featured as a co-author for *Success Blueprint* with renowned sales coach and author Brian Tracy.

The greatest joys in Rebecca's life involve what she's most passionate about. She loves working for their family farming business, growing the *Texas Farm Girl* brand, playing tennis, and spending time with her daughter Acie, her "mini me." Together, they enjoy traveling, attending movies, and sporting events. Rebecca is also committed to Family Farms Charities (familyfarmcharities.org), an organization that she personally adopted after they helped her after her loss. They are dedicated to using farming practices and principles to help those in need.

Find out more about Rebecca at:
- www.RebeccaCrownover.com
- www.TexasFarmGirl.com

CHAPTER 24

PUBLIC SPEAKING: WHAT YOU NEED TO SUCCEED!

BY MOHAMED ISA

When I was thirteen, I delivered the worst speech of my life in a jam-packed city hall. I was forced to deliver the speech by an older person who said, "Mohamed, you have great grades in school. It's time to shine in your own community. Here is the speech you must read tonight."

"Do you mean now?" I asked him.

"No," he replied, "in ten minutes."

And I did deliver the three-page speech, if you could call that a speech! Far from the bolstering experience it was meant to be, I felt nothing but shame, disgrace, and humiliation. To add insult to injury, most of my relatives and friends were in the hall!

After this disturbing experience, I hated, dreaded, and avoided public speaking for many years until I got into university. And along the way I missed countless speaking opportunities in my schools and community. I missed opportunities to make an impact on others. I missed opportunities to inspire the next generation of young speakers. But that was then; now I can speak to hundreds of people without any fear. I came to realize that the fear of public speaking could be cured through continuous learning and practice. In this chapter, you will learn the blueprint to becoming a successful speaker.

In 2008, I came across a powerful quote that captured the essence of public speaking in just forty-nine words. You will pick up great speaking lessons from this anonymous quote. And it goes like this:

> The speech sounded very much like an economics lecture. It had no oratorical eloquence, and did not use many stories, jokes or illustrative references to give the speech human interests. You couldn't do much worse than that, could you? The speech was the first of a young orator named ...

I will dissect the quote into seven distinct speaking lessons that you could apply for all your future speeches so that you get laughter, applause, and your message across! And I promise by the end of the chapter, you will know the name of this mediocre speaker too. So here we go:

1). The speech sounded very much like an economics lecture.

Did you study economics in school or university? I studied five economics courses, and most of my colleagues did not like the subject because it was dull and dry. I imagine that our speaker in the quote used too much industry jargon and too many technical terms that alienated the audience. He made it very hard for the audience to follow his speech. Whether they listened or not, it made no difference to them. His words just flew over their heads.

The Lesson: Express. Do not try to impress.

2). It had no eloquence.

The Merriam-Webster dictionary defines *eloquence* as the ability to speak or write well and in an effective way. You will only become eloquent if you engage in a program to expand your vocabulary and language skills and then apply and practice what you learn so that your spoken words become like symphonies and musical notes whenever you speak. Unlike jargon, eloquent words will command the audience's attention. In my mind, I admire two eloquent speakers whose vocabulary mesmerizes me and makes me listen to their speeches again and again: Malcolm X and Nelson Mandela. Both of them embarked on the same journey in the ocean of words for many years.

The Lesson: Expand your vocabulary to engage your audience.

3). And did not use many stories.

If you want your speeches to become memorable, tell the audience some stories—and preferably tell them your own personal stories. I do not appreciate it when speakers get up onstage only to tell some stories they picked up from the Internet. Yes, they might be powerful stories, but they are not yours. You may say, "But I don't have any good personal stories." Your stories do not have to be profound to be effective. Your stories should support your arguments and serve as anchors to your points.

I strongly suggest that you start a personal story file whether using a journal or a computer. Don't try to write the full details of the stories; just focus on the key characters, key conversations, place and time, and finally the moral of the story. Keep building up this file and you will be surprised at the many stories you have.

Stories bring emotions and emotions help you connect with the audience. Here are three exercises for you:

- Think of stories that brought you happiness, sadness, anger, joy, jealousy, or fear. We all share and feel these emotions.
- Think of your failures, frustrations, and flaws. These will be the fastest way to connect with your audience. And that is why I shared with you my first failure in speaking.
- If you could travel back in time to have a conversation with someone, who would it be and what would you talk about?

Here are four more thoughts on how to become a master storyteller:

- Do not just tell your story, relive it. Use dialogue (or conversations) to bring life to the story. Let the audience see and hear the characters of your stories. Give your characters a voice. The dialogue helps you bring out the emotions of the characters.
- Include conflict in your stories to grab the attention of the audience. If you have no conflict, you have no story. It is just like a movie; when the script is flowing smoothly, you lose interest. Have conflict and escalate it. The audience will be hooked.
- The more specific the story, the more terrific it becomes. Give the

audience more details. Which is better, to say he had a red car or to say he had a red Ferrari? Did you just see that red Ferrari in your mind? I bet you did.

- Do not always be the hero of your stories or speech. The audience should not get the message that you are better than they; instead they should feel that you are one of them. You are not there to brag about your achievements, you are there to help them grow and prosper. This way you will connect better.

The Lesson: If you do not have a story, you do not have a speech!

4). Did not use many ... jokes.

Humor is a very important speaking tool, but most people are afraid to use it. There is no feeling like telling a joke that falls flat. In the speaking business, they have this saying: You don't have to use humor unless you want to get paid. Humor is very important because when you make your audience laugh, they like you and are likely to listen to you.

Here are some thoughts on humor:

- Do not tell jokes. Yes, no jokes please. Jokes are not that good. As with Internet stories, the audience may have heard your jokes before. If you use these and then do not get a laugh, you lose some of your energy, and you will end up having an uncomfortable time onstage.
- Do not add humor, weave it in. Many speakers try to make the audience laugh by bringing jokes or punchlines to their speeches. They digress from their speech just to get a laugh. This is not an optimal practice. The humor should flow naturally in your speech through your points or stories.
- When you weave humor in, you can move on. One of the advantages of weaving in humor is that if your punchline did not work, you can move on as if you did not actually intend to make the audience laugh.
- When you manage to make the audience laugh, let them laugh. You should not step on their laughter because if you do, you are sending them the wrong message. In a way, you are telling them "you are not supposed to laugh." In April 2008, I delivered a speech to an audience of more than four hundred people. I made them laugh during the entire speech, but there was one big laugh that lasted for

fourteen seconds. I stood on the stage silently. I said nothing. I just enjoyed watching the audience laugh!

- Finally, you can always weave in humor in your introduction. When the meeting organizers ask you for a written introduction, make it witty. There is no better situation than to face the audience while they are smiling or laughing.

The Lesson: Humor connects humanity. Use it whenever possible.

5). And did not use many ... illustrative references.

Analogies are great for illustrating your points and making them unforgettable. For example, in a management meeting I used a prop to illustrate my viewpoint on a critical decision. The company received many plaques and trophies for sponsoring various events, and one of them was a miniature boat. I placed the boat on the table and asked, "If this boat were sinking, what should you do? Accept more load or off-load goods to survive?" They all said, "Of course, off-load." Here, I retorted: "Exactly. But what the company is doing now is the opposite. We are making the company sink faster."

The Lesson: Do not just throw ideas, illustrate them creatively.

6). To give the speech human interests.

Does your speech have human interest? What is in it for the audience? Why would they listen to you? The audience should see the benefit in listening to your speech or presentation. To generate human interest, you should use statements or questions that heighten their interest. For example:

- Ladies and gentlemen, this is important to you because ...
- Ladies and gentlemen, what does this mean to you? It means ...
- Ladies and gentlemen, why am I telling you this? Because ...

So how do you do this in real life? Start with the foundation for preparing for any speech: audience analysis.

Whenever I am invited to speak, I ask the meeting organizer to answer specific questions about the event, the audience, and the venue. You can see a sample of my pre-event questionnaire on my website. In addition, I call the organizer to clarify any doubts I may have.

Here are two interesting examples on how audience analysis helps:

- One time I was invited to speak to military personnel. I sent my questionnaire to the event organizer and asked him to fill it in. I had many phone calls with him, and in one of the calls I asked, "Does the audience like to laugh?" He answered, "No, no, no. They do not like to laugh. They are very serious." I thought, *I must remove all the humor from my speech.* But then I thought, *I will keep some and if they do not laugh, I will just move on. If they are serious, I will act serious too.* They never laughed. And I was lucky to have done some research so that I did not become disappointed.
- Exactly one week later, I delivered the same program to a group of students and they were laughing all the way through the entire speech. The same speech produced different audience responses.

The Lesson: Analyze your audience and make your speech interesting to them.

7). But who was this speaker?

To know who it was, read the full quote:

> The speech sounded very much like an economics lecture. It had no oratorical eloquence, and did not use many stories, jokes or illustrative references to give the speech human interests. You couldn't do much worse than that, could you? The speech was the first of a young orator named John F. Kennedy.

If you take only one point from my chapter, it should be this point. The mediocre speech we talked about in this chapter belongs to the former president of the United States, John F. Kennedy. He started as a mediocre speaker but ended up being one of the top speakers in the history of the world. What does this mean to you? It means a lot. No matter how you rate your current speaking skills, you could improve them significantly. Apply the blueprint I shared with you and you will become a more successful speaker!

About Mohamed

Mohamed Isa is a fiercely-committed coach and speaker who helps executives and their teams achieve more sales and productivity so they can enjoy higher levels of satisfaction as they pursue—and achieve—their dreams and desires. With more than fifteen years of experience in coaching clients to achieve remarkable success, Mohamed will help you get more laughs, receive more applause, and send your message across to an enthusiastic audience.

His path to becoming a speech coach emerged at an early age. In the early 1990s, when Mohamed was a business student at the University of Bahrain, he was the go-to person when it came to the preparation and practice of class presentations and case studies. He coached many students on how to deliver presentations that engaged their audience in an undeniable way.

Clients say remarkable things about the impact of Mohamed's coaching and speaking on their lives and business success. Check out the testimonials at his website. Similar benefits await when you decide to invite Mohamed to serve you in the powerful ways that can support your success.

What lights him up about this work is knowing that this is his life's calling: to guide his clients to achieve their dreams and desires through becoming charismatic speakers who can grab the audience's attention and hold it to the end, whether they are raising funds for a charity or selling products or services.

What sets Mohamed apart from other coaches and speakers is that he has a real business experience in several areas including finance, human resources, information technology, risk management, legal affairs, compliance, corporate governance, and investments. He gained this experience with the multinational giant Unilever and then by becoming a Chief Financial Officer (CFO) of a startup company, where he and the executive team took that business from a humble value of USD $63 million to USD $528 million in four years.

Over the years he has learned how to dazzle audiences at conferences in the Gulf, Europe and U.S.A. Mohamed has shared the stage with some of the top speakers in the world, such as Tom Peters, Tony Buzan, Shep Hyken, John Gray, and Doug Lipp among others. In a nutshell, your time is precious. Allow him to spare you the trial-and-error and the frustration that go along with learning a new skill.

Mohamed is a co-author of the Amazon bestselling book, *World Class Speaking in Action*, in the categories of Presentations and Public Speaking Reference. He is also a co-author of *Heart of a Toastmaster*, which won the Best Anthology Award by the International Book Awards, in which he documents his transformation from being a mediocre speaker to a world-class speaker.

Why not explore how he can accelerate your growth? He will guide you to achieve the results you desire and the life you imagine, quicker!

You can connect with Mohamed at:
- Mohamed@3DSpeaking.com
- www.linkedin.com/in/mohdisa
- www.facebook.com/mohamed.isa3
- @mohamed_isa

CHAPTER 25

SUCCESS IS PERSONAL

BY DAWN S. KIRK

I believe, as a society, we are highly focused on external factors as the barometer for success. We often define success by how much money we make, what kind of car we drive, the size of our house, our title, and the list goes on. But is this true success? I have observed people who have "achieved success" and they are burned out, unfulfilled, and burdened with guilt and regret. Why? I believe many of us have abandoned who we are for the outward appearance of success. Let me share a personal example.

In 2004, I was appointed to a newly-formed director role which required my first relocation. In my heart, I knew I shouldn't take the role. The timing was not right, the culture was not a fit, I was a brand new mom with a husband who traveled, and I had no personal or professional support system in the new location. I took the role because I was externally focused on title, status, and compensation. It was the most challenging two years of my career. I lost confidence, I was angry with myself, I didn't perform well in my role, and I had a great deal of guilt which manifested itself in panic attacks. Why? I let others define success for me, I got caught up with the external appearance of success, and I was not true to myself. My life was inconsistent with who I was. As a result of this experience, I have a renewed outlook on success. I believe success is personal. You must define it, own it, and live it. My definition of success is when my personal life and professional life are in alignment with my core values. Or, as I like to say, the audio matches the video.

As I look back on my journey, I have identified ten key lessons that have contributed to my personal success thus far.

1. **Define your Core Values:** Core Values are guiding principles that define who you are, what you stand for, and determine your behavior and action. Your core values formulate your decision-making compass of life. They help determine to what you say yes or no. This is where you explore who you are, what you want, and why you want it. I had my epiphany in a training class in 2006. I was forced to define and write down my core values. I had avoided doing this because I knew I would then be accountable to myself. It was at that moment, I realized I had been putting my career ahead of what was important to me. I am now clear on my core values which are faith, family, friends, wellness, leadership, learning, and inclusion. From that moment forward, I have made decisions based on my core values.

   Action: Sit down and write out your core values. What are those things that are non-negotiable about you? Compare this list to how you are living your life. Are they congruent? Would people know what you value by observing your life? If not, what changes do you need to make?

2. **Be a Servant Leader:** A servant leader is one who removes obstacles and simultaneously equips and guides others to achieve their optimum level in their chosen profession. I have held 16 different roles in 24 years and I attribute this to my servant leadership philosophy. I was able to break down major barriers of being the only woman, the only African-American, and/or the youngest leader by serving before leading. People knew I cared about them personally and professionally. This enabled me to build trust, credibility, and knowledge to enable their success rapidly. By the way, this works whether you have a leadership title or not. I believe when you help others get what they want, you'll be elevated in the process.

   Action: Start by asking questions of those around you. How can I help/support you? What is one thing I could do to make your job easier?

3. **Develop and foster a learning mindset:** It is important to be open to new experiences, learn all aspects of the business, and be an active knowledge seeker. In order to add value to others and your organization, you have to grow. Growth is intentional and does not happen by chance. You have to proactively and purposely invest in yourself. When is the last time you read a personal development book, attended a seminar, workshop, or class? How about taking a lateral role to learn a new area of the business? If you are stuck, could it be that you're not growing? I mentioned earlier that I've had 16 roles in 24 years. Eight were lateral moves in different areas of the business. For example, I gained experience in the areas of finance, marketing, operations, and customer management. I am truly a better leader as a result of these varied experiences.

Action: Develop your personal learning plan. What books will you read? What courses, seminars, and workshops will you attend? To what professional publications will you subscribe? What competencies are you developing?

4. **Learn the art of networking:** Networking is a scary word for many people. My definition of networking is simple. Networking is building mutual relationships. The key word is mutual - a reciprocal relationship. I avoided networking early in my career because I viewed it as a waste of time. I paid the price almost 10 years later when I relocated to another market. I thought my track record of performance was enough to come in and establish credibility with my team and co-workers. I was so wrong! I had not built any relationships outside of my previous location. As a result, I ended up working twice as hard to get things done. The U.S. Department of Labor reports that 70% of all jobs are found through networking. As a result of networking, I was recruited to Coca-Cola at an executive level. A recruiter reached out to a former boss and asked who did he know that would be a good fit for the role he was sourcing. My former boss gave him my name, he called me, and the rest is history. There is not a day that goes by that I am not involved in some type of networking.

Action: Who is in your network? Who would you like to be in your network? The next time you are attending a networking event take some time to find who will be attending. Pre-determine who you would like to meet, come prepared with 2 – 3 questions, and be prepared to add value to the conversation. My secret to networking is getting the other person to talk. People like to talk about themselves and that takes all the pressure off of you.

5. **Master the art of communication:** In this high tech age, communication is becoming a lost art. Everything communicates. Your verbal, non-verbal, written communication, what you say and what you don't say, all matters. You either gain or lose credibility with every interaction.

Action: Evaluate how much time you spend thinking and planning how you are going to communicate. What's your message? Determine if your message should be delivered in person, via phone, or email. Are you frequently connecting with your team and co-workers? How are you engaging them?

6. **Own your career path:** I learned early that you need to decide what you want from your career; set goals, and revisit these throughout the seasons of your life. I remember on "Day 1" setting my goal of becoming a Zone Sales Leader at Frito-Lay, Inc. It was the first executive level role in the field organization. Every role I took was deliberate and provided me the necessary skills and critical experiences to reach my goal. I find that people are frustrated and disengaged with their current careers. However, when I ask, "What do you want to do?" they can't clearly articulate what they want. People can't help you if you don't know what you want.

Action: Map out your career goals. Understand the skills and critical experiences necessary to achieve your goals. Develop a plan. Do you have a mentor? I recommend more than one. Do you have a sponsor? If not, get exposure to Senior Executives. Increase your exposure by getting involved in high profile projects, take on key strategic roles, and be a consistent top performer.

7. **Create an Onboarding Plan:** The first 100 days of any new role is critical to your success, not only in that role, but within the organization. Instead of waiting on the organization to provide you a plan, I highly recommend you develop your own plan and present it to your leader for feedback. The biggest mistake people make is

thinking that onboarding starts the day you start the job. Wrong! Onboarding starts the day you are offered the job. Your goal is to contribute and add value to the organization as quickly as possible. Unfortunately, I learned this the hard way. I had just been promoted to a newly-created Director role in a new market after 13 years with the organization. I showed up on the first day expecting to receive this nice organized training plan and that did not happen. I was completely lost and had no idea what to do next. As a result, it took me too long to ramp up and have an impact. To make matters worse, this was a turnaround situation and there were expectations of driving change quickly. As you can imagine, this was a challenging experience and one I vowed never to repeat again.

Action: Do you have a framework for on boarding? If not, here are three key questions to ask:
    (i) People - Who are my key stakeholders up, down, and across the organization? What are the strengths and opportunities individually and organizationally?
   (ii) Process - How does work get done? What's the infrastructure?
  (iii) Culture - What are the values/norms of this department/ organization? What is the current situation of the team/ organization? How are decisions made?

8. Be a part of the solution: It is easy to point out and complain about problems, but it actually takes courage and leadership to be part of the solution. John Maxwell's definition of leadership is influence. Nothing more, nothing less. Whether you have an executive title or not, solving problems increases your influence and subsequently your leadership. There are no shortages of problems. However, there is a shortage of people willing to dig in, identify root causes, and create viable solutions.

Action: What are the repetitive problems, pain points, or complaints in your organization? How will you become part of the solution?

9. Solicit feedback often: It is critical that you are aware of your strengths and opportunities from other's perspective because we all have blind spots. Don't assume that no news is good news. You want to take a proactive approach in this space to minimize surprises at review time or when you are not selected for a role that you wanted.

Action: Do you have regular meetings with your manager? I recommend bi-weekly or monthly. Do you have personal advisors who will give you candid feedback? Periodically ask co-workers to provide three things you do well and three opportunities to make improvements. Request '360' feedback annually. This allows you to get feedback from multiple levels of the organization and serves as input to your development plan.

10. **Deliver Results:** This is pretty self-explanatory. In order to progress in any organization, you have to demonstrate the ability to get things done individually and collectively through others. The key is to always understand how your role fits into the big picture metrics of the organization: Revenue, Profits, Costs, and Share. Never lose sight of your metrics and ensure that you are spending the majority of your time on the work that delivers against your metrics.

    Action: Write down the metrics you are evaluated on. Pull out your calendar. Do the activities on your calendar reflect the activities that support delivering your results? If not, what adjustments do you need to make?

As a result of these ten key lessons, I am enjoying a rewarding career and a cohesive relationship with my family.

Make success personal... Define it! Own it! Live it!

About Dawn

When someone shows you who they are,
believe them the first time.
~ Maya Angelou

Any initial encounter with Dawn S. Kirk is tantamount to greeting the epitome of spiritual fortitude, graceful exuberance, and uncompromising determination. These are gifts bestowed upon her from a lifetime of yielding to a still small inner voice that whispers inside her indomitable soul. Her moral compass has guided her from an early age into the values of church, with an indelible reliance upon her musical, sports, and entrepreneurial spirit. The combination creates a perfect storm for the twenty-four-year corporate veteran who uses her artistry and erudition to combat competitive corporate challenges.

The resume of Dawn S. Kirk unfolds like a book with pages of corporate excellence and company elevation that has garnered her a reputation for successful endeavors at work and on the home front. She matriculated and graduated from the University of Iowa with a degree in Accounting in 1991. An apt pupil in and out of the classroom, this wife and mother juggles the nurturing of her family with an impressive corporate climb in the most internationally-renowned and esteemed businesses. She spent eighteen years of her illustrious career as a Senior Executive with the number one snack company, Frito-Lay. The last six years have catapulted her career into new heights as Senior Executive with the number one beverage company, Coca-Cola. Her philosophy that "leadership starts with personal development and increases through serving others" was the catalyst for her business, DK Associates, a company born from her desire to share her knowledge with others. She carves through the niches of community service while paying homage to her religious fortitude with leadership roles within her church and in organizations, including Network of Executive Women and Jack and Jill of America, Inc.

Her acknowledgments for excelling in the business arena are numerous and continue to mount. In 2013, she was awarded the Corporate Phenomenal Woman Award by The Black Women's Expo in Chicago, Illinois. In 2014, she was listed in *Georgia's 100 Most Powerful and Influential Women* by Women Works Media Group in Atlanta, GA. She is certified as a speaker, trainer, and coach with the reputable John Maxwell Team. 2015 is the year she was inducted into the VIP Woman of the Year Circle by the National Association of Professional Women. In 2016, she was featured in the *Atlanta Tribune*, selected as a speaker for the National Sales Network (NSN) national conference, and selected as one of America's PremierExperts.

Dawn S. Kirk is a proud denizen of Atlanta, where she shares her life with husband,

Tony Kirk, a retired Corporate Project Manager and two sons, Kendall and Kristopher. Dawn S. Kirk is the vision of a successful leader – one whose transparent heart transfixes your spirit the moment you meet her.

You can connect with Dawn at:
- www.JohnMaxwellGroup.com/DawnKirk
- www.Twitter.com/Learn2LeadwDawn

CHAPTER 26

MONEY GONE MENTAL

BY DANA MUSAT

Bernard Shaw once remarked: If you teach a man anything, he will never learn. Shaw was right. Why? Just studying without practice will not take you anywhere. The two subjects we will explore and forever enjoy from this day on are Feelings and Finances. Logically, this is a statement that prompts the questions:

- Should managing your money be easier? – YES to handling our Finances!
- Should Life be less stressful? – Yes to managing our Feelings!

From here on forward, all lies and myths are out the window. Why? Faking a positive attitude is a lie. Telling yourself "everything will be ok" when you're truly terrified, is a myth. Pretended optimism is a lie. Dreaming without clarity is a myth. The truth is that we are scared and defensive. We feel terrified about Death, Taxes and Wars (as internal battles for the purpose of this chapter). And deep down we know we have to handle it, but we keep saying "later" or "tomorrow" or "another time." Why? Because we don't know how! We lack the strategy to handle them! Allow me to step in and help with procrastination.

Formula for Success = *Sparks of Belief + Dash of Courage to Act NOW + 100% Self-Honesty Foundation*

What do Death, Taxes and Wars have in common or have anything to do with Finances and Feelings?

- *Your Money Situation affects your Mental State.*
- *Your Mental Affairs affect your Money Potential.*

They all require strategy. Yes, I know, it's a vicious circle, a perfect example of a reciprocal cause-and effect sequence in which two or more elements intensify and aggravate each other, leading inexorably to a worsening of the situation.

But we live in a world of what is… not in one of fairytale dreams. We silently battle our own wars. We have nightmares about money and taxes. We fear we'll die too soon. We worry about everything and never appear to be ready for anything.

You see, many years ago I embarked on a rollercoaster ride. Little did I know that I was in the middle of a harsh "Life Quake" experience. Comparable earthquake damage to real-life experiences. Suddenly, my lovely days turned into living nightmares. If any of the following strike a chord in you, then you know what I mean. And I am really sorry for your pain! I was not ready for Death, Despair, Doubts, Divorce, Depression, Damage, Disorder, and Deprivation. And when they all decided to attack me in rapid succession, I found myself feeling powerless and hopeless. I was feeling this disturbingly calm attraction to the powerful negative. It had become my purpose in life. Misery, stress, chaos and pain took over what used to be me. My smiley, attractive, full-of-life, decision-making, driven personality was now just a foggy and hurtful memory.

How did I managed to turn dark into light again and you could, too? I started implementing Professional Conduct into my Personal Actions— strategic decisions steps. I stopped being my worst enemy. I started treating myself as if I were my only 'most valuable client or customer.' I promised myself to never ever lie to myself again. The sooner you start implementing these steps, the brighter your tomorrows will be.

My programs: *Money Gone Mental and Life Entrepreneurs*
. . . were designed with you in mind.

Unlike a Business Owner, a *Life Entrepreneur* takes charge of all aspects of Life and Business, the Personal-Individual side and the Professional-Business side. Harmonious interactions of Feelings and Finance lead to overall success – similar to being the Commander-in-Charge of the successful execution of military operations, strategically committed and determined.

You should not be embarrassed about not feeling "peace" when dealing with Finances and Feelings. If most people were honest about their true feelings and admitted their own financial struggles, the majority of your friends, neighbors and co-workers would say the same thing, "Feelings and Finances are almost impossible to manage together." One must keep them apart and deal with them separately. Why?

Each monetary amount has an emotional trigger. This is why I will show you how Tax Returns, Emotions and War/Battles can and will affect your everyday life and decisions for a better future. You have two choices:

- Embrace and enjoy it all or
- A forever fear of finances

Which one do you choose? Think. Desire. Trust. Decide.

You will learn how ATBM (Accounting Principles, Audit Procedures, Taxes, Business Management) and MDMP (Military Decision-Making Plan) play the most important role in your Life Owner journey. Work-Life Harmony is possible and achievable if you commit to implementing just a few simples steps into your daily, weekly, and monthly routine. Routine can be exciting, should you choose wisely. Strategy is key. Remember these two: ATBM and MDMP!

If there's one thing I hope you will learn today, it is that your main desire becomes:

Freedom = Feelings + Financial.

(Similar to basic Accounting Equation: Assets = Liabilities + Owner's Equity.)

These recipes for success cover a span of over 20 years of experience and education, professional and personal. I have come to realize that as in Business, applying this set of conduct rules to Personal life, proved to be what saved me from "chaos" and brought me back to life. Be brave and focus on allowing yourself to steer towards a happy, healthy, profitable life journey.

1. Alive and Thriving ☺ Accounting for Life.
2. Planning for Success = Strategic Steps
3. Using Fear for Learning. Feelings Management. Audit of Thoughts.

About a year ago, I said "ENOUGH!" That was the end of the "Life Quake" hustle. April of 2015 was the beginning of owning my life instead of allowing life to happen to me. I looked at myself in the mirror and said, "Haven't you had enough?" Yes, I have. And I want to change and feel better and be happy again, but I am stuck in this flow and don't know how to get out of it. I take one step forward and many steps back (Life Dancing) .

So I did what I do best. I looked at myself as if I were my only best client. I talked. I listened. I took notes. I felt so much better. But now what? What am I going to do about it? How am I going to win my battles? And it just came to me, effortlessly: "What do you do when you meet with a new client?" "I gather information, evaluate options, draft a summary plan, list all actions to be taken and deliver solutions for desired results." YES! And that's what I did, successfully!

How does it feel to lie in bed at night and smile at your accomplishments? How does it feel to wake up every morning energized and ready to tackle your day? How amazing is it to embrace all your challenges and struggles? If you answered "I don't know" to any of the above questions, it's ok. I am here for you. I will help you use your fears strategically in order to gain clarity, and account for and report thoughts and actions properly, monetary and emotionally.

What do I mean by "use your fears"? Let's use the most obvious example we all know:

Are you afraid of an IRS audit? Well, then plan properly and get educated... *and thus reduce stress and fears!*

I am not going to lecture you about taxes nor impose foreign terminology on your already-busy brain. My intention is to get you enthusiastic about taxes by explaining the process and how you can implement certain steps towards making your life easier and generate extra cash in your pocket. Extra cash in my pocket you say? Now that I've got your attention, YES, you do have a say on how your income and taxes are being handled, if only you knew.

I get all kinds of questions throughout the year when it comes to taxes. But whether at social gatherings, sporting events or even business networking functions, two of the most common ones I receive are: "Can I write this off?" and "How can I end up with more money?"

Well, allow me, today, to set the record straight on all of this for you. In my experience, there are three primary mindsets of people out there:

Mindset 1: People who want to write off everything, whether it's legal or not, and figure the cost of an IRS audit won't be "that bad." Or else they think they can't ever get caught. They are invisible, or so they think.

Mindset 2: These folks don't want to write ANYTHING off. In fact, I've known some who will tell me that they want to purposely overpay their taxes. But the IRS doesn't take bribes. This plan doesn't work either.

Mindset 3: These are people who want to pay less in tax, but they are cautious. They still want to sleep at night. I've got good news and bad news about this one. First the good: it's easier than you might think. Now the bad: you really have to do it right.

All deductible expenses must have a business purpose. The expense must be "ordinary and necessary to the production of income." But that's about all the guidance you're going to get. And that's the reason why so many people get stuck, especially in the beginning. What's deductible? It depends!

If you can prove that this expense helps your business, you're covered. This is pretty much a no-brainer. No receipt = No deduction. When you're out, use your phone to take a picture of receipts. It's a whole lot easier to keep track of pictures than it is loose slips of paper. Then, if you paid for the deduction with cash, check or credit, you've got the deduction. Make sure you properly report them on your tax return.

Strategy + Implementation + Reporting = Steps for Success (eliminate fear of IRS audit and start enjoying the upcoming Profits).

The actual Tax Return is the Final Part of your annual strategy The same definition of "ordinary and necessary" expense applies to your everyday life strategy as well. The same "steps for success" should be applied to your fears, feelings, thoughts, actions and decisions.

Find your Honest "WHY" to ALL your DILEMMAS. Once you know your true "why," you can proceed with the repairing process. Allow yourself Time and Patience. Implement MDMT (Military Strategy) and ATBM (Business Management) steps that I mentioned earlier, in any situation, and I guarantee successful accomplishments. Let's find your WHY!

I was asked to give exact examples on how to complete the following 8-Step Solution Recipe, but I found it difficult to pin-point a single "example" because we can't just change one thing without changing everything... a decision to change is a chain reaction of "many changes." You will get better at Chain-Reaction-Change as soon as you start implementing these 8-Steps. Similar to Taxes and Accounting, seeing the whole picture along with all the little steps needed, is necessary and ordinary in your journey to reach your dreams and goals, one by one and all together. These steps are meant for all of us to become more grounded and intentional. Honesty and judgemental-less are the main keys here for the entire 8-Step process to flow smoothly.

1) Decision and Initial Contact – I already know something must change but not sure what and how?

2) Brainstorming Step and Research – Buy a notepad and write everything down. . Write down all your thoughts, feelings, actions and fears. No judgments. Just observe and write. Uncomfortable is necessary to reach comfortable.

3) Meeting or Introduction – Allow yourself 1-week or 1-month for step #2. Set specific day, date, time and duration to review info. Yes, you set up a meeting with yourself and you make sure to be on time. Bring your notebook, pencils and your "I can do this" attitude.

4) Analyze and Review Situation – After you read everything in your Initial Meeting, organize information by categories:
   - Personal (Routine) and Professional (Requirements)
   - Necessary (Work/Money) and Ordinary (Study/Improve)
   - Likes (what/who you like/love) and Dislikes (what/who you like/love less)
   - Now (Actions to START Now) and Future (Growth Path – Ongoing Progress)
   - Real (Goals) and Unreal (Dreams)

5) Determine Goals and Desires – Based on your above categories, determine what you can do right now and what you can do later and what you need to learn. Write a time frame next to each Desire and Goal. Be honest with what you can and cannot do. CALL today to schedule appointment with Strategy Consultant/Business Advisor; Set Up Monthly/Quarterly Pre-Paid Meetings as motivational solution to get organized;

6) Draft Temporary Action Plan – Take one Goal/Desire and turn it into a plan. Feel what you want. Think how you could do it. Acknowledge what you have, want and need. Who can help you. Write down each step you consider necessary. Write down possible outcomes and how to handle when/if they happen (maintain self-honesty at all times). Set cap on losses, when to stop. Use this "Cap" on ALL Losses: Time, Feelings, Money, Sanity! Know when to stop and re-arrange plan/path to travel. (Money gone Mental)

7) Set Rewards at each Destination – Praise yourself for each little achievement. Celebrate each step forward. Use that movie ticket as a gift for being on time to meeting(s), instead of just going to the movies. Buy those shoes for filing tax returns on time. Exercise to celebrate your body abilities. Plan that overdue vacation trip as an award for sticking to your new healthy financial habits! You get the picture... use ordinary actions to turn into extraordinary achievement awards.☺

8) Commit. Start. – Repeat All Steps for any decision from now on. Start now. Don't judge yourself, instead analyze "WHY do I feel this...? Why did I do that...? Why do I want/desire...?. Feel. Think. Write. Review. Analyze. Modify. Commit to Start now. Repeat all steps 1 – 7 over and over again.☺

We adult-practitioners need schedules, step-by-step instructions, discipline and commitment in order to achieve our goals. (Are you a grown up kid as well?) I recommend the above 8-steps for any decision, difficulty or direction in your growth journey, either personal or professional. When you also add a life detox day for sanity reboot purposes (no gadgets, no electronics, no social media, no emails, no phones, no TV), or at least 15-minutes daily (or several 15-min. time blocks per day), the above 8-step solution-driven formula will exceed your expectations and effective results.

As always, make it a smiley and efficient day,

Dana Musat ☺

About Dana

Dana Musat serves Life Entrepreneurs throughout their journey for personal, professional and financial fulfillment.

She describes her strategy here: When an experienced teacher, seasoned accountant, knowledgeable tax professional, and a determined Life Survivor are "hired to team up" for the sole purpose of brainstorming for solutions to their own "soul eating" and "financial aching" problems, rest assured that priceless formulas and recipes they create can be applied to anyone – regardless which path of life stage they are.

Remarkably, substantial growth can be unlocked from a very simple formula:

Success = Knowledge + Strategy + Implementation + Reporting (Personal & Professional)

Dana started this business out of her need to "survive" what she describes as her *Life Quake*: divorce, relocation, death, illness and the inevitable financial fall(s) that threw her into a completely confusing complex chaos. To her own surprise, a basic plan of action and steps for intentional implementation not only drew her through and out of these inevitable life trials, into a life of tremendous financial, professional, and most importantly, personal life of joy and fulfillment.

Dana is determined that this harmonious life can bestow anyone, and has committed herself to sharing her strategies, experiences and expertise through her stories and growth journey. She does not believe that everyone needs to go through the pain, effort and hardship of her experiences. Instead, she offers, for the open-minded, step-by-step personalized action plans for success.

Another easy recipe for success is: change your questions, amend your vocabulary, and you will receive more powerful answers and discover the possible solutions you were looking for.

Over the years, Dana has learnt that people want MORE (not less) from their Tax Accountant in terms of communication and relationship. She realized that, in her initial selfish pursuit to solve her own Life-Crisis, she was actually selfishly helping clients and friends to win their "Own Wars" = "Internal Battles" + "Financial Fears"+ "Emotional Distress." She was adding value to them without even knowing it, nor charging them high consulting fees. Helping others has been healing and a win-win for us all!

From there on Dana became intentional in investing in profitable relationships. She started investing time, money, effort, feelings, thoughts, dreams, patience, and sanity in helping others help her grow and return that wealth of expertise back to them in form of Consulting Services, via "How to..." sessions and personalized steps such as: "Turn Complaining Session into Gratitude Opportunities"; "Understand that Profits is not just a Money-Term." Profits apply to all investing opportunities, not only to your wages, salary or business net income itself. The reason why Dana Musat titled her upcoming book content: *Money Gone Mental.*

Dana's Holistic Consulting approach is her passion, her philosophy, and has already impacted countless individuals, families and businesses on how taxes, spending, investing and emotions are inextricably linked and affect our daily lives and our futures.

Dana resides in NYC and continues to invest in growth and expertise, by traveling and learning directly from the best, such as: Brian Tracy, John Maxwell, Brendon Burchard, Lisa Sasevich, Mark Bowness, Tony Robins and a myriad of other experts, clients, friends and family members. She offers you this unique inspiring combo of experience, skills and expertise for you to unleash your desires, goals and passions.

CHAPTER 27

BLUEPRINT FOR A SUCCESSFUL CAREER

BY AYOBIYI SHOTE

In the course of my career, one of the common mistakes I have seen people make is taking on a job or a career for the sole purpose of paying bills and for survival. What happens then is that apart from the monetary gains, there is no other factor to continually drive performance and encourage the employee to keep developing his/her potential. The resulting effect is stagnancy in terms of performance and in the role being occupied in the chosen career. Apparently, in the event of any economic meltdown, such a career will be the first to bear the brunt of any consequential decisions made, for instance downsizing, redundancy, etc. This prevalent mistake has inspired me to educate people on the need to build a sustainable career as well as the process to build it.

The first step to building a sustainable career will be acquiring a knowledge of what your individual purpose is. A knowledge of what your purpose is, will help you determine what you want. Is your focus making money only or do you want to build a sustainable career whilst bringing value to those around you? A money-oriented person will not focus on improving his or her skillset and will consequently run out of the requisite skills needed to ensure sustenance for any given career. A key success principle for any employee, or entrepreneur, is to build a career that is iron-clad enough to withstand cataclysmic changes. This chapter is focused on teaching you this.

WHAT IS MY PURPOSE?

As a human being created by God, your purpose can only be found in Him. Your purpose is your unique assignment on earth or your job description. You will need to have an understanding of your passion and your gifts in order to know what your unique God-given purpose is. Knowledge of this makes you understand your inborn and innate skills. Maximizing these skills towards living out your purpose will ensure adequate fulfilment in any chosen career. Hence, you will not just work for the purpose of making money, but would take on jobs that suit your chosen career and enable you to impact others positively – while maximizing your potential.

A knowledge of one's purpose will aid in determining the core values necessary for its realization. Getting what you want out of your chosen career will then be dependent on the values and qualities that you exude. For instance, your ability to withstand pressure and perform adequately, might see you being assigned projects that require such a skill. In the end, you acquire more experience at a job in the chosen career than you will ordinarily be privy to than a colleague who is there just for the purpose of making money. Core values that help project an influential charisma such as integrity, diligence, orderliness, time management, etc., if deciphered at the early stages of a chosen career, can be improved upon. Improving your core values will ensure focus on a career dependent on these core values. Understanding your core values will help you make decisions in your chosen career. Employers will recognize that your personal values are somewhat independent of the contract of employment, deeming you as a reliable employee.

Being armed with an understanding of your purpose, you will need to ask yourself what you want out of your career. Your answer should have sustainability as its foundation, as your decision will determine the job you choose. Any job you choose should be viewed as part of the bigger picture of your overarching career goal.

PERFORMANCE, POTENTIAL, PROMOTION!

Upon determining your overarching career goal, the next question to ask will be: *"What can I do to increase my performance and potential?"*

Performance is the ability to execute and deliver desired outcomes, whilst Potential is the ability to handle bigger tasks and deliver better outcomes, moving beyond your current level of performance. The English Thesaurus lists synonyms for potential as ability (noun), Capacity, Possibility, Aptitude, Capability, Promise. Therefore, a focus on developing potential is to work on increasing your capacity, aptitude and capability to do more. It is also showing promise that you can grow and take on more responsibility. A combination of performance and potential therefore determines your ability to get promoted, improving your chances of success, and enabling your advancement up the corporate ladder or becoming an expert in your field.

Promotion is neither based on the length of time you have spent in a role or a company, nor is it based on seniority in your chosen career. It is based on your performance and potential. Developing and executing a structured personal development plan is principal in developing potential and maintaining a high level of performance. To craft a realistic personal development plan, a clear understanding of your purpose and career goal is inevitable.

YOUR PERSONAL DEVELOPMENT PLAN.

To craft a personal development plan, understanding the age-old Greek maxim "know thyself" is critical. According to Wikipedia, Personal Development is a range of activities that improve awareness, develop talent and potential, build human capital and contribute to the realization of dreams and aspirations. Therefore, undertaking psychometric and personality tests will help you determine the strengths and weaknesses you exhibit. According to a McKinsey Institute report, "human beings all too often lack insight into what they need to know but don't," leading to biases that "can lead people to overlook their limitations and be overconfident of their abilities."[1] Therefore for you to overcome this bias, you need to understand who you are. Examples of questions you will need answered by taking these tests are noted below:

- What are my strengths?
- What are my weaknesses?
- How do I react under pressure?
- Am I more effective and productive as a team player than when I work solo?

- What is my style when working in a team?
- What is my learning or leadership type?
- Etc., etc.

Answering questions like these will help improve your understanding of your personality, learning, leadership and teamwork styles. This knowledge is essential in determining the areas that require improvement and development and in crafting your development plan.

You can develop a plan at any age or stage in your career. However, when you are crafting a plan, there are several things you should have resolved in your mind: who you are, why you are on earth, the values you want to be known for, and the goal you are setting out to achieve. These should be answered before commencing the process of crafting a ten-year personal development plan. Ten years is the magic number as it is not too long for you to lose interest in it, while it is not too short to achieve. I got the idea of a 10-year plan whilst having a conversation with one of my mentors in 2005.

From my experience, there should be two aspects of an effective personal development plan. However, before we talk about the two aspects, it is critical to talk about the most important question you should ask yourself: *"Where do I want to be in 10 years?"* Asking this question is vital to commencing the crafting of a development plan. When I embarked on this process for the first time in 2006, I followed the process specified by Brian Tracy, when he advised: *"Assume you have all the resources you need in the world, then determine what you want to do."* I determined I wanted to run organizations as a chief executive officer, either in paid employment or as an entrepreneur. That was my starting point.

When you have an idea of where you want to be, it is essential to study the profile of individuals that are already doing this same thing and are successful at it, so you can shorten the learning curve; while you are at it, take notes. Identify the skills and competence that your subjects have exhibited in the role. Identify, the issues and problems they had and how they overcame them. It is also essential to learn why they had these issues in the first place, as from experience I have learnt that the gaps in your skillset and competencies can be the reason. As you identify this information, you need to be able to match them to your identified skills and competencies, then identify the gaps in your skillset and competence. It is important to do this with your mentor.

I would advise that a personal development plan should not focus exclusively on your career. It is important to ensure that a proper work-life balance is built into the plan, as "all work and no play...." The plan should be a living plan that can be updated and adjusted as your priorities change. While the first part should focus on your entire career as a whole, the second part should focus on the career and development path you envisage in the company you are currently working in.

While crafting this plan you will need to ask and answer certain questions, to make the plan realistically achievable. For instance:

- Where am I now?

- Where do I want to be in this time frame?

- What skills do I have now?

- What skills do I need in order to be at the desired level within the time frame I want?

- What do I need to develop these desired skills?

- Are there any skill sets to unlearn, which hinder my performance?

Furthermore, a personal development plan aimed at building a sustainable career must take cognizance of technical and professional training. There must be a plan to develop yourself through professional courses, knowledge acquisition and improvement, in order to acquire the competence and skills required for your chosen career. In some cases, a short course that will not strain you in your current role will suffice. Reading books about the chosen subject is also an excellent strategy to consider. Considering the fast pace of innovation and the continuous evolution of principles, theories and technology relevant to the world today, developing a reading habit is essential. This will ensure that you remain abreast of developments in your profession, giving you an edge over a monetarily-inspired career.

It is more efficient to break your plan down into bite-sized chunks, because this makes it easy to organize your plan into short, medium and long-term milestones. From my experience, the timeline for these milestones are:

- Short term: 1 – 2 years

- Medium term : 3 – 5 years

- Long term: 6 – 10 years

What remains vital in this plan is working through it with diligence, bearing in mind the overarching goal of excelling at a chosen career while being indispensable in a current role.

SKILLS DEVELOPMENT

Considering that the goal of the 10-year plan is a process, it is necessary to maximize current opportunities towards ensuring the realization of the overarching goal. One of the most cost effective ways of developing skills is to look out for extra responsibilities and projects to volunteer for, that would enable you develop the required skills needed.

What sort of jobs or projects would you embark on to develop critical skills? Employers are naturally drawn to high performers with potential, as they can be entrusted with the realization of the corporate vision, which is not restricted to just delivering a profit, but delivering value to all stakeholders. High performers are usually the last to be considered for release, if at all, in the event of the consequential problems from adverse economic conditions. This is why your efforts at developing skills should be focused on developing potential.

READING AS A STRATEGY

Reading is a personal development strategy that is often overlooked. Brian Tracy once said; "If you decide to read one book per week on a specific subject, in a year, you would have read 52 books on the subject and you will be a subject matter expert." A consistent focus on developing specific skills makes a difference, not only in improving performance, but developing potential.

This is why it is also important to continue to develop skills needed in your current role. Search out knowledge on how to improve at your job and increase your performance. To develop potential however, needs a little bit more! Reading a wide range of subjects and authors develops a person's ability to think outside the box, challenge conventional wisdom and developing the ability to deal with ambiguity whilst increasing your capacity for innovative thought.

The personal development plan should be a live document that can be reviewed and updated as the specific targets and milestones are achieved.

MAKE LEADERSHIP A CORE COMPETENCE

Leadership development is critical for a successful career. Leadership, whilst not a function of your position in the office or in your business, is a function of the influence you exert within your immediate sphere due to the relationships formed with peers, team members, colleagues, stakeholders and others. A lot of managers erroneously believe that they are leaders by virtue of their functional roles, but you can be a manager and not be a leader. Yet, an effective leader is a more effective manager, as leadership deals more with influencing people, crafting a compelling vision, and motivating team members to achieving the team goal irrespective of each individual circumstance. Leadership as a core competence should be included as part of your development plan.

CONCLUSION

Although opinions on the best approach to sustaining a chosen career might vary, one fact remains that consistent focus on personal development plays a vital role in ensuring career success. It is also an indicator of personal drive and ability to adequately wield authority and accept accountability. These are all factors that constitute a blueprint of a successful career.

References

1. http://www.mckinsey.com/business-functions/organization/our-insights/the-four-building-blocks--of-change?cid=other-eml-alt-mkq-mck-oth-1605

About Ayobiyi

Ayobiyi Shote, immediate past Managing Director, Baker Hughes Incorporated, West Africa, is a management executive known for his leadership skills and strategies which have contributed to the growth of the organizations he has been a part of. His people management, interpersonal and consultative leadership skills have seen him form dynamic partnerships with employees and customers that have given rise to innovative solutions and eventual sustained operational growth. Over the years, he has developed advanced business strategies that drive consistent organizational growth.

In addition to his ability to maximize profits, he has also reinforced operations through strategic decision-making, resource management, and cost containment. He wields the dynamic ability to motivate employees towards delivering on operational expectations, inadvertently increasing customer satisfaction.

With a background in Engineering, he has over 19 years of cumulative experience in the global oil and gas industry, spanning Sales, Marketing, Applications Engineering, Operations, and Strategic Management. He has worked in several countries, notably the United Kingdom, France, and Oman in differing Management roles. He has an MBA from the University of Liverpool and a Master of Arts 'Leading Innovation and Change' from York St John University, UK.

He is a Fellow of the Chartered Management Institute and a member of the Institute of Directors, both in the UK. He is also a Fellow of the Institute of Credit Administration, Nigeria.

Ayo who is also an ordained pastor is married to Ogechukwu, his wife of 18 years; they are blessed with Ayodeji, Wuraola and Oyindamola.

- For more information, pls. contact: shotea@icloud.com

CHAPTER 28

SUCCESS HEADPHONES
— CANCEL OUT THE NOISE AND FOCUS ON THE POTENTIAL

BY VAMEGH ASKARI

What we carry inside of us, we take with us everywhere we go.

In my life, I've had the joy of working in many different types of businesses as an MBA degree holder. Regardless of where I am or what I am doing, I've found that there is always a need for awareness of how we respond internally to everything that is happening externally. We cannot avoid what we are feeling because it dictates the flow of our moment, our day. When we think of the actions we take in life, we know we do them in hopes of gaining something better and to find a more fulfilling place, but we often struggle to get there. This can change.

Never one to shy away from self-reflection, I've always sought out those sources which make me better. People. Places. Opportunities. Knowledge. Ways to focus on self-improvement are everywhere when we look for them, and in everything we do. I think that's a beautiful thing, and it is my passion for this that really inspires me. I haven't really tapped into anything "new" in the new age world, but I have found a way to align personal harmony and fulfillment with a corporate world that is oftentimes riddled with stress, anxiety, and uncertainty in the pursuit of rising to the top. People wonder how I've done it, with keeping this calmness about me. It's noticeable, mostly because it's authentic. It's driven by my approach to life, not the words I choose. You can't fake fulfillment for long to others; and your time is even shorter for how long you can fake-out yourself. Eventually, you'll press your hands over your ears, trying to block out the anxiety and negative noises, but they resist you. They are so loud!

I had noises once upon a time, but I was able to filter out all that didn't enhance my life so I could better focus on what did. How? I found my headphones, and through their use I've come across something great. It's a fusion of my passion for self-improvement and the engineering skills that are also an intricate part of who I am. I've grown into a Life Engineering Coach, dedicated to helping people find their headphones, dusting them off, and starting using them. And the great news is—you cannot leave home without them! They are in you; they are in all of us.

BECOME A STATE OF THE ART "YOU" BY USING YOUR HEADPHONES

The illiterate of the 21st century will not be those who cannot read and write, but those who cannot learn, unlearn, and relearn.
~ Alvin Toffler

When we think about life, the beautiful thing it's meant to be, we can easily identify that it cannot be complete without embracing change. This change comes in many ways, both large and small, but ideally, it takes you in the right direction. We all seek to become more "complete" and to do that, it's important to seek out the positive paths, words, and thoughts that will move us forward. The easiest way to cancel out the distracting noises in our lives is by putting on our headphones. By doing this, we can better choose how and where to focus our energy. Visualize this…

- ᪥ That individual who is writing a check in the line, just ahead of you, doesn't make you tap your foot in impatience. You are able to be patient, recognizing that moment doesn't have to be wasted—it can be focused on something positive. . . perhaps the chat you had with your child that morning or the meeting you have worked so hard to earn that's coming up.

- ᪥ Everyone around you is bickering, draining you of your focus and tasks at hand, and you are able to cancel out that noise and accomplish what makes you better.

258

🎧 Instead of worrying about what has happened or what is yet to be, you are embracing the moment for what it is – whether it seems favorable or not does not matter, as it is something you must tend to in order to grow and move upward and forward.

**We average 50,000 to 60,000 thoughts per day.
98% of them are the same.**

If we take the advice of Alvin Toffler and relearn better concepts for us, replacing the ones that don't help us grow into our full potential, we can find the strength to move our mountains, whatever those mountains may be. By being tapped into our spiritual and mental power concurrently, we are capable of greatness that exceeds anything we may have experienced up until this point in our lives.

*As infants, we learn to speak and listen; and as adults,
we must learn to be mute and deaf in a positive way.*
~ Vamegh Askari

Thomas Edison had an advantage with this because he was nearly deaf. But often enough, he expressed gratitude for this, as it allowed him the opportunity to better focus on his experiments. Where would we be now without those wonderful experiments and inventions? All 1,000+ of them.

What do our headphones offer us, really? They offer us the ability to be both silent and deaf. To recognize that everything that rains down on us does not have to weigh us down; rather, it can help us to grow. Headphones are the recognition that we don't have to carry the concerns of the world on our shoulders, while also struggling to learn who "we" really are. The best "us" can only show its presence when we recognize that our need to be whole is the foundation to making all those other changes we long to see around us, or at least expressing our views in a more meaningful way.

Change our thinking. Change our outcomes.

Does a life that is free of the noise and static of the world around you sound appealing? Would you like to calm your mind and find clarity? If you see the value in these things, you are on your way to understanding all the benefits that come with learning to use your headphones—headphones that are hardwired for success, by your definition of what success is to you.

BENEFITS OF USING YOUR HEADPHONES

If you insult me or even put a curse, I will respond only in praise.
~ Hafiz Shirazi

There are three areas of our lives where using our headphones is as strategic a move for self-improvement as it is an act of self-love, to show yourself that you know you deserve more than the clutter that's around you. Your very soul is longing for this place of contentment, where there are no winds and storms that throw you off course. Finding that place for even one minute in a trying time will keep the doorway open so you can easily travel there anytime you need.

🎧 Bring out your "Success Voice":

Our age of instant access does bring us wonderful benefits, such as access to the voices of the masters who have given us knowledge and guidance from years—even centuries—long past that still apply to us today. The reason it still applies to us today is that the human spirit does not change, our fundamental needs to be whole, complete, and at harmony in our environments cannot go away.

We must stop our inner critical voice and help it relearn a better approach to our success by having it become a voice of praise that is genuine to your greater good and positive energy in this world.

Be still. The quieter you become the more you can hear.
~ Ram Dass

🎧 Cancel out the Noise:

Learning to cancel out the noises that distract and hinder us from feeling contentment and happiness, or pursuing our paths and passions is essential. We need to block out those outside voices that think dreaming, pursuing, and finding internal bliss is all a fantasy, a desire that cannot be fulfilled. Because it can. One of the best ways I've found to cancel out the noise is through meditation. This can be just in the moment, visualizing something that is positive and moves me forward, or it can be something longer, in a quiet place where I can acknowledge my thoughts, addressing what I must, and celebrating how I've grown from that experience itself, as well as the experiences of my day.

> *Don't waste your time with explanations; people*
> *only hear what they want to hear.*
> ~ Paulo Coelho

🎧 Do not let anyone disturb you:

The power of focus is a wonderful power that is waiting to burst through inside of you, breaking through the noise that is disguised as a dead end or brick wall that is blocking you from your passions and purpose. Once you see your passion and your inner voice becomes your biggest advocate for success, you will find a laser focus waiting for you that cannot be disrupted for anything. Then the rewards of mastering your headphones begin to show themselves.

Nothing can stop the man who chooses focus over distraction, for he
will be consumed with good intentions and positive actions.

Imagine waking up in the morning and feeling excited to start your day. You can feel your body gaining energy and excitement from the good things that are in store. It may be finishing a tough project you've been working on. Perhaps you have a wonderful meal with family and friends that evening. Or maybe, you are eager to read that next chapter of that book that has truly impacted you in some way. Feeling this way is contagious in the most positive of ways, and a large part of achieving this type of moment comes from using your success headphones. They come with a lifetime warranty, too!

CARING FOR YOUR HEADPHONES

The things we cherish most are those that we should
make every effort to take wonderful care of.

Our avenues to caring for the headphones that are working so hard for our betterment are threefold; each having a specific purpose to helping us, and all of them, when working together, help us to achieve success, as we define it. For me, success comes from teaching others on how to use their headphones and watching as they transform, their true inner beauty coming out and their destinies clearly ahead. For you, it could be something different, which is wonderful. After all, we're unique and wonderful in our own way—all of us.

🎧 **First, we need to understand "how" to care for our headphones.**
We all have access to at least one, if not all, the ways to care for our headphones. These options include:
- Meditation: study the types of meditation out there and find the ones that work best for you. You can meditate when you're walking, waiting in line, or even for a minute when you first wake up in the morning. Use this wonderful gift to yourself to stay focused on the positive steps you can take every day.
- Seminars: events that range from an hour or two, to an entire day or weekend are out there. Each is designed to help connect people with messages that will transform and help them seek out what they are missing. Follow your favorite "thought leaders" to learn where they may be so you can have the joy of experiencing their energy in a live venue. Every time I have done this I have left with a few "moments of awareness" that I haven't previously had, and quite often, also a smile that shone from the inside out.
- Multimedia: books, audio books, movies, short videos, and blogs are also wonderful sources of getting a daily touch of inspiration and motivation to help your headphones stay charged up for you.

🎧 **Second, we need to learn "when" we should put our headphones on.**
This is the easiest thing to do with your headphones—know when to use them, because you can use them anytime! If you are awake and you need your headphones, put them on. It will help you to take care of everything more efficiently, effectively, and if it's particularly tumultuous, with more grace.

🎧 **Third, we must recognize "where" we can best use our headphones.**
Really, the answer to "where" is "everywhere." However, a few places that those I help and myself have found great joy with our headphones include:

- *The car:* take advantage of an audio book or just enjoy the scenery around you; with practice, even stand-still rush hour traffic can be a positive experience for you internally.
- *The gym:* fitness and self-awareness make for a beautiful combination. There is a reason that many people are euphoric when they are done exercising—it physically triggers our bodies to feel that way. Add in the power of your headphones in that moment (relearning, remember) and you will give yourself the fuel you need for success.
- *Shopping malls:* for many people, shopping isn't fun. There is impatience, whether on the part of those around you or you personally, and that means wasted time in negative emotions. By putting your headphones on you'll find that you take care of what you need to do just as quickly, and with a sense of contentment in your heart.

I get so excited when I see how something that we all have within us can be brought to light, creating significant changes that make one's life better and more fulfilled. My passion for it is endless and the rewards that happen in my life by recognizing my dreams grow more wonderful every day.

Being a Life Engineer Coach has really helped me to take this desire to the next stage, talking to people individually and in group forums. As I hear the stories of those who open up to me I see eyes of hope. People want inspiration for change, and I recognize how blessed I am to contribute to this. And with each blessing I receive, I learn and grow, too. In a world where life isn't always "easy," I'm now contributing something of value that will help others take the steps to find the quiet behind the noise. This is the path I'm meant to be on, and now I ask you: "Do you know where your headphones are?"

About Vamegh

Vamegh Askari is a life engineering coach who provides private consulting services in Canada, United Arab Emirates, Iran, and via the Internet all around the world. He earned his Master of Business Administration at the University of Phoenix, and prior to becoming a life engineering coach, he worked as a material science engineer and translated self-improvement books between English and Persian. He is the co-author of *Success Blueprint* along with Brian Tracy and was selected as one of America's PremierExperts™. Known as an effective communicator, Vamegh is passionate about forming transcendent connections with people in which deep and lasting growth can take place and also about witnessing that growth as it takes place.

Vamegh operates at *reLearn Centre* under the slogan "Stay Current." As someone who is cognizant of the ever-changing modern world, he is a proponent of remaining in a constant state of adaptation. He believes that success comes to those who live their lives aware of their surroundings and willing to acknowledge their own shortcomings, and when he works with his clients, he encourages them to unlearn the old, outdated rules and learn the new rules that fit their environment more neatly. Intent on breaking you out of our comfort zone, he will teach you how to challenge all assumptions in order to build forward momentum in your career and in your life.

As a life engineering coach, Vamegh offers a variety of services, including Mind Mapping, Smart Reading, Memory Improvement Techniques, Goal Setting, Time Management, and Peak Performance. Everything he does, he does with the goal of personal development in mind, breaking you out of your bad habits when necessary and illustrating positive habits for you as well. He has seen over and over the dramatic change of which people are capable, and he has become an expert in replicating that dramatic change in his clients, eliciting their best work, eliciting new levels of organization and analytical brilliance, eliciting more powerful thought processes and more solid self-belief.

In addition to co-founding reLearn Centre, Vamegh is the founder of Vamegh Success Academy, through which he offers the educational courses based on classic books such as, *Think and Grow Rich*, *The Richest Man in Babylon*, and *Acres of Diamonds*. All courses come with several questionnaires and mind maps that will give you the opportunity to read the books line by line and digest the information. He also offers time-tested business promotion services, which are said to be known for establishing start-up companies in their respective industries and expanding established companies beyond their projected growth potential. Based out of Oakville Ontario, Vamegh lives with his family and his favourite pastimes are reading, hiking and traveling.

You can connect with Vamegh at:
- info@vamegh.com
- info@relearncentre.com

CHAPTER 29

CLIMBING THE PYRAMID OF TAX EFFICIENCY
— BUSINESS OWNERS AND PROFESSIONALS: YOU CAN MAKE IT BUT DO YOU KNOW HOW TO KEEP IT?

BY PETER HIBBARD

Every owner of a business or profession reaches a point where they wonder, "Has it been worth it?" You've struggled to become successful and you are among peers who are now in their 50s and 60s. You've taken all the risks of your profession in stride and met all your business and family obligations with pride. The kids are out of the house, the house is paid or mostly paid for, and the business is now mature. You lay awake at night wondering if all you've put into it will now return financial security in retirement to you and your loved ones. You wonder if you will be able to build on your financial security when continually faced with all the financial hurdles. The biggest hurdle is comprised of all the taxes you face at so many levels. You can make it, but something always seems to take it.

I want to tell you the story of Paul and Lisa. Before I get into the story I want you to realize that the integrated solutions to Paul and Lisa's problems are not just solutions available to medical professionals. They are solutions for all types of professionals as well as all types and sizes of commercial businesses.

Paul was a successful 55-year old physician. Lisa ran the office. Five years ago, Paul finally came to see me. Actually, Paul was one of my doctors and he had a general idea around what I did for clients in his situation. However, for many years prior to that meeting, Paul would almost always say at the end of my visit in his office, "I have to meet with you." He would say this right after he said," I'm paying too much in tax and my tax adviser doesn't have any viable solutions for me. I think it's affecting my ability to retire when and how I'd like."

During our first business meeting, I learned as much as I could about his personal goals and some details about the financial aspects of his practice. After he sent me the additional documents and data I needed, it was easy to conclude he was right. He was paying too much in tax and it was robbing him of the wherewithal to retire when he wanted and how he wanted.

At our next meeting, I asked Paul if he knew that the Federal Internal Revenue Code statutes, regulations, and case law exceed 70,000 pages in length according to the Tax Foundation (taxfoundation.org). I then asked Paul who or what is leveraging off him? At first he didn't understand the question. I knew Paul was an avid fisherman. So I asked him why he didn't just catch fish with his hands and not use one of the his many fishing poles. He said, "Well, the fishing pole is more efficient." I said, "Exactly, the fishing pole is a form of leverage. Another example of leverage is Wall Street's use of the media. Wall Street constantly pumps out positive news as it wants you invested in the markets (their casino) for as long as it can get you to do so. That way the Wall Street casino can extract fees from you for a lifetime. As you can see, Wall Street leverages off all of us."

So I asked, "Why might the Federal tax code and regulations have grown to over 70,000 pages? Perhaps it's so the Government can leverage off you, to do what it needs to get from you and to do whatever it wants." All those pages allow the Federal government to take what it will from all citizens.

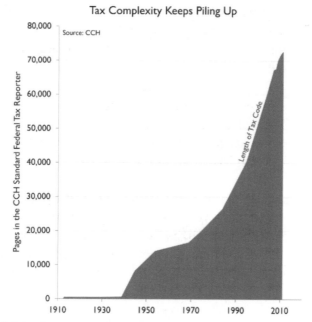

Tax Complexity Keeps Piling Up

I told Paul it's time to talk about reducing the government's leverage over him. I further explained that hidden in those 70,000 pages are gems that could be mined to reduce tax burden, grow net worth and increase financial security.

While we're talking about taxes, where do you think tax rates are going in the future? As you can see from this chart, we are at relatively low tax rates historically speaking.

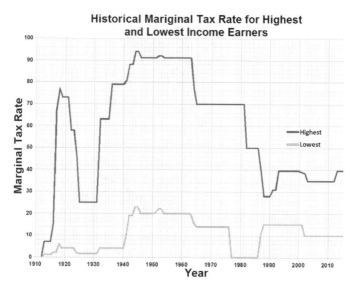

Historical Mariginal Tax Rate for Highest and Lowest Income Earners

As you are also aware, our nation has historically high debt nearing $20 trillion dollars. What is not frequently talked about is the size of unfunded liabilities we face as a nation. The liabilities I'm referring to are all the Federal programs that don't have funds backing current and future benefits. These liabilities are calculated to be in excess of $100 trillion dollars (source: www.usdebtclock.org). The total US unfunded liability includes Social Security, Medicare Parts A, B and D, Federal Debt held by the Public, plus Federal Employee and Veteran Benefits (Source: U.S. Treasury GAAP Accounting).

Let me now ask a simple question, where do you think tax rates are going? Frankly, most of my friends and clients think tax rates are going up. Paul agreed and also realized now was the time to act before he was out of time to secure his retirement. The future of his profession looked bright, the future of government leveraging off him was quite frightening.

I told Paul that to a good extent, paying taxes is a voluntary exercise. There are hundreds of opportunities (programs if you will) hidden in the 70,000 pages of tax code that Paul could take advantage of. Remember the tax codes gems I mentioned above? Let's mine some of them for you so that you can climb the Pyramid of Tax Efficiency. When climbing the pyramid, you should examine each gem as a three-dimensional opportunity. This triad perspective will help you consider each opportunity as it progresses through three dimensions.

Tax efficiency has three dimensions or phases: Contribution, Accumulation and Distribution. In the contribution phase, the tax efficiency we seek is having an annual tax deduction against your personal or corporate income. This deduction should be as large as your profitability and cash flow allow. The second phase is the accumulation phase. In this phase the tax efficiency we seek is to have your money grow tax deferred or tax exempt. Finally, the third phase is the distribution phase. This phase is essentially the retirement phase where you are drawing down your accumulated funds to support your desired lifestyle. In many cases this phase is as important if not more important than the first two phases. The ultimate tax efficiency we seek is to have ongoing income which is tax favored throughout retirement. As we discuss Paul's case, I'll show examples of how Paul achieved tax efficiency in each of the three phases.

In summary, you should have the opportunity to contribute, accumulate and distribute your money in a tax efficient manner in all years. Climbing the Pyramid effectively earns you a higher probability of your money outliving you.

Paul's practice had matured but was still growing. In addition to his salary, he was being taxed on the large corporate profit passing through to his tax return. Paul was very tired of writing really large checks to Federal and State tax authorities. This is typical of many business owners and professionals, who, in their 40s, 50s and even early 60s have hit their stride in success and profitability. They've put their kids through college, have the home they want, and have paid off most or all of their debts. Now there's a new hurdle coming they knew was out there but little they'd done about it. They are staring at retirement and the tax man is standing between them and their desired retirement goal.

Paul's tax professional had told him that his practice's 401(k) plan was the only qualified plan he needed because the cost of using any other type of qualified plan was too high and he'd get little benefit from it. What I found most absurd was his tax advisor's comment that there was little he could do and he'd just have to suck it up and write the government tax checks. Fortunately, not all tax advisers are like this, but many are.

I told Paul we were going to begin climbing the Pyramid of Tax Efficiency together. Although there are many steps in the pyramid my job was to select which of the many tax efficiency gems were to be mined. Of course, we made sure each selected gem was relevant to Paul's situation. Next we will examine the three gems Paul picked up as he stepped up the Pyramid. The first gem allowed Paul to install a specialty-designed qualified retirement plan.

THE BIG PLAN

The BIG plan is a unique retirement plan because it allows much higher contribution levels than a traditional 401(k) or defined benefit plan. Remember that Paul's then tax advisor told him not to use these plans because the employees would receive most of the contribution. He was told he and his wife would not get much of the plan's contribution. We reviewed the demographics of Paul's firm and determined he had the opportunity to contribute up to $1,000,000 to the BIG plan design.

That's a nice number, but what was even better was that over 90% of this contribution was going to fund Paul and Lisa's retirement. In other words, less than 10% of the overall contribution went to other employees and administration expenses. Now that's tax efficiency by any standard! This large deductible contribution has been made for over 5 years and has saved Paul over $2.5 million in income tax. Where did the money go? It was moved into his future, to be delivered at his and his wife's retirement.

CAPTIVATE YOURSELF WITH THE CAPTURE OF YOUR OWN CAPTIVE

As Paul was reaching maximum accumulation in the BIG Plan, his allowable contribution to the plan began to decrease. Paul needed another gem from the steps in the Pyramid. Paul was still working hard, was still very profitable and still needed tax relief. Our next step was to discuss the business and professional risks inherent in his practice. Many of the risks were insured and had traditional professional liability insurance, worker's compensation insurance, business interruption insurance, etc. However, there were many not-so-obvious business and financial risks that were not insured, because there was no traditional commercial property and casualty insurance available. As a result, Paul decided to form his own insurance company to insure the practice's additional risk.

My firm provided Paul with an actuarial risk study that quantified the additional risks that needed to be addressed. The type of risks identified were Cyber/HIPPA Liability, Legal Expense and Administrative Actions to name a few. Our actuaries were able to price these real risks, as well as others we identified. Make no bones about it, to form a Captive you must transfer risk by paying your insurance company a premium and it assumes these real risks and insures against them. The result in Paul's case was an additional annual deductible insurance premium of $775,000. By the time Paul is expected to retire, his Captive will have saved Paul another $1.2 million in taxes.

Assuming Paul continues to run his practice successfully and is not hit with insurance claims that drain funds from his captive, he will be able to sell or close the captive at a tax efficient capital gains tax cost. Paul is now building a tax efficient second pool of funds to support his retirement.

THE PRESTIGE PLUS STRATEGY – USING OPM (OTHER PEOPLE'S MONEY) FOR RETIREMENT

Paul was also concerned about his family if something should happen to him. Paul asked if there was a tax efficient way to protect his family and at the same time supplement his retirement income. In response, we introduced Paul to the Prestige Plus Strategy (PPS) and the living benefits of life insurance. What are the living benefits of life insurance? Most people view life insurance as death protection only and the premium is viewed as cost. Paul's view of life insurance was traditional in that he was convinced life insurance only provided death benefits and that it was expensive. As Paul learned, that view was not at all accurate. He learned there are potentially significant living benefits available with properly structured modern life insurance policies. Paul elected to use bank financing (OPM) to fund a policy for both he and Lisa. Using this concept, Paul will be able to retire earlier and wealthier. Here are some of the benefits Paul acquired by implementing our Prestige Plus Strategy.

1. Retirement income that is tax-free when properly structured.
2. Life insurance to protect family and business as well as business succession.
3. Liquidity to pay estate and transfer taxes at Paul and Lisa's passing.
4. Employee retention in the form of a one-of-a-kind retirement protection.
5. A business cash account, earning more than CDs and Money Market accounts.
6. A "sinking" account to finance other business opportunities that may arise.

[For more information on this strategy, please visit my associates and myself at websites following in my bio below.]

The PPS will deliver to Paul and Lisa a supplemental tax-free retirement income over $1 million in income during their retirement years. He also enjoyed tax favored contributions while funding the PPS. This feature saved Paul an additional $500,000 in taxes during the contribution phase.

SUMMARY

Over Paul's working years he legally reduced his tax bill by over $3.0 million dollars.

Tax Summary for just three "Climb the Pyramid of Tax Efficiency" steps

Plan	Contributions	Accumulations	Distributions
The BIG Plan	Tax Deductible	Tax deferred	Taxable
Captive Plan	Tax Deductible	Tax favored	Tax favored
Prestige Plus Strategy Plan	Tax favored	Tax exempt	Tax exempt

These three strategies are found in the 70,000 pages of tax code and regulations. Just imagine what else might be hidden in all those pages! After reading a book published by The Brookings Institution in 1978 called, *A Voluntary Tax?* I had an epiphany.

The Brookings book reviewed studies of wealthy families in an effort to try and understand how the use of sophisticated estate-planning techniques helped these families avoid the estate tax in an era of relatively high estate tax rates. Specifically, the book talked about the DuPont family and how its wealth transferred from generation to generation, paying an estate tax of less than 5% in an era where the Federal estate tax rate was near 70%. The book's conclusion was there are many factors that account for eliminating or at least reducing the amount of estate tax paid. However, the driving factor was the use by these families of a special breed of legal and financial advisors who not only knew about the tools to be used, but more importantly had the ability to time, combine and sequence the tools to implement the tax reduction strategies.

Have you discovered the right advisors? Paul did!

About Peter

Peter Hibbard has been in the financial services business since 1971. In 1978 he founded Columbia Benefits Consultants,Inc. DBA CBC Retirement Partners, Inc. (CBC) which is an independent consulting firm advising clients and their advisors on the advanced tools and techniques needed to create total financial and retirement security. CBC brings a unique series of services that holistically assists business owners and their employees to achieve their retirement goals. CBC may be engaged to provide actuarial, administrative, recordkeeping and advisory services for companies to establish and manage quality retirement plans for its employees. In addition, CBC's retirement income and compensation planning divisions help clients design their compensation systems in a way that properly aligns the owners and their key employees' vision of their future to grow the company profitably.

Following graduation in 1967 from Rutgers University, Pete was commissioned and served as an officer in the United States Marine Corps. During the Vietnam War, Pete was an infantry platoon commander and was decorated for his leadership in combat. He is also the recipient of a Purple Heart. He is a member of The Forum 400, the Society of Financial Services Professionals, American Society of Pension Professionals and Actuaries, The National Association of Actuaries and Consultants, and the Association for Advanced Life Underwriting. He has earned the professional designations of Chartered Life Underwriter (CLU) and Chartered Financial Consultant (ChFC) conferred by the American College, Bryn Mawr, PA. He speaks nationally to organizations of tax and investment professionals.

Pete and his wife Beth have two children and four grandchildren and reside in Columbia, MD. His daughter, Kerri, is a busy mom of four boys. Pete's son-in-law, Tim, is CBC's President, a registered investment advisor and plays an integral part in the firm's compensation planning, exit planning, and wealth transfer planning work. His son, Jamie, joined the firm as a financial advisor and is involved in all the planning needed by our clients. Pete also serves on the board of directors or chairs the finance committees of several local charities including Howard County General Hospital Foundation, a member of Johns Hopkins Medicine. He is also a member of the Board of Directors of First Financial Resources, a firm comprised of some of the top financial advisors from around the nation.

For more information on the Prestige Strategy, please contact us at:
- info@columbiabenefits.com
- www.coolspringsfinancial.com.

You can connect with Peter at the following:
- phibbard@columbiabenefits.com
- www.columbiabenefits.com
- www.cbcdaily.com

CHAPTER 30

START BY READING AND LEARNING TO ENTER THE WORLD OF BUSINESS

BY ROBERT S. CHMIELEWSKI

Dreams of today are the achievements of tomorrow.

You can achieve success very easily, the only tasks you have to do are to read, learn and take action.

Road map for achieving success is very simple:
1. Read *Rich Dad, Poor Dad* by Robert Kiyosaki.
2. Read *Eat That Frog* by Brian Tracy.
3. Complete *Success Mastery Academy* by Brian Tracy and take action.
4. Exactly define your goals in all areas using *Life Makeover Coaching* by T. Harv Eker.
5. Find the right mentor and start to realize your dreams, your vision, build a company, live a level-10 life, etc.

Of course you can choose Brian Tracy or Tony Robbins. There are great leaders and mentors in America and in every country around the world. You can find the best one for you. Start at once. If you are just starting, begin with the road map above. Just do it!

Main principles of success by Robert S. Chmielewski. - Strategy expert in creating blue oceans:

1. *Implement excellence, because excellence is not high cost; convert and implement your best ideas into reality and improve yourself and your business. Ask yourself how I am able to realize it successfully and solve it like those before. Solve every challenge using creativity. Find the right root-causes and solve like those before with success.*

2. *Solve your challenges by visualization. When you can see them, you can start finding solutions. Visualize all your challenges, so that you conquer them easier, from managing the company to greater challenges. One of my mentors once said "...it is very easy..." I try to remember these words every day.*

Please find my new tool called "Leader Desktop" to manage your company.

MARKET WINDOW	ORGANIZATION WINDOW				KNOWLEDGE WINDOW
INFORMATION	STRATEGY				NEW KNOWLEDGE
INFO SERVISES	MISSION	VISION	VALUES	CORPORATE CULTURE	STRATEGY JOURNALS
	GOALS	KEY SUCCESS INDICATORS	LEADERSHIP	CANVAS MODEL	
INNOVATION INFO	PERFORMANCE				RESEARCHES
	BALANCE SHEET	PROFIT & LOSS ACCOUNT	CASH FLOW	ADDED VALUE GAP, ADJUSTMENT GAPS	
TRADES	TACTICS				TRAININGS
EXHIBITIONS					
	PROFIT CENTERS	BUSINESS UNITS	PROJECTS	PRODUCTS	
BENCHMARKING	OPERATIONS				CONTINOUS IMPROVEMENT
GOOD PRACTICES					EXCELLENCE IMPROVEMENT
	QUALITY	TECHNOLOGY	COST	LOGISTIC	
	KPI - PPM			KPI - LPI	

LEADER DESKTOP ™

© Robert S.Chmielewski

The Leader Desktop Tool consists of three windows:

   I. The Market window provides knowledge about current market trends, competition.

   II. The Organization window delivers a global view on the company.

   III. The Knowledge window makes available new know-how and the latest research on strategy.

3. *Learn from the best worldwide, read, train and ask, always improve.*
Growth is like breathing, people need clean air; successful people
need new knowledge to strengthen their auto-motivation.

4. *Help other people to achieve their goals and businesses. They will*
help you.
At the beginning of every meeting I ask, "How am I able to help you
in realizing your goals...?"

How to achieve success through reading and study?

'What does not kill us, makes us stronger.' What if it made us stronger
over the last 5 years? I did not know the practical answer for the last 5
years, until I had a nice conversation with the company's owner I have
been working with for the past 5 years.

One possible answer from experience: the company's owner may propose
you take the position of CEO or you can try even harder to start up as an
entrepreneur with your own business.

I have been also offered a management position at **BOZAMET LTD**
(www. bozamet.pl), a strong, developing company on the industry
market with great future possibilities. We have been searching for big
global business partners with high added-value projects to develop with
each other due to investing in Poland with spectacular cost reductions
for big investors and implementation of the newest business management
tools. We offer over 43,000 m^2 in operating halls and over 200,000 m^2
of grounds to invest. **BOZAMET** hires 420 employees. Our highly
qualified managers have a strong technical background in cooperation
with global leaders in automotive, construction, defense and aviation,
energy and environment, machining, industrial manufacturing, medical,
printing, parking and the railway industry and take care of transfers or
new projects. **BOZAMET R&D** has been cooperating with leading
German Research and Development Institutes.

My passion for reading started in my childhood. I read hundreds of books.
My interest in business started from my passion to play "Monopoly" and
"Fortune." I really liked business. My passion for business is connected
with sports: basketball, running and swimming.

I am the firstborn of my siblings, and I had to do everything first. This meant getting my driving license first, my first car and my motorboat license – all of these were a big challenge for me. Unfortunately, my Dad died very young at the age of 43. So starting from birth up to age 14, we always had the strongest support from my dad. After his death, I was so sad that, for half-a-year, I tried to remember everything he taught me during his lifetime. From this difficult time on, I tried to find support in sports heroes.

In 1991, Polish television rebroadcast the NBA finals. Believe me, watching Michael Jordan in action was something really incredible. He was my sports hero along with Larry Bird and Magic Johnson. I must say that I am lucky, because I started rooting for the Bulls when the march began for six championship titles. Even now, after 20 years, these sports heroes are my inspiration in business and winning. Business' enormous pressure is similar to sports, but a little easier, because you have more time to prepare a game plan.

Learn from the best worldwide players, businessman, speakers, rulers or kings of sport. Look carefully how they play, this is a good strategy model to follow. Although it is better to invent your own strategy and achieve goals like no one before you. My passion to learn will continue as long as there are new things to learn. I had the good fortune to work in very well-managed companies, and I analyzed their financial statements in connection with the observation of corporate culture and operations.

From 2004 to 2011 I worked as a technical sales representative. Then in 2011, I decided on trying the Manager position. I thought that I would try it for half a year... with an option to go back to my previous position.

> *When an opportunity comes, take the opportunity and*
> *then learn how to do it later!*
> ~ Richard Branson

A production company with high-end customers was my next challenge. The next two years were very challenging, starting from the end of 2013, with a very challenging new project with the printing leader.

At the same time, we also conducted a new project with the global Italian leader in the parking business, **FAAC S.P.A.** In addition to these projects, I was in the middle of finishing my EMBA studies at Oxford

Brooks University – a Polish Open University. The only thing I could do was to try harder. Thank you very much to all my teammates who worked to complete the project.

Alberto Manfredi, my contact Purchasing Supervision Manager at **FAAC**, is the best negotiator I know. He is really amazing as a person and negotiator. After the project implementation, we sent the "Oscar samples" of the PARQUBE Parking Cabinet to our Italian colleagues as a 'Thank You' for participation in the project. As a result of our cooperation, business improved, and our project in common was successful for both companies.

I am in the middle of my business journey, and I would like to be an example of a person who can motivate and inspire, but with my biggest successes in front of me.

My future plans are very challenging as well as the level of challenges is higher. Working as a manager, I have been constantly saying: "What does not kill us makes us stronger, but what should be done if it made us stronger over the past five years." Now I know the answer.

My next plan is to start my own company named **INNOGATE** (Gate to innovations: www.innogate.pl) and to give strategic advice to Fortune 500 companies. My next challenge is to find a good mentor who can advise me how to achieve it. My aim is to help using knowledge, leverage and the potential of Brian Tracy and other great Americans. I think it is achievable.

I am going to publish my EMBA dissertation: "Strategy Workbook for Top Executives." My aim is to help business owners, CEO's and business managers to visualize their businesses and create high quality strategies. Another business project in my plans could be a book about product optimization to reduce costs to compete even with really low-cost suppliers.

As a strategy expert, please evaluate my support for "You" as an "Executive" in the area of strategy. Your valuable feedback would be highly appreciated on: robert@innogate.pl.

"Strategy Workbook for Top-Executives" will be a future top-selling position about strategy and how to create Blue-Ocean Strategies and defend vs. Blue-Ocean Strategies.

John Francis Welch, called the Manager of the Century, longtime President and leader of General Electric who built the company value from $12 billion to $500 billion, asked himself: "How do we want to win in this business?"[1]

Welch said: "If you do not have a competitive advantage, do not compete." Based on this finding, each leader must build the company's strategy to guarantee success in the next decade. Take a helicopter view of the complete market and then plan how to win.

Competitiveness against creativity.[2] David Brooks announces the coming of the "Creative Economy"[3] where greater value is constantly creating new value-added for customers, rather than expanding competitiveness. Do you agree with this statement?

Time horizon: Do not try competing in a three-year time frame as most companies do. Compete in a time-frame of seven years or more, because only a few companies can do that and there is less competition and your chances are greater. This is an opinion expressed by Amazon managers.

Today's developed strategy will work tomorrow, but the day after tomorrow the market can change and strategy may need to be modified. Leaders must analyze the situation in the global market from day-to-day, and change the system of work and strategy. Strategies can't be fixed but should be based on solid, lasting values.

Timing is also crucial, due to the transfer of military technologies that can be used as civil and commercial solutions. George Friedman in his book, *The Next Decade*, presents the perspective and the ability to penetrate specific types of modern technology for the commercial market. The strategy is to determine and correct the right course. The strategy is closely related to leadership. The owners of the company provide appropriate leadership, and are inspired to make significant changes. Leaders have to stand out to change the world; everything starts from leaders. Leadership has a huge impact on the success of your organization.[4]

For the company and its leaders, the mission statement and vision of the company is important. Leaders must have a future vision of their company.

A look at strategy from the perspective of the leaders of the country creates new opportunities. His Highness Sheikh Mohammed bin Rashid Al Maktoum, Vice President and Prime Minister of the United Arab Emirates, continued the realization of the vision of their predecessors in his book, *My Vision: Challenges in the Race for Excellence.* He describes the challenges experienced by his country in its efforts to achieve excellence and raise its status from a regional center to an international economic hub.[5] The reader is surprised by the vast knowledge of the business author who led the flowering of the country by creating a vision, demarcation of objectives and defining strategies and objectives for economic prosperity.

Specific objectives are monitored by key performance indicators and strict controlling.

Management of the country with the use of modern business knowledge proved to be the key to success and enabled the cooperation of government and business on an unprecedented scale.

The transformation of society into a 'knowledge-based society' plus support for entrepreneurship in young leaders, has already resulted in huge business success. All decisions must be accurate and responsible, and bring added value to the company. The strategy is closely aligned with the direction extending from the company's mission to its vision. All activities must be closely synchronized through a strategy.

The enormity of knowledge used by global companies like Samsung, Canon, and Toyota allow them to lead the market by using appropriate strategies. In the twentieth century, the changes were huge surprises, but the twenty-first century promises to be even more interesting. *The key will be the right people, the know-how, the response time to changes, and most importantly, the creation of the changes.* The available amount of knowledge in the world doubles every two years, which also creates new opportunities in development strategies (tools and techniques of management). *The Demand for the right people will be unlimited; the right people in the next decade will be the key.*

I have been conducting research on strategies used in production companies in Europe between 2014 and 2016. In strategy research, we came to one conclusion, the business world creates new sectors and new markets in the economy, breakthrough products and innovations, and from the other side, the world of science discovers new models and theories sometimes ahead of the business world. Otherwise theories and models are implemented into business and create blue oceans and spectacular business successes. Both these camps complement each other and the world of science and the business world together create progress for humanity. Results are interesting, but besides good results there is a need to implement strategy and knowledge in organizations to create even better results.

Interviewed executives expressed very interesting thinking about their strategies:

"...Strategy models are not of value themselves, models cannot replace reality, but listening to the customer can. The customer creates reality, and the base is creative, but models play a secondary role. It is more important to listen to the customer's voice in his challenges and propose solutions to meet them. We should adapt our services to customer requirements."

Leaders in production companies do not accept world reality, so they create their own business reality as they change the balance of power on the market. They are oriented according to blue-ocean strategy for "non-customers." They ask about customer problems and how we can solve them and building new standards and creating new blue oceans.

Few leaders have paid attention to the concept of time reduction from Rajan Suri: **QRM – Quick Response Manufacturing** well known from the American market. **"Industrial Internet of things"** and **Manufacturing 5.0** are currently implemented in operations in manufacturing companies as well as virtual speed and simplicity in production.

The most urgent topic is now the **"Blue-ocean gap"** between inventing companies and followers on the market. Companies implementing blue ocean products are creating a blue-ocean gap between them and other companies present on the market.

In my next book, I will try to answer how to radically close the blue-ocean gap. Listening closely to the market is greatly important, so as not to miss reaction time. There are at least three solutions in order not to miss it.

Professor **Vijay Govindarajan** and **Chris Trimble**, the main experts in innovation strategy are presenting the concept "Reverse Innovation"[7] by conducting the innovating process in low-cost countries and selling in EU and US markets. Reverse innovation not only reduces cost in low-cost countries, but also offers huge added value in good pricing. Please focus on *Monetizing Innovation* by Madhavan Ramanujam and Georg Tacke.

The philosophy of the leading manufacturer on global markets is to bring added value through the entire duration of action. If action does not bring added value, do not do it. There is the strategy of growth through acquisition of other companies, through accumulated savings.
Being an owner of the big business, go into excellence, because excellence has no finish line. Create blue-oceans. Always improve yourself, help to grow your people, your businesses and products.

The key strategy is speed and learning how to implement the changes, and going against current trends. Good strategy well executed should give spectacular wins.

[*Acknowledgment: I would like to express my great thank you to Mr. Brian Tracy and all the great friends from DNA Agency for their help in the creation of this book.*]

References

1. Jack Welch, Suzy Welch, *WINNING*, Studio EMKA, Warszaw, 2014, pg.12
2. http://www.forbes.com/sites/stevedenning/2012/04/25/david-brooks-competitiveness-vs-creativity-ge-vs-apple/; 2014-09-28
3. http://www.forbes.com/sites/stevedenning/2012/04/25/david-brooks-competitiveness-vs-creativity-ge-vs-apple/; 2014-09-28
4. Cynthia Montgomery, *Strategy*, Warsaw, 2010, audiobook
5. Mohammed bin Rashid Al Maktoum, *My Vision: Challenges in the Race for Excellence*, Motivate Publishing, Dubai, 2014.
6. Brian Tracy`s trainings.
7. V. Govindarajan, C. Trimble; *Reverse Innovation: Create far from home, Win everywhere*. HRB Books, 2012.

About Robert

Robert S. Chmielewski is a CEO of P&K Project and startup owner of INNOGATE company specializing in strategy training and development of individuals and organizations. He is the owner of two companies headquartered in Siedlce, Poland.

Robert's goal is to help you achieve all your personal and business goals, specializing in creations of blue-oceans for companies.

Robert S. Chmielewski has been consulting with companies and people throughout Europe. He has studied Business Management at Oxford Brookes University/Polish Open University.

Robert has an Executive MBA degree and his research is in strategy and economics. He is a best selling co-author of a book written with Brian Tracy and other successful authors throughout America called *SUCCESS BLUEPRINT*.

He is also the author of a forthcoming book, *STRATEGY WORKBOOK FOR TOP EXECUTIVES*, a future top selling position about strategy and how to create Blue-Ocean Strategies and defense vs. Blue Ocean Strategies. Robert is planning also to write a book ,"GIVE YOURSELF A PROMOTION" – presenting all tools and training which help you in getting promoted. His third planned book is: HOW TO OPTIMIZE PRODUCTS, CUT COST DOWN AND BE COMPETITIVE?

Robert speaks to corporate and public audiences on the subjects of Strategy and Manager Development and Professional Development, including to top executives and staff of many large European corporations. He has traveled and worked in over ten countries on three continents, and speaks four languages.

Robert is happily married and has two children.

Please feel free to contact Robert to discuss the strategy for your organization and re-design it into spectacular successes. If you have any questions about Robert S. Chmielewski's learning programs and services, please email: support@innogate.pl or call 48-604 660 101.

To contact Robert S. Chmielewski:
- www.innogate.pl
- www.innogate.pl/AboutRobert
- robert@innogate.pl or robertsch@interia.pl
- phone: +48 604 660 101.

CHAPTER 31

WHAT'S *YOUR* EXCUSE?

BY ROB ROWSELL

So there I was, kneeling on the ground with the door open on the passenger side of the vehicle, my head tucked inside where the passenger's legs sit, fighting with what's left of the broken glass crack pipe I had just discarded out of the car window a block away. My wife, Claudia, is in tears in the driver's seat, pleading with me to get up and come inside the building. I was burning my lips and my fingers as I attempted to take just one last hit of crack before I surrendered and walked through the doors of the drug rehab., which had already agreed to admit me.

That is where my disease had taken me. I was homeless, toothless and unemployable. I was a compulsive gambler who was addicted to crack cocaine, crystal meth and alcohol. I was a shoplifter, a fraudulent schemer - a thief - to support my habit. I was missing a lot of my teeth, my face was sunken in and I was 40 pounds under weight – I looked and felt like walking death!

Every waking moment was dedicated to committing the crime to get the money I needed to get the drugs, getting the drugs, doing the drugs or sleeping for 2-3 days because I had been awake for 4-7 days from doing the drugs. It was a never-ending cycle that rarely ends well. The date was November 22nd, 1999.

I knew what my choices were. They were:
  1. Get help (drug rehab)
  2. Prison or
  3. Death

Prison and/or death were right around the corner, and even I was aware of that. I already had two probation officers at the time, one for a DUI on crystal meth and one for domestic violence. There was no way that I could meet the requirements of either probation while still actively using drugs. Having that probation revoked and doing the time, 2-4 years in prison, was inevitable if I continued the path I was on. Death was just one crack hit or one crystal shot away and really the only question was when. By the Grace of God, I was able to get up from that last hit of dope and walk through the doors of the drug rehab at that very moment. I have not picked up a drink or a drug ever since!

Fast forward to 2016. I am a homeowner now for 13 years, I am a multiple business owner for twelve years with my beautiful wife Claudia, and I am an involved parent of three and I have the marriage of my dreams! I am actively involved in my church that we've attended for 12 years, where I have been a youth leader, Sunday school teacher, Board Member, and many other roles. I have been actively involved in numerous local Chamber of Commerce groups, my local REIA (Real Estate Investment Assoc.), BNI (Business Networking International) and Kiwanis.

So how does an out-of-control drug addict with an 8th Grade education go from homeless, toothless and unemployable to living the life of their dreams in a short period of time? How does the transformation from caterpillar to butterfly begin, continue to manifest itself daily, and then follow through to the finish line?

Those are great questions, and the answers to those questions are likely more than I could ever possibly cover in this one chapter, but let's lay the foundation for a successful beginning as I share four principles for success that I live by daily, and which have catapulted my achievements beyond my wildest expectations. Would that be good? Fantastic, so let's get going.

Principle #1 – You have to be a good student. The day that I decided that I wanted more out of life than I could possibly achieve by working for somebody else is the day that I got busy seeking out the education, and the motivation, necessary to expand my thinking to what's possible in life. For me this happened in my first year of recovery in 2000.

I started devouring everything that I could get my hands on from authors such as Zig Zigler, Rick Warren and Joel Osteen, just to name a few. I listened to motivational/educational cassette tapes (ask your grey haired co-workers what those are, if necessary) and CD's everywhere that I drove. My car was, and still is today, the college classroom that I never had. I watched videos on every category of real estate investing that you can think of.

As I mentioned earlier, the last year of formal education that I completed was the 8th grade. I wouldn't recommend this path to anyone, but for me it's part of my story. Drugs and alcohol became more important than school in the ninth grade. So I dropped out of school to pursue my addictions.

But this principle applies to everyone, no matter what level you have achieved in formal education. We must continue to feed our minds the same way that we *should* be feeding our bodies, with a good quality high protein, low fat, diet. We wouldn't think of skipping too many meals (although some of us sure could afford to!), but yet we'll go days, weeks, months or even years without feeding our mind with what it needs to inspire us and lead us to the lives of our dreams. Isn't that amazing!

One of my mentors explained to me two things that I have never forgotten – which has helped me to this day. He would say: "There's no difference between someone who does not read and someone who cannot read, none at all." He also would tell me: "The only difference between where you are now and where you are going to be in five years is the books you read and the people that you meet." We'll talk about the "people that you meet" (Law of exposure) part in another principle, but are you starting to get the picture?

I know that for some of you this as basic as it gets, because you are reading this book already, and it's one of many that you'll read this year. I would be so bold as to assume that if this is true in your life, and has been for some time, you have already achieved success at levels beyond the average person, or are at least on your way there, because you are a good student. It's that reliable.

Principle #2 – Respect The Law of Exposure. The Law of Exposure says "What I expose myself to I shall become" – period. This law is as reliable as the Law of Gravity!

It's why people in Boston "Pahhk the Cahh in the Hahvahhd Yahhd," it's why people of the South say "Ya'll." It's why your kids act just like you in certain situations (regardless of their age). It's why fathers/sons and mothers/daughters end up in the same careers and it's why the majority of businesses I own today are auto repair shops. My grandfather and father exposed me to it all my life. It's "in-my-blood".

Did your mom ever tell you, "If you hang around that street corner with those hoodlums you'll end up just like them?" Well, neither did mine, but it is very good advice! My mom was, however, very protective about whom I was allowed to play with in my younger years, I only wish I had listened in my teen years! It could have saved me years of wasted time because I ended up just like those I chose to hang around, doing drugs. I did not understand this principle yet.

For those of us that are parents, are you "selective" about who your kids are allowed to be around? Of course you are, I know my wife and I are. Why? Because we are all "molded" by the environment we are continually exposed to, good or bad. We know that it's our job as parents to protect our kids from predators of all shapes and sizes, so we are constantly on guard for threats. Well, we also have to be constantly on guard for the threats that are holding us back from being the best that we can be, from living the life of our dreams. They are subtle and difficult to recognize as threats.

There is something inside us that instinctively knows this, yet you will listen to talk radio that is filled with filthy garbage and useless rhetoric on the way to work every day and end your day with the negative newscast, while eating dinner, every night. You will attend R-rated movies, heck, rated PG nowadays, and think that it doesn't negatively affect you. You'll hang around that guy or gal, or group of people, that is going nowhere, doing nothing and pretty convinced that there is no use in trying to better yourselves, the people that are just existing, simply because it's convenient since you work with them, or you've known them since you were kids, or because their kids hang around your kids. You'll browse questionable websites, or watch videos online that you know are inappropriate. What's the harm, right? Who will know?

Don't get "faked out" into believing that these influences do not affect your thinking, your attitude and, especially, your behavior – which in turn affects your destination. I've learned this Law the hard way. Everything affects our destination, EVERYTHING! A friend of mine would often say to the youth in our small group; "Show me your friends and I'll show you your future."

I know that if I hang around bikers, I will become a biker. If I hang around skinheads, I will become a skinhead. If I hang around cowboys, I will become a cowboy. If I hang around bank robbers, I will become a bank robber. If I hang around God-fearing Christian men that won't settle for being less than God has gifted them to be, in every area of their lives, who are convinced that we are constantly being prepared for the next level that He has in store for us, then *that's what I will become*. The Law of Exposure is as reliable as the Law of Gravity.

Principle #3 – You've got to continually play Offense. It's very easy for anyone that has achieved any level of success to "lay off the throttle" and coast. How do I know this? Because I've done it, and I bet that I'm not the only one. It has restricted my growth for short periods of time as I played defense, forgetting that in order to get more "points on the scoreboard" that I was going to have to play offense again.

Examples of success that could get us distracted from continuing to play offense can be anything from graduating college and landing the job you wanted, to getting the girl (or guy) of your dreams, to starting/buying your first business (or second or third or . . .), to winning that seat on the board, to selling your business(es) or being recognized as the top in your field. The list is endless.

There are times where it is completely acceptable to stand on the patio chair in the backyard and pound your chest while singing, "We are the champions" at the top of your lungs. (Hopefully when the neighbors are not home so you don't go viral on YouTube!)

Celebrating your successes is a must. If you don't celebrate, your subconscious mind will wonder what you're doing this for and want to quit. The length of the celebration will depend on the success. A day, a week, a month, that's up to you. Once the celebration is complete, though, it's time to "get the gear back on and get back out there and fight!"

Prosperity breeds complacency if you are not careful. I encourage you to

Google the phrase "rest on your laurels." An early mentor of mine would say, "You can't win this week's game on last week's performance." You may want to write that one down somewhere that you will see it every morning. My kids have it memorized. Essentially it's saying to get your head out of, um-m-m-m, . . . the clouds, and get back to work. You've only reached a new plateau, *not your destination!*

Another mentor would say that a tree does not get to decide when it stops growing, why does man? To be continually playing offense in the areas that are important to you – your Spiritual growth, your marriage, your role as a parent, your social life, your health, your career, your finances or anything else – you have got to be setting goals that you can monitor and see your progress on. And remember that a need, once satisfied, no longer motivates. So set those goals big, and adjust them as needed to keep you excited.

Principle #4 – Without God it's all pointless. Well, I couldn't write even a small chapter without giving God the Glory for anything and everything that I've been able to achieve in my life. He is the foundation of anything good that is accomplished.

There is a phrase that I often say, and if you've known me for any length of time, you've probably heard me say it, and the phrase is "Praise Him!" I have it on the back of our cars, our motorhome and above our Corporate office entrance. It's a reminder to me that no matter what might be going on at that moment, no matter what stressful thing that I am currently experiencing, it is very likely a result of a past prayer answered, and I just need to praise Him! Living in an attitude of gratitude is fairly easy for me. I praise Him on the way to work and on the way home, as well as countless times throughout the day.

My personal belief is that this life I live today is a Gift from God, and I certainly do not deserve it. (I pray that I never get what I deserve!) I also believe that what I do with this life is my gift back to God, and I do NOT want Him to be disappointed with what I've done with this Gift of a second chance. This is why I refuse to settle for just "good enough." He provides me with the gifts and the talents, the opportunity, the resources, the people and everything else required for me to succeed. This is known as the seed, the sunshine, the soil and the rain. The miracle of making all of these things come together at the right time can only be done by God

Himself. It's easy to overlook this fact if we are not careful, but without God's involvement it's all pointless.

This is the most important principle that I could suggest to you that I live by. I know what a difference it has made for me. I know that I have tried it without Him, under my own power, and you already know how that turned out!

Reach out to me if you'd like to discuss this any further, I look forward to it.

May God Bless you the way that he has me!

About Rob

Rob Rowsell has a truly incredible story! Rob was living on the streets, homeless, toothless and unemployable back in 1999. Addicted to crystal meth and crack cocaine, Rob was living the criminal lifestyle, shoplifting and stealing to provide for his drug habit. At the direction of one of his probation officers, Rob admitted himself into a 30-day drug rehab. By the Grace of God, he has been sober since that day.

Upon graduation from that drug rehab, Rob had no job, no driver's license, no car, no place to call home, no credit, two probation officers for unrelated matters, owed $15,000.00 in traffic fines before a license would even be considered, owed $8,000.00 in restitution for bad checks that he had written and owed $40,000.00 to the IRS in back taxes.

- Rob was able to get his driver's license back by 2001!
- In 2002, three years to the day that he got sober, Rob was able to close escrow on his first home!
- In 2004, Rob was able to buy his first auto repair business (#1) with his wife Claudia.
- In 2007, they attended some real estate classes and started their second business - buying, fixing up and selling houses. They were inducted into their real estate school's "Hall of Fame" in 2009 for their accomplishments in real estate.
- In 2010, they were able to purchase their 3rd business, auto repair shop #2.
- In 2014, they were able to start their fourth business, auto repair shop #3.
- In 2016, Rob is publishing his first book!

Rob has helped many people in numerous ways. From coaching people on getting their credit fixed and purchasing their first home to coaching people on how to start their own business, and how to take their existing business(es) to the next level. His breakthrough coaching sessions have changed many lives in many ways!

Rob is best known for his heart for people. Coming from where he does, with the odds against him, and seeing what can be accomplished by an average guy with only an 8th grade education, he wants to see everyone accomplish what they are capable of achieving and not settle for less.

All of these life experiences have taught Rob some very unique strategies that have contributed significantly to his success. He is able to share them in his book in an entertaining way, mixed in with his real life story that is truly an unbelievable journey!

Rob's book is called: *Addicted To Life! How I Went From Homeless to Extraordinary Success and Happiness In A Short Period of Time.*
Your 8-Step Formula For Achievement.

What you will learn from reading his book:

- How *anybody* can own their own business!
- The only thing stopping you from achieving your dreams is **YOU!**
- Fear is normal, you DON'T have to be paralyzed by it anymore!
- It's not always going to *feel* like you're making progress!
- It does **NOT** matter where your starting point is!
- You're striving for progress, *not perfection!*
- How the "Law Of Exposure" is affecting you every day.
- Taking "Massive Action" is a mindset that can be learned.
- You have to be DONE with settling for "Good Enough"!
- You'll get the confirmation that you're looking for IF you are making the right decisions!
- How to be sure that your achievements do not hinder your Main Objective.
- Why "Full Rounded" success is the only way to true happiness.
- How the timing for you to take it to the next level will **NEVER** be perfect!

For more information on his book – *Addicted To Life! How I Went From Homeless to Extraordinary Success and Happiness In A Short Period of Time.*
Your 8-Step Formula For Achievement.– go to: AddictedToLifeBook.com

- Rob can be contacted at: Rob@RobRowsell.com

CHAPTER 32

MAINTAINING THE MOMENTUM
— PRACTICAL STEPS TO DEFEAT STRESS AND ACHIEVE SUCCESS!

BY DR. DEBRA LINDH

STRESS

Everyone experiences stress. Some stress is good. It gives us an adrenaline boost to go the extra mile or to finish that last minute project. An unfortunate reality is most people are experiencing good stress as well as bad stress. Continued stress. Chronic stress. Continued and chronic stress is a global epidemic. *In fact, the World Health Organization declared stress a global epidemic.* A Global Epidemic! Now if that fact does not shake up the need for change maybe some other astounding facts will.

Workplace stress is costing companies in the United States over $300 billion annually.

Employees are absent from work due to stress-related symptoms. Co-worker relationships are strained and conflict is on the rise. Employees may be physically present at work, however, they are constantly distracted about personal stressors resulting in a decline in innovation, creativity, and productivity. All of these consequences negatively affect corporate profitability, growth, as well as the most important investment – the people.

Stress is at an all-time high, causing physical, emotional, energy and mental drain. Stress is known to cause obesity, heart conditions, high blood pressure, intestinal disorders, and even death; feelings of low self-worth and self-esteem, hopelessness, frustration, insomnia, withdrawal, rage and conflict, as well as depression, anxiety, and sometimes suicide.

No one is immune to stress. People are so desperate seeking relief from stress that they are coping with drugs, food, alcohol, video games and self-harm. As one client shared, "I needed to drink to numb the pain." While another client shared, "I pick, I pull my hair, just to feel something and know that I'm alive."

These unfavorable actions create a never-ending vicious cycle. People are seeking for that "something" that will bring normalcy back to their lives. They want something to stop the heart palpitations, mind from racing, fights from happening, the crying to stop, and frankly, for life to be better and happier.

This chapter will help you reduce and in some cases, eliminate your stress, and quickly get your life to be better and happier.

Whether you've just picked this book up by chance or you're desperately seeking a solution to the stress problem, this is a blueprint for getting your life back. Think about it – what if you could be more than just 10% happier, what if your week was 6:1 where 6 days are awesome and one day had some stress, and stress that didn't affect you like it does now? What if those awesome days added up to months and months added to a year, then two years, going from some of the time, to most of the time, to a majority of the time? Can you imagine a life like that? Can you see yourself living a life like that? Imagine it. See it. Now let's do it!

PMBSR

Over the past 5 years, I've created and refined a process that can get you there and I'm going to share it with you now. The process is called *Practical Mindfulness-Based Stress Reduction (PMBSR)*. There is some theory in this chapter as I've formally studied human behavior for over 25 years, earning a bachelor's degree in Philosophy and Organizational Communication, a master's degree in Organizational Leadership and Strategic Management, and a doctorate in Organization Development where my award-winning doctoral dissertation applied research focused on Employee Stress and Mindfulness.

This process was originally created for myself. I am a survivor of PTSD resulting from child abuse, neglect, and chronic stress. It wasn't until after having children that I started recalling past memories and experiences that negatively affected my life and wellbeing. I knew I needed a solution and the available options presented as solutions weren't viable, in my opinion. I wanted a drug-free solution that I could use whenever I needed it, not be codependent on a psychotherapist or other provider; something that resulted in me being in control of my life.

The reality is when we need help, we cannot pick up the phone and get help from our therapist real-time. I wanted something that I could use whenever and wherever I needed it, that was simple, easy, practical and, most importantly, produced ongoing results. So, I used myself as the guinea pig, testing and exploring traditional and alternative techniques. Coming across mindfulness, I put myself in an out-patient mindfulness-based stress reduction (MBSR) program, created by Jon Kabat-Zinn which is clinically proven to reduce stress.

My stress levels did reduce. However, this program was in a controlled environment. All the things I learned, I couldn't use real-time. All throughout my doctoral studies, I was gathering data, experiences, and keeping track of what worked, what didn't work, supporting research and applications; both positive and negative. My dissertation research used mindfulness training to reduce employee stress in the workplace. I knew I was on to something when my experiences and the experiences of the employees matched. Aside from the data, and more importantly, my life and the employees' lives had improved. And not by some mere 10%, but significantly – mind, body, energy, and emotion. Relationships improved, stress levels minimized, and the usual stress triggers no longer had a controlling grip. Life was great!

PMBSR is an investment. The biggest investment you can make is in YOURSELF. There's plenty of work involved just like with any accomplished success. The PMBSR blueprint is rooted in science and proven effective. It's the "what" and the "how" of a proven, tested system.

THE AFTER STATE

I'd like to share a secret. Well, it won't be a secret for long, but here it is… how we imagine and see ourselves is what actually happens in real life. If we see ourselves confident, successful, productive, and competent – then those thoughts become part of our subconscious, our brain's cellular memory, and those subconscious thoughts are the drivers of our behavior which then manifest in real life. Another secret, becoming who we desire, wish, and hope to be, are doable and very possible. *All changes, improvements, and transformations to our outside world starts with changes, improvements, and transformations internally.* All the change and transformation begins as an inside job that connects to your outside world.

Once we create a visual image of what and how we want to be, next we need to learn to develop new ways of thinking, new ways of doing, new skills, and new habits. And we do that through PMBSR. When you develop yourself as a whole – mind, emotions, energy, and physical body – and when putting those developments into consistent, repeatable action, you will be on your way to producing the desired results in your life and career.

Overall, PMBSR involves steps: incremental steps, foundational steps, and revised steps.

STEP 1 IN PMBSR: DCA – DECIDE, COMMIT, ACTION

Making the *decision* to do this is not as easy as it sounds. The decision is a decision you make based on a plethora of choices. To do or not to do. Remember, as like Yoda said, "There is no try, only do." Once you make the decision, you make the decision to do. To be all in. Then, *you need to commit.* You do this for you. Not for me or anyone else. So, do whatever you need to do – write down the commitment on a piece of paper, tape it to a wall, or put it someplace where the commitment is visible every day. Lastly, *take action.* You may notice that all three steps are inter-connected. If one is out of balance, then the rest are affected. Action is key to your success with PMBSR. You don't use it; you don't get results.

People who experience PMBSR success decide, are all in, and take consistent action; every day.

Daily action can look different from person to person and from day to day. *What is important is taking consistent action.* So, when does PMBSR not work? While PMBSR is *for* everyone, it does not *work* for everyone. PMBSR is not for the person who wants a quick-fix, to cut corners, the egotistical know-it-all, as well as the excuse maker.

To be great, a person needs to think and act great.

STEP 2 INVOLVES GPS: GOALS, PLANNING, AND SUCCESS

Success is possible to achieve with realistic goals and planning. How much time can you invest? How is this a priority? *Create a list of goals.* What is it that you want? What do you *not* want? Then pick the top three goals and work with those. Once you master those three goals, move on to the next or new top three goals.

Create a plan that reflects all your goals, interests, values, and interests. If you do this step, then you'll be more likely to take action. When we prepare with realistic commitments, we then are more likely to stick with our decision. Dipping your toe in the water doesn't make you a swimmer. Figure out what to do, why do it, and stick with it. Remember, we are our own worst enemy and greatest competitor. So, run your own marathon; your own race. Compete against only one person – YOU!

We have covered the "What to do" now for the "How."

This "how" is awareness. It's the "M" part of PMBSR – Mindfulness. Currently, Mindfulness is everywhere. Mindfulness is in schools, corporations, the military, magazine covers, and endorsed by athletes, coaches, and business executives. Mainstream mindfulness has many definitions, however, in PMBSR, *mindfulness means awareness.* And like any skill, as we develop our awareness, we move from knowing to understanding. Sound simple? The concept is simple but the work is challenging and doable. In awareness skill development, I want you to remember these two questions:

1. Where did that come from?

2. Who said or told that to me?

Because everything we know and do is learned. Everything.

Once we identify the "who" and the "where" we can evaluate: Is this something that fits with me? How does this behavior or action represent who I am, who I aspire to be? Or is this something I need to get rid of?

FOUR COMPONENTS TO AWARENESS ARE: MIND, BODY, EMOTIONS, AND ENERGY

Through awareness we can identify: How is my mind…is it focused or distracted? How is my body…tense or relaxed? How are my emotions… angry/sad or happy/calm? Lastly, how is my energy? Do I feel depleted and exhausted or am I full of life – revved up and ready to go? Through your new awareness and continued awareness skill development, we reflect, revise, and retake action. If it doesn't' match up to those questions, seriously reconsider the decision to keep those things in your life. Once this awareness surfaces, then people feel empowered and they take action. Again, if you take away one thing from this chapter, it should be *Awareness Skill Development* using those questions.

CONSEQUENCES

Every action we take will have an outcome or a "consequence." Now, consequences can be both positive AND negative. Consequences are important to address because while you're on the road of PMBSR, the changes you experience will affect those around you. And frankly, some will be celebrating along your side and others, well, they won't be. So, be mindful that as you experience changes, these changes will affect your relationships for the better or worse. *Here's the Key: Some people are in our life for a lifetime, others for a season; all for a reason.*

SUCCESS AND SETBACKS

Now everyone enjoys reading about successes but not many like talking about setbacks. Everyone has experienced setbacks and disappointments. Here's the key to setbacks. All setbacks are temporary and a set-up to something greater. We need to see and appreciate the value of setbacks. Everything has value. Even manure has value. Each setback, challenge, disappointment – they all have value. Sometimes we cannot see the value. We are too close to the situation, too emotional, and unable to be at peace to see the value. Remember: Quick fixes provide empty promises and set people up for failure. Like a phoenix rising from the ashes, with PMBSR successes, we transform chronic stress into post-stress growth. An all-in commitment to PMBSR and celebrating successes while seeing setbacks as temporary and a setup for something greater, impacts our awareness as well as our emotions, mind, body, and energy. This mindset keeps the main thing, well, the main thing. Celebrate successes – any win, no matter how small. Every win is a win and small wins turn into big wins and big wins turn into massive success. To keep the momentum going, focus on the wins and connecting all wins. Keep track of all those daily actions supporting the momentum. Every day take actions that link directly to those goals, to using PMBSR, and produces results.

WHAT NOW?

Maintaining the momentum is good but thinking longevity is great. Momentum gives us energy; it fuels us to perform. Keeping an awareness of longevity keeps our mindset connected to long-term results. Remember, PMBSR is a marathon not a sprint. You're going to fall off the program, slip up, and have a setback. These things can and will happen because life is uncontrollable and unpredictable. What we can do is prepare for the unexpected. For example, coming down with the flu or overstraining a muscle can be a setback. Remember, setbacks are temporary that we can prepare to overcome.

So, when a setback happens, prepare with the 5 R's: *Reflect, Regroup, Recommit, Retake action*, and *Repeat*. I want you to reflect, regroup, recommit, retake action, and repeat. Reflect takes a look at what happened and why did it happen; regroup takes a look at your plan and adjusts the plan according to the reflection; recommit circles back to your "why:" retake action means exactly that – get back in the game and take action; and repeat means to take incremental daily and consistent actions as well as reflect and adjust as needed.

No matter where you are at, no matter what challenges and struggles you face, you can always go higher, and PMBSR will take you there. It's not easy. But if you want proof that PMBSR works, just ask my clients. They all started here and I'm going to ask you the same thing I ask my clients: Do PMBSR as it's given to you and give it your all. That's it. If you can do those two things, here's what you'll get in return:

1. Effective skills for improved stress reduction

2. Increased energy, awareness, concentration, and focus
3. Mental resilience and longevity endurance
4. A relaxed, calm body
5. Stressor, trigger, and reaction prevention
6. PMBSR guidelines for improved results
7. Effective rest and renewal
8. Improvement in your overall life

PMBSR works. PMBSR is designed for everyone who is committed to results, and are willing to make the commitment to produce results. Are you willing to get serious about your life and discover that life you dream, pray, wish, and hope for? If you're serious, if you're ready, if you're committed to doing the work every day, then you're on a journey that will set you apart from the mediocre and improve your life like you've only imagined possible.

About Dr. Deb

Dr. Debra Lindh (known as "Dr. Deb") helps her clients transform stress into positive growth. A survivor-warrior, leader, and advocate of PTSD, Dr. Deb passionately focused on the world of stress management and practical mindfulness. A third generation entrepreneur, Dr. Lindh launched the Mindful Effect® by offering Practical Mindfulness Based Stress Reduction (PMBSR) as a drug-free option to develop skills to defeat the negative effects of stress.

Dr. Deb's company is centered on her philosophy of "everything has value." Her goal is to help her clients build automatic skills to defeat stress reactions real-time and produce long-lasting results and longevity growth. Once those skills are developed and mastered, then clients experience significant results and positive growth. Dr. Deb also created the PMBSR process which teaches her clients how to build skills quickly, easily, and practically and use those new skills in their careers and personal life.

Dr. Deb is known for customizing training programs for organizations of all sizes and has positively affected people and organizations worldwide. Fortune 500 companies, entrepreneurs, non-profit organizations, and adults, teens and children use Dr. Deb's PMBSR techniques and systems to defeat stress and increase their success.

Dr. Deb is a graduate of the University of St. Thomas, Minneapolis, Minnesota. She is the President of Mindful Effect®, a training and consulting company and has been speaking to audiences around the world for over twenty years on innovation, success, strategy, stress management, ADHD, mindfulness, and motivation. Dr. Deb's dynamic energy and authentic delivery keeps audiences engaged, intrigued, and involved. She has received many awards and is globally recognized for her pioneering contributions to organizations such as PsychCentral's Top 21 to Follow on Twitter, Mashable, University of Arizona School of Medicine, American Psychological Association, Working Mother Media, Minnesota Department of Education, Organization Development Network, and is an author of a forthcoming book with Brian Tracy. Dr. Deb was also recently selected as one of America's PremierExperts™ and has been a regular contributor and quoted in PTSDChat and Bullying Recovery.

In addition to her passion for helping her clients achieve the life they desire and deserve, she enjoys spending time with her two kids, collecting vintage books, cooking, fitness, Australian red licorice, espresso, and traveling.

You can connect with Dr. Deb at:
- Debra@TheMindfulEffect.com
- www.TheMindfulEffect.com

- www.DebraLindh.com
- www.twitter.com/DebraLindh
- www.linkedin.com/in/debra-lindh-ed-d-298b143

CHAPTER 33

THE FIVE VIRTUES OF SUCCESS

BY EDUARDO CHOLULA

*Those who live without change are good, while those who adapt
to change are better, but whoever causes these changes is a winner.*

I like to share this phrase in my lectures, because it triggers important
and impressive changes in your life. I have known hundreds of people
who think they are the owners of all the problems of the world, but
despite their critical situation, they do nothing to overcome it. I'm going
to describe some of my background, but not to complain, nor to pity
myself, but as a reference. Some years ago, I didn't enjoy life because
of my low self-esteem. Though later, life itself taught me in a wonderful
way how to appreciate it. I was diagnosed with polio in my left leg at two
years old. I was abused physically, mentally and emotionally in those
times; I was traumatized, I just didn't want to live.

Fortunately, I began to reject those negative thoughts which in turn began
to increase my self-esteem; firstly, I achieved the ability of being able to
laugh at myself, then discovered that I was totally responsible for my own
thoughts, feelings, actions and outcomes. This allowed me to abandon all
of my lamenting and further raised my self-esteem. My childhood and
youth were loaded with painful experiences, but in the end opened my
eyes to see my true value; life was preparing me for a great change.

I had the good fortune of being able to start a family. I was doing all
right, but honestly, despite the challenges, my life was quite ordinary

until I faced an adversity which caused a 180 degree turn in my life. I'm a proud father of five children, the third one was born premature after five months of pregnancy, weighing a pound with many health complications with his liver, kidneys, lungs, and with a strong anemia. Even today; he still has to receive blood transfusions every 2 weeks to keep him alive. He has slowed his physical and mental development and if that was not enough, he also lost his sight, and on several occasions the doctors said he would not live long. On top of his critical health, I lost my job and I was subsequently evicted from the house we rented, thus virtually overnight we were on the streets with nowhere to live.

Those difficult situations did not overpower us, on the contrary, it empowered us. We were filled with strength and came together like the family we were. I learned a valuable lesson when I met my newborn son in the incubator, he was full of connectors and IVs and was moving energetically. As I stared down at him, I perceived his message: "Look at me daddy, I am struggling to live, but what are you doing with your life?" It was then that I decided to publish my first book, then others; now I have become a best-selling author.

I learned that every day I have at least two options. <u>Option number one</u>: I stay in a dark corner and claim to be the victim and complain about everything. <u>Option number two</u>: I get up again and again, with positive energy, taking one step at a time towards a better quality of life. This taught me that:

In an adversity, the pain is inevitable, but the suffering is optional, and you decide what to live for each day.

What has more worth to you? That you stay down and cry about life, or that you be thankful for this precious moment and enjoy it intensely with your loved ones?

I do not know what situation you are facing right now, but I am sure that your self-worth is more valuable that any situation that you are confronted with. In addition, I know you have the capacity and the potential to be successful if you at least apply these three words: Decision, Action and Persistence.

For example: To complete my book, first *I decided* to do it, then *I wrote down* my goals, being as detailed as possible when planning it all out. I planned things such as the book size, front and back cover, themes, how many pages, chapters, the date and time that I wanted it to be ready, etcetera. I realized my dream when I had no money, had too many difficult situations in my life, a time when nobody believed in me, when the adversities hit us time after time, and when I really felt uncomfortable with my quality of life. However, I have always appreciated every precious moment of my life, and I now take action. Now I'm persistent and I remain persistent until achieving my goal. So, if I could take a step with my injured leg, you can also take a million steps easily.

If you've ever thought that everything you plan, say or do has no value or merit, it is because you believe it to be that way. But if you have achieved and are successful in your goals, it is because you have decided to accomplish something and have stuck with it from start to finish. However, if everything in your life seems to be a failure or a problem, and you feel constantly faced with adversities, it is also because you have convinced yourself that it's so.

In the past, I was at the peak of bitterness, feeling like a victim chained to the bottom of a ravine with my self-esteem below zero. I didn't like who I was, and consequently couldn't see the value of myself or others, nor could I see the great opportunities that were all around me. My life took a turn when I learned that I was in total control of myself. It's true, once you take responsibility for your decisions and actions, then you will discover a wonderful world of joy with its fruits, and the harvest will be vast and infinite if you at least apply these three words to your life:

1. Decision
2. Action
3. Persistence

If you have reached your goals and you have an excellent quality of life, it's because you have <u>decided</u> to do so, and you have taken <u>action</u> and have been <u>persistent</u>. If your life is ordinary and full of problems, it's because you have allowed it to be this way as well. You haven't taken action to change it, neither have you been persistent. You surrendered without putting forth the effort to make yourself shine once again.

If your life has been routine, ordinary and empty, it is because you may have a bandage in your heart that hasn't allowed for the healing of your emotional wounds. This allows you to see nothing but bitterness and pain all around you. If this is you, perhaps you need to bandage your eyes to allow your other senses to perceive the wonderful and great opportunities that are always around you, waiting to be exploited by your great potential.

What has happened in your life shouldn't limit you. On the contrary, it should push you to want to live in total harmony. Perhaps you wonder, how do you live in harmony when the world is so overwhelmed with problems? But what is important isn't what you need physically, the important thing is to do wonders with what one has, which is more valid than being one of those who complain about everything, but do nothing to overcome it. I don't know of anyone who has declared with strong conviction: "I want to be the best failure in the world, and have the worst of the worst." On the contrary, we all want and deserve the best of the best—on that we are going to focus.

The reason some people only see misfortunes around them is because they are paying too much attention to their shortcomings in life, instead of cultivating their virtues and their great potential. When you decide to pay more attention to your virtues, you will naturally exploit your potential and will be unstoppable in everything that you do.

I repeat, if you ever wonder why, despite your best efforts, desires and hard work, you fail to obtain the success you desire, it's because there is a disparity in what you say, think and do. There must be consistency between what you think and feel. You must fully engage yourself in your thoughts, actions and your being, in order to become an unstoppable success.

If there are any discrepancies between what you say and what you do, it is because you have been pre-programmed, and you are willing (unconsciously) to fail, because your mind is already addicted to that way of thinking. And believe it or not, the thoughts that you are used to may even give you pleasure. This will only continue until you reprogram your mind with positive habits that you promote with creative thoughts, rather than negative and destructive ones. It's perhaps why you avoid changes, although those changes would be of great benefit to you, though unconsciously you will continue to choose failure and poverty until you must realize that you can control your own thoughts, feelings and actions.

Every day we are surrounded by great opportunities and valuable changes.

You must decide and take action toward coming to the full realization of the potential of your life. Perhaps, if you do not feel ready to take control of your life, don't worry, nobody is sufficiently prepared to succeed instantly because the learning never ends. But the sooner you decide to make the change, the sooner you'll realize the happiness and the feeling of accomplishment you attain by moving up level after level. If you wait forever to get the perfect climate, circumstances, economy, you will end up wasting your life without ever taking maximum advantage of your strength and talents. When you wait for all the planets to align in order to be happy, you will realize that is too late – everything has a process, and you must learn it and enjoy it. Remember this: "When you make a decision, immediately take action, otherwise your dreams will bury you alive."

To have wealth, health and to be successful, I suggest you abandon your old beliefs and clichés that only limit you; you need to reprogram your being, senses, and increase your knowledge; be creative and stay active.

Now, if you are wealthy, enjoy perfect health and tremendous success, congratulations. If you aren't on the way to the realization of your dreams and goals, you'd better start now! Wealth is obtained by taking action, certain risks, being creative, disciplined, innovative and having a financial education. Success doesn't happen overnight. You cannot get from point A to point B in an instant either; it takes time. Thus the accumulation of wealth requires patience, perseverance, creativity and continuous learning, so take your success one step at a time.

No matter what happens around you, what is important is that your being is totally impregnated with self-worth and that you make the *decision*, *act* and be *persistent*. Remind yourself that if you are facing adversity, you might fall, bend or break, but never should you ever surrender. You must be as visionary as the eagle, astute as the fox, strong as the tiger, persistent like the wolf and as patient as the turtle.

I know that you have the ability, and that you are willing to make the decision to achieve great changes in your life. I will share with you the five virtues that helped me to create a better quality of life, and if I can do it, so can you. Study the application of these **Five Virtues** to free your great potential:

#1 - The Virtue of Love: When you have love and share it, you feel the magic of completely enjoying life. True love is the ingredient that ignites life; it's intangible but can fill each corner, it's so powerful that it inspires the creations of the most wonderful works in the universe. One who has love in his heart isn't afraid, has no doubts or envy. Love is like the energy that drives you to share, enjoy, teach, learn, and live. It is peace, harmony, happiness, joy, fullness and abundance. *Love enables you to attract and have the feeling of fullness, it's the maximum expression of creation.*

#2 - The Virtue of Gratitude: Gratitude opens endless doors to wonderful opportunities for the taking, and boosts your unstoppable success. You should never ask the universe for what you lack, rather you must thank the universe as if you already have it, and believe me, with your action and persistence, you will obtain it in due time. Always be grateful for all that surrounds you and the universe will bless you for it.

#3 - The Virtue of Forgiveness: Forgiving wholeheartedly, regardless of the matter (offense, abuse, insult, contempt, poorly understood, hatred), will break any chain that keeps you captive in mediocrity, continued failure, and pain. If you have not had the success you want and do not live to your fullness, it is because you have some or many thorns in your heart that are piercing your beautiful being. You haven't forgiven some event(s) in your life and this prevents you from advancing to the next level. Forgiving will save you many headaches, besides giving you a better quality of life, and it will bless you with health and happiness. *The choice is yours.*

#4 - The Virtue of Health is a healthy coexistence, a perfect balance between your being, body, mind, actions and outcomes. Watch what you eat, feel, hear, think, say and do. This will bring you a healthy advantage if you focus positively, and add habits that you can promote to be better every day. Be always thankful; for example, say: "I thank the creator because my cells regenerate: strong, healthy and happy."

#5 - The Virtue of Wealth: Instead of focusing on excuses, lamentations and on your shortfalls, focus on wealth. It is completely healthy and natural to desire wealth at the time that you feel the flow of your greatness and creativity. Your life would be unbalanced even when practicing the virtues of love, gratitude, health and forgiveness if your life is in economic distress. How could you help a loved one or yourself if your pockets are empty? Therefore, always have thoughts of an increase in wealth and of an improvement in all aspects of your life: health, wealth, happiness, etcetera.

In my opinion, based on my personal experiences, the study and the application of the Five Virtues undoubtedly moves you toward having a better quality of life, just as it has done with me – a man who went from mundanely ordinary to a bestselling author. I invite you to make a **Decision**, take **Action** and retain **Persistence**; you and I are merely two people with great potential, advancing in different ways and are taking different steps, but with the same goal in mind. . . To live intensely.

I wish happiness, health and abundance to always be your faithful companions.

About Eduardo

Eduardo Cholula, author of ten inspirational books, has captivated the public with his humble and inner strength, and his promotion of human values, prosperity and excellence. He is an international key note speaker on topics of personal growth. His books and lectures have inspired thousands of people to a better quality of life by developing high self-esteem to reach personal goals and success. He humbly carries the flag of eternal learning, love and gratitude for all that surround him. He has been an event host, personal life coach, actor in a movie and theater plays. He was president of HIT (Hispanic Inspiring Talent), an association of Latin writers in California. Presently he writes scripts for movies, articles in newspapers, local magazines, and is an internet radio commentator.

He was diagnosed with polio and now is the father of a son with physical limitations who is blind and has a rare blood syndrome, which requires blood transfusions every two weeks to keep him alive. Due to his inspirational messages he has been special guest on different mass media, including newspapers, radio and television.

Eduardo's professionalism, life story and powerful positive messages have led him to be one of the best authors and speakers of our time. Eduardo Cholula has captivated the public with his simplicity and internal strength. He is a model of success through his mentality of encountering adversities as real opportunities of growth. His audience is simply captivated by the power of his inspirational messages.

You can connect with Eduardo Cholula:
- author@eduardocholula.com
- www.eduardocholula.com
- www.facebook.com/eduardo.cholula.7

Today is a great day, never surrender!

CHAPTER 34

LIVING IN A HOLOGRAPHIC UNIVERSE

BY ILONA SELKE

Let me invite you on a journey into a different kind of universe, one that allows for parallel universes to exist side-by-side. This story contains the secret behind how we create success.

Imagine you are sitting down in an airplane, a Boeing 777, with its small video-display right in front of you. To your right-hand side sits a pediatrician, who has taken this flight to Washington, D.C. many times, and he's on his way to give a lecture in D.C. You're on the flight to Key West, Florida to attend a conference and you have a short layover in Washington Dulles Airport.

However, instead of going to land in Washington, D.C., after flying in a holding pattern for half an hour due to thunderstorms, the captain announces that the airplane has been re-routed to Baltimore, Maryland.

The pediatrician next to you tells you with 100% certainty that this always happens, every single year, due to the weather in the summer on the East Coast. The pediatrician also tells you in great detail that you will be deplaning in Baltimore Maryland, then you will be shuttled by bus back to Washington D.C., where you will most likely arrive much too late to catch your connecting flight. And worst of all, he makes the dire prediction that you probably won't even make your connecting flight until the next morning. He's been through it many times and he knows how it goes.

Even the small video monitor in front of you shows you the new flight path now as a bright red line, heading straight to Baltimore, Maryland.

"This can't be true!" You exclaim in your mind. You **need** to be on time for the conference in Key West, as participants depend on you!

For some magical reason, you had found a fascinating book in the seat pouch in front of you that you had started reading since take off. It was about *Time – Space Shifts*, and about *Parallel Universes.*

Based on the new understanding of quantum physics, you had learned that this universe is *consciousness interactive*. It appears to act much more like the *Holo-deck* did for the crew of *Starship Enterprise*. For those who are not *Trekkies*, let's just say that the universe acts more like a holographic picture show in which your thoughts, your visions, and your focus, all become 3-D reality.

Needless to say, you had become very fascinated by the possibilities that quantum theory offered. You had already been reading books about how success is created by having clear goals in your mind and by imagining a positive outcome.

You knew that you pre-create your success by imagining yourself in your own successful future in advance. You had already been practicing some of these steps in your own life and already created good results. And you felt you had mastered one of the master keys for creating your success in advance: To **feel** what it would feel like if *your goals or wishes had already been realized and fulfilled*. This brings about the creation of your success faster and with greater ease.

Landing in Baltimore, Maryland, as the flight purser had just announced, and being late for your conference, was just not an option. This book on *Time – Space Shifting* and *Parallel Universes* had you intrigued and you were ready to try out some of the techniques outlined in the book.

Not taking no for an answer, you made yourself comfortable in your seat and simply closed your eyes. You knew that you needed to have a PERFECT BLUEPRINT in your mind before you can manifest the desired external result. **You started** by imagining being at a beautiful beach. The anxiety began to leave your body and you started feeling much more at ease.

In your mind you now recalled the steps:

The first step is to STEP BACK, o*ut of the picture of your current experience.*

This allows you to TAKE A LOOK at the situation, as if you are outside of the problematic situation. And as you begin to get an overview of the situation you start feeling even more relaxed.

The second step is to define your goal. This way you start taking on the position of being the director of your own life's film, and you RE-FOCUS on what you REALLY want. To do this you DESCRIBE the goal clearly:

You land on time in Washington Dulles Airport in order to catch all your connecting flights, in order to participate at a conference in Key West, Florida, tomorrow.

The third step is to IMAGINE and FEEL exactly what it is that you REALLY WANT as if it already had happened. *You imagine yourself arriving in Key West, just in time for the conference to start the next day. You can already feel the warm, balmy air of Key West caressing your skin as you arrive on time. You can see how everything re-aligns itself perfectly.*

In the last step, you feel the end result as having already happened! *You continue holding the vision of your future fulfilled until you can feel manifestation of the final vision with a 100% certitude in your bones.*

Since success is built upon success, it is best to start with small miracles and work yourself up to expressing greater visions in time. This builds self-esteem and helps you create trust that the universe is really listening.

These steps are creating the PERFECT BLUEPRINT for your SUCCESSFUL experience.

Let me fast-forward the movie for you and tell you how it went for me when I was in exactly that same situation. I did what I'd learned to do, in order to create success and results: I pre-envisioned the success, and also transformed any blocks that were in the way, such as negative beliefs, doubts or fears.

Obviously, this wasn't the first time I had re-envisioned my universe and tried my hand at shifting into a more successful parallel universe. Over time I had already built up a series of successes and was able to muster up enough certitude in my focus that day.

When we landed I was so sure what we were going to land in Washington Dulles, that I congratulated my husband who was sitting next to me before the announcement by the flight crew! To my dismay the purser of the flight announced that we had just landed in Baltimore, Maryland!

"This is not how it was supposed to go," I thought to myself!

The pediatrician next to me felt proud, because his prediction had come true, just like he had predicted it would. He preferred to believe in Murphy's Law.

Instead of being flustered and upset, I just closed my eyes again and re-created the future-experience that I really needed and wanted. "We do live in a holographic universe," I kept telling myself, "and many parallel dimensions exist." I continued in my mind "My perfect parallel dimension in which I successfully land in Washington Dulles airport equally exists. Contrary to what it looks like, I am not really in a solid universe!"

You may want to know that our thoughts have not been able to be measured as of yet, but thoughts have been observed to have effect on our physical word. In the scientific community the idea of alternate universes was first proposed in 1957 by Hugh Everett III, a young Princeton University doctoral candidate and one of John Wheeler's students. He called it the "Many-Worlds Theory" and used it as an explanation as to why quantum matter behaves erratically.

At one of the **Prophet's Conferences**, I had the privilege to share the stage with Dr. Michio Kaku, a physicist, professor and bestselling author. I was honored to be invited numerous times to speak alongside presenters such as the late astronaut, Edgar Mitchell, and thought-leaders such as Barbara Marx Hubbard and Jean Houston. Michio Kaku said in 'highly scientific' terms: "There are probably other parallel universes in our living room. There are vibrations of different universes right here, right now. We're just not in tune with them. This is modern physics.

This is the modern interpretation of quantum theory, that many worlds represent reality."

Professor Steven Weinberg, who earned his Nobel Prize in Physics in 1979 states: "*There are* an infinite number of parallel realities coexisting with us in the same room." He goes on to explain: "There are hundreds of different radio waves being broadcast all around you from distant stations. At any given instant, your office or car or living room is full of these radio waves. However, if you turn on a radio, you can listen to only one frequency at a time; these other frequencies are not in phase with each other. Each station has a different frequency, a different energy. As a result, your radio can usually only be turned to one broadcast at a time. **But there are an infinite number of parallel realities coexisting with us in the same room, although we usually cannot tune into them.**"

In order to shift into an alternate outcome of a better kind, I took a few moments of deep relaxation, and started refocusing my mind again on the desired outcome of landing in Washington Dulles Airport. Creating a powerful blueprint of a future event takes a little practice. However, all of us create these blueprints, all of the time, mostly haphazardly. We manifest our expectations all around us on a daily basis, albeit mostly subconsciously.

Today I simply *refocused on what I really wanted* (and really needed) at this moment, which was to arrive at Washington Dulles Airport.

Just when I felt this feeling with 100% certitude in my bones that this possibility was real, the purser announced with a great surprise in his voice:

"Dear Ladies and Gentlemen, I was just informed that we actually landed in Washington, Dulles Airport!"

In jubilant joy I turned to my husband and shook hands with him in affirmation that parallel universes and time-space shifts do exist. We do live in a holographic universe, just like many scientists are trying to tell us now.

Imagine now that it was you who had just heard to your amazement that you had landed in exactly the reality in which you had wanted to land in.

How would you feel?

What you had done was follow the simple steps of creating the BLUEPRINT of SUCCESS in your mind. Instead of being dismayed at reality around you, you simply acknowledged the fact that this universe is indeed much more mysterious than you could've ever dreamed of, *and you refocused and imagined what was really important to you.*

Life will hand us enough opportunities to refocus on what we really want. **There are two options:** We can either give up and give in, or we can be proactive and pre-create life as we wish to experience it.

Let us review the five steps of creating a SUCCESS BLUEPRINT:

1. **TAKE A STEP BACK** from the event that isn't going exactly the way you want it to.
2. **TAKE A LOOK** at what is going on, to get an overview.
3. **RE-FOCUS** on what you REALLY want to experience.
4. **PRE-IMAGINE your SUCCESS** and what you really want to experience, until you can really feel this goal or wish being fulfilled, 100%.
5. **Then LET GO** and let the larger universe re-arrange itself for the highest good of all concerned.

I have been teaching this system of Living From Vision®, a course that teaches how to create from the inside out successfully, to business people, laypeople, therapists, teachers, children and teenagers, worldwide, in six languages for the last 25 years. These laws are universal and point to radically new ways of understanding life.

Life will teach us, either by giving us pain when we are refusing to cooperate, or by giving us pleasure and joy when we are cooperating with life. *Either way, we will learn and grow and expand beyond the horizon of what we thought was possible.*

Our reality appears to be solid, but it is acting more like a dream. You are the director of your dream life, and you can create the kind of outcome that you really want.

In the process of discovering the laws of the holographic universe, you will probably discover that there is a greater source of life that is at the center of all creation. Some call it the **Source of All That Is**, some call it **God**, and some people simply call it the **Life Force**.

By learning how to cooperate with the higher laws of the universe, and connecting your goals with the highest source, you will discover that you are much more than a three-dimensional body. *You are here on Earth to discover what this greater YOU is about.* Your successes and failures are the feedback which life gives you in order to teach what works and what does not work.

In time we realize that we are more akin to a light bulb in a projector which illuminates the film, rather than the actor in the film. To the degree that we learn to connect to a higher force, we awaken to the greater power within us, which in turn allows us to create more beauty, happiness and fulfillment.

The future has arrived, and you are one of the pioneers, learning how to co-create a shift in your time-space reality with your consciousness. Welcome to the future! Let us create a better world for ourselves, our children and family, and the world around us.

And foremost:

BE THE LEGACY YOU WANT TO LEAVE BEHIND!

About Ilona

Ilona Selke is an international author and seminar leader, lecturer, and musician. She has written four books and has 25 CDs to her name, and has been quoted in numerous books for her work. Her books and teachings have been translated into English, German, French, Spanish, Chinese, Russian, Polish, Czechoslovakian and Hindi.

Since 1987, Ilona Selke has been teaching personal growth seminars in Europe, the Americas and Asia to therapists, teachers, doctors, business people and laymen alike. During the last 30 years, Ilona Selke has inspired thousands of people worldwide to discover the power of their consciousness and how to create a successful life.

She has appeared on TV and on Radio, on the well-known **Hay-House Summit** in English and German and has appeared as an inspirational speaker on many tele summits. She has also been a favorite speaker at many conferences, such as the *Prophet's Conferences, the Quantum Energy Conferences, the Global Sciences,* and *the Global Spiritual Scientist,* etc.

Ilona Selke and her husband Don Paris, Ph.D. are co-founders and directors of *Living From Vision*, a company committed to teaching about the holographic nature of the universe and how human consciousness can intentionally interact with the 3-Dimensional world.

The **Living From Vision®** course, available online or in book form, teaches methods of goal setting, creating success and manifestation skills through a holographic whole-brain method. The LFV course has been translated into six languages and has been taught worldwide through a network of LFV Teachers and Coaches since 1990.

Additionally, Ilona Selke and her husband have been involved in the research of a quantum tool called the **SE-5 1000** since 1987, for which her husband received an honorary Ph.D. in 2000. (http://www.se-5.com)

In 2007 they built the inspiring **Shambala Oceanside Retreat Center** on the Northshore of Bali (www.baliseminars.com); as well as a **Wellness Spa** called **Shambala Spa** in Ubud, the heart of Bali (www.ubudmassage.com) with a total of 30 employees in Bali, which they still run to this date.

From 2004 – 2014 Ilona Selke and her husband owned a Dolphin Watch Boat in Key West, where they still offer **Wild Dolphin Encounters**. Numerous articles and Ilona Selke's books chronicle the astounding research and discoveries she made with the dolphins in her over 1000 hours of underwater contact with wild dolphins.

Ilona Selke and her husband divide their time between their home in Bali and their home on an island in the Pacific Northwest in the USA.

You can contact Ilona Selke at:
- info@ilonaselke.com
- www.livingfromvision.com

Office Tel: +1 387 5713 PST in the USA

CHAPTER 35

MASTER THE ART OF RELEVANCE

BY GREG W. REID

In networking settings we're constantly on the lookout for that magical connection that launches a thriving business relationship. At times, we find ourselves missing the magic potion that brings it all to life.

The key to that magic begins with honest self-assessment and mastering an understanding of the art of becoming relevant. What do I mean by that? How you approach building a business relationship is in part determined by the importance, applicability and significance you have established.

Let's consider that every person you meet in life is a new Client. That includes a contact, business target, a boss or even a potential business partner. I will outline the concepts and approaches that I have used throughout multiple successful careers and business startups to help you master an overlooked component in business networking – *Your Relevance.*

WE ALL SEEK RELEVANCE

I equate a Client relevance assessment to an online search result. With every Google search you make, you are looking for answers to problems. Search results are determined by *relevance of the content* that the webpage offers based on your search keywords.

The next time you go to a networking environment, think of each person in the room being in the same search situation. They are looking for an answer to the problems they have, the items that keep them up at night. If YOU were a living human web page, how high would you rank in their search results? When Clients meet you in person, you are the living version of a landing page that they analyze, assessing whether your value proposition matches what they are looking for. But unlike static company pages, *you have the opportunity* to craft your *personal value proposition* and tailor it based on the needs you uncover each time you meet someone new.

Companies spend millions improving their landing pages to be featured high in the results list. Where are you in your commitment to communicate your value to your Clients in a networking setting?

THREE REASONS WHY NETWORKING EFFORTS FAIL

1) YOU DON'T KNOW WHO YOU ARE

Take a complete inventory of your experiences, achievements, training and professional network resources. Are you an Introvert or Extrovert – Connector or Maven? Knowing yourself leads to an understanding of your role and place in virtually any networking scenario. Failing to *know thyself* is a path toward consistent failed networking encounters.

2) YOU DON'T KNOW WHAT YOU HAVE

From the moment people meet you they are trying to determine if you have a level of trust from your career competence to be a part of their professional circle. Your skills, experiences and a belief in your vision are resources that must be at a level that measures up to your Client's expectations. What do you bring to the party? Think of the times you failed to convert a networking connection that you really wanted and honestly ask yourself where you fell short. What personal resources did you fail to utilize or develop, that could have lost the connection?

3) YOU DON'T KNOW WHAT THEY NEED

Save your *elevator pitch* and focus on having simple *organic* conversations. In order to become a valued resource that is relevant, you need to spend more time asking and less time talking. The goal is to understand your Client's *goals and current strategies* they are using to "get there." You can't be a solution to the problems for your connections if you aren't inquiring what their current pain points are. Without *acquiring the information*, you are missing the opportunity to give yourself a chance to become uniquely relevant to them.

FIND YOUR VALUE PROPOSITION

Psychological studies reveal that **Trust** and **Competence** are how people evaluate you in a business situation. The fastest way to establish trust is to deliver on a value proposition.

A *value proposition* is a positioning statement explaining what benefits you provide for who and how you do it uniquely well. It describes the problems you solve, and why you're distinctly better than the alternative. Everyone is seeking answers to problems. What problems are you able to solve and what solutions can you deliver based on your available personal resources – the skills, experience and insights you have acquired?

As a comedian, I spent thousands of hours crafting my set to become a professional. After winning competitions and booking significant paid television roles, I gained *credibility* with my Clients and opened the door to have more engaging conversations leading to potential business opportunities. I was able to showcase a developed skillset that was unique to other people. That skill helped generate a level of trust built on my competence as a professional entertainer and actor.

Your expertise can range from international finance to professional drone racing. On either end, highlighting these special skills puts you in a position where your *expertise transfers into trust* - a trust that you *perform at a high level* and are likely able to repeat.

THE POWER OF CONTINUOUS LEARNING

Personal value is built from every book you read, every class you complete, every trip you take and every person you encounter in life. With a mindset of continuous learning, you are always acquiring new skills and validating your understanding of concepts that make you a little more interesting with your Clients.

Take the time to learn from all of your personal interests in life. What you learn brings more interesting discussion topics in your future conversations. All of this information and experience gives you a databank of perspectives and potential topics at your disposal to bond with your Clients and develop trust.

Do your homework for life and career and watch how your network will grow one organic conversation at a time. Taking the time to acquire skills or master a philosophy brings knowledge that becomes a *conversation link* (a Bond) your Client uses to *anchor* a potentially deeper relationship.

THE IMPORTANCE OF RELEVANCE

A historic social evolution study by Robin Dunbar suggested there is a *cognitive limit* to the number of people with whom one can maintain stable social relationships. *Dunbar's Number* sets that limit at 150. In the business and professional world, you want to remain in the exclusive 150 group and maintain your intimate relations by establishing trust, competence and a resource value proposition. Ultimately, as your Client's needs change, they will seek answers from inside their network. If you continue do the work, *they will think of you first*, thus getting you a *seat at their table*.

BUILDING THE BOND

Likeability is the core of initial connections.

Likeability = Relevance

Being likeable isn't a popularity contest. It results when you show enough genuine interest in your Clients. It comes in the form of two relational categories that I call **Passive Relevance** and **Active Relevance**. Passive Relevance is achieved in the background of your interactions with others. It comes from the people that click with you and become someone *you like to have around*. It could be someone you admire for their stylish dress or simply because they have celebrity status, a unique presence or sense of humor.

Passive relevance is also established when you have *shared experiences*. You both survived the same public school education, you conquered Mt. Kilimanjaro or amazingly had the same medical procedure. Because of that, there is an immediate bond that *aligns you to them*. As a psychological condition, it gives you an open door to go further and find a resource-driven strategy for your contacts.

Active Relevance, on the other hand, comes from the *efforts you put forth* to be a reliable resource that is indispensable to your Clients. Here are ways you can do it.

BECOME THE SOLUTION

Meetup settings such as tech co-founder mixers and Hollywood coffee shops are filled with *connection seekers* looking to be "discovered" in a sea of handshakes and awkward conversations. *Their Goal* is to find out who you are and more importantly, *who you know.* However, new Clients are often wary of giving people access to their closest contacts for fear of losing the quality of their established relationships. *Your Goal should be to prove your worthiness.*

(i)   *GIVE THEM THE INFORMATION*
Until your Clients have earned YOUR TRUST and showed a value proposition you may want to restrict access to your NETWORK, but it shouldn't keep you from adding value in other ways. It's your chance to put your learning and experiences to use and be of service to them first.

I met with a tech investor to pitch a project. I mentioned my professional baseball background with the Oakland A's which immediately established a form of Passive Relevance and kicked in some fun story telling. In hindsight, I wasn't ready for the meeting but like many before me, I didn't even know it! While we weren't a match to work together, because I showed some level of likeability, he took the time to provide me references to websites, books and TED videos that would be helpful to *developing* my CEO mentality. I followed his advice and after a few months, he was comfortable extending an invitation to join some of his investor groups pitch meetings.

He protected himself and his contacts by directing me to information first. I took his resource offering and did the extra work, which *earned his trust* from my *acquired competencies* and allowed me to have access to his intimate client circle.

(ii)   GIVE THEM THE BLUEPRINTS

Helping your Clients with tough problems, financial advice, the golf swing and even practical ideas are invaluable acts of business kindness that show your personal value. Be willing to offer your solutions to their non-business related challenges without the expectation of quid pro quo.

While in sales at a large pharmaceutical company, I had a physician customer that didn't have a bond with me. He needed some direction on a home remodeling project that was a major pain point for him. That year, I happened to complete a monumental home improvement project, which gave me experience with contractors and expense management. I shared detailed insights with my Client and saved him thousands of dollars. *I became a trusted resource.* The resulting interactions took us into a deeper intimate bond that persisted and secured future business deals and a great friendship.

(iii)   GIVE THEM SOME CONNECTIONS

The holy grail of networking is getting to the right people. I could write another chapter on this topic alone, but my humble advice to you comes in two forms. Be open to sharing with your contacts – with the caveat that you only open your power group to a person that has passed YOUR Trust/Competency test. Again, since you are already in their trusted resource group, you should be expected to find them Clients that also honor the code of being a valued resource with a service-minded sensibility. It sets your new introductions up for success.

You may have Clients that aren't quite ready so beware. We have all made the mistake of finding someone likeable; allow them a warm handoff to an established connection, only to find they weren't quite ready for primetime.

PUTTING IT ALL TOGETHER

The most exciting part of the work ahead is meeting and working with new and exciting people. It's the reason we move along a sales cycle, increase our wealth and ultimately brings us happiness.

The Trust you build from your development and learning efforts give you a *Competence* that creates a value proposition that is a better resource than any million-dollar bankroll can bring. People bring you the answers, the solutions and ultimately, more people. Bottom Line. It is the discovery of *relevant relationships* that make business dreams come true, not an algorithm delivering search results or Internet how-to-videos.

Think about it. We want every person we encounter to be the answer to our problems. We are searching for dynamic individuals that are obsessed with building great things and seeking partners that deliver a value proposition that is anchored by your *Relevance.*

That person should be you!!

About Greg

Greg Wendell Reid has an eclectic professional background that encompasses careers as a former professional baseball player, award winning director/actor, top-performing sales professional and startup entrepreneur.

Greg currently manages a multi-million dollar sales division at St Jude Medical, launching a revolutionary device, The CardioMEMS HF System, the world's first wireless Heart Failure monitor to effectively fight the growing epidemic of Heart Failure in America. He started his medical sales career at large multinational pharmaceutical companies including, Abbott Laboratories, Merck and Gilead Sciences with a focus in Cardiology and Healthcare Economics. He's a two-time winner of the Rep of the Year award while at Merck and Abbott Labs, along with multiple regional awards while at Gilead Sciences. His roles ranged from business development, contract management and creating local marketing initiatives.

While in sales, Greg followed his career interest in entertainment. His successful career run in the entertainment industry includes over 25 guest television appearances as an actor/comedian appearing on Emmy award winning shows like, *The Young and the Restless, The Practice, CSI: Miami and Comics Unleashed* to name a few. Greg began co-producing digital shorts when online videos were in the infancy. As a writer/director, Greg won multiple online video contests including the Assassin Creed video game competition with his short, *Ultimate Weapon*, which also aired nationally on the IFC channel. He also co-created *The Comedy Blips*, a short-form branded comedy show that aired in over 17 million homes on Colours TV Network. He also studied improvisation at Groundings in Los Angeles and took his standup comedy talents to the Hollywood Improv, Comedy Store, Pasadena Ice House, and to competitions like the Seattle International Comedy Festival.

Greg comes from a family of entrepreneurs. After completing his Marketing Degree at Cal State Los Angeles, he launched his first company, Oggo Gear, a patented baseball cap technology featuring interchangeable display logos. The company successfully launched by inking custom order deals with companies like Universal Television and retail pilot projects with Nike Sports Specialties and Upper Deck. He currently satisfies his zest for technology with his partnership at Tymlyn Labs, Inc. a small mobile/web app consultancy company where he offers his expertise in marketing for early stage app developers.

Greg achieved one of his childhood dreams when he was drafted by the Oakland A's and embarked on a brief professional baseball career in the early 1990's. Multiple injures contributed to an early end to his career, giving Greg an unsettling feeling of being dispensable. This modeled his belief that in a rapidly-changing world, we must continue to evolve by investing in ourselves to turn talents and interests into income-generating opportunities.

Greg's mission is to build great things and inspire people to convert their passions into fulfilling careers. He resides in Los Angeles and shares his entrepreneurial background in mentoring opportunities with youth whenever possible.

You can connect with Greg at:
- Twitter.com/GregWendellReid
- Facebook.com/Greg Reid

CHAPTER 36

INTENSIVE CLEANING AS HOME ENVIRONMENTAL MEDICINE

BY GREGORY RYNARD HUNTER

"I don't know WHAT you did to my mother's house but she's eating again, and she hasn't been eating regularly for months. I'm calling you just to make sure this will not be just a one-time visit, and that you don't drop us from your regular schedule...this is really unusual, but I like your results."

I was happy to hear those remarks. Her mother's appetite had returned and it was triggered by something related to my cleaning session. I expected the behavioral change because years ago I made some remarkable discoveries. Now, after two decades of inquiries from my clients about my esoteric intensive cleaning services, why it makes them behave and feel like it does and why I have a never-ending stream of demand for my services, I have decided to talk. I discovered that indoor home environments are matrices of visible and invisible activity that affect human physiology (the physical and chemical activity of the cells, tissue and organs of the body) and psycho-physiology (the interrelationship of mental and physical phenomena). I probed deeper and discovered that the activity of the indoor environmental elements can be directed and used medicinally to shorten in-home outpatient recovery time. This maximizes caregiver's focus and performance, eliminates caregiver burnout, and reduces hospital readmission rates caused by contaminated, deteriorated indoor environments.

The new paradigm of the home cleaning and health industry is here; it is called Home Environmental Medicine. Home Environmental Medicine (HEM) was conceptualized, created and branded in 2001 by Gregory Rynard Hunter, Founder, Owner and CEO of Hunter Cleaning Services (HCS) of Takoma Park, Maryland, USA.

My unique niche brand was born when I married my passion for architectural industry technology and compassion for mankind to my fascination with cleaning industry technology. The result was the creation of an extraordinary method of intensive home cleaning that has a medicinal application. This multisensory, multidimensional procedure utilizes the dynamic interplay of the spectrum of indoor environmental elements to access the receptors in the brain, turn neurons on and off, synchronize the activity of both brain hemispheres, lower blood pressure, reset a patient's circadian rhythm, and open a gateway for the body to repair itself. All through my intensive cleaning process.

You may say, WOW!!! If you did, you are not alone. I got a lot of WOW'S from my clients and even WOW'S from myself. I was amazed by what I was doing. "This is incredible and fun" I often said to myself. I like to help people and the fact is, for many years I knew I was *doing something* that positively affected the demeanor and health of my clients in that special space they call home. It was something that was very different, but I didn't have a name for it. I just worked quietly and observed the changes.

My peculiar journey as an intensive home cleaner has enabled me to put a spotlight on the burden that unclean indoor home environments put on the immune system, the respiratory system, the circulatory system and the brain, all with adverse effects on in-home outpatient outcomes, the over-all health of the community and healthcare cost. Gregory Rynard Hunter is pioneering the mission with HEM to close the In-Home "Outpatient Rehabilitation System Gap" (ORS Gap).

Before I answer the two questions that I'm asked most about Home Environmental Medicine and how you can use it, let me share with you who has been requesting this service, why they are calling, and how they benefit from my unique niche brand.

Who's calling? Case managers; assisted living agencies; geriatric care managers; social services agencies; health and human services agencies;

social workers; live-in nurses, certified nursing assistants, in-home health aides; adult companion care companies; rehabilitative therapists; behavioral therapist; physical therapist; personal care agencies; professional home organizers; stroke recovery experts, smoking cessation practitioners; caregivers; hospital discharge planners; clinical psychiatrist; outpatient care centers; elder law and estate planning firms; healthcare professionals; eldercare services; aging life care managers; home care agencies; and relatives and loved ones of patients soon to be or recently discharged from a hospital or rehabilitation facility. Well, you get the idea, it's a lot of people.

And why are they calling Hunter Cleaning Services (of Takoma Park, Maryland)? What exactly do they want? They want *The Medicine.* They want a healthy work environment and environmental relief. They're in a crisis, in dire need of help. One of the many calls for help that I received went like this. "Gregory, PLEASE, PLEASE, PLEASE CALL ME!! My live-in caregivers are threatening to quit in 3 days..." Why? Because the home they were assigned to work in was unbearable and unfit for human habitation. What were the details of that situation? There were two client-patients in the same home, an 84-year-old mother with Dementia and her 30-year-old Autistic daughter who was functioning at the level of a six-year-old child. The house was absolutely filthy. Both women were extreme hoarders and incontinent. This gut wrenching and heartbreaking scenario was made more dreadful by the two dogs that lived inside. They defecated and urinated throughout the house at will. The home was an environmental disaster, a health trap to everyone in the home, and a morale destroyer for the live-in aides whose passions are in patient care. This in-home outpatient environment was causing physical anxiety symptoms and extreme mental stress to the live-in aides.

Psychophysiologically speaking, the broad dynamics of that environment were bombarding all of their senses, re-wiring the neurons in their brains, and triggering the release of chemicals that were eroding their immune systems. The home was so rancid that one of the live-in aides spent most of her time with a blanket over her head to shield herself from the stench. When it was time for her to eat, she went outside and ate in her car. Harsh and miserable home environments do not bring out stellar performances from home health aides. Furthermore, if the aides quit the patients won't get any care.

The filthy home environment is a major community health issue especially among the senior population. With this in mind I responded to the emergency. When I arrived, it was her declared exit day. However, I had a remedy for the situation. My mission was twofold:

1. To intensively clean and rid the environment of all the hazards to human health, and
2. To construct an atmosphere of wave activity that removed the aides desire to quit while enabling them to execute their work with passion and care, at peak performance levels of focus, concentration and efficiency.

To accomplish this, I would have to access the master control center mechanism in her brain. This is always my plan. By the time I was 80 percent complete with my (HEM) procedures, the aide was on her telephone calling her relief coworker. She spoke with exuberance and declared, "You don't have to quit now! You won't believe how clean and fresh your room is now! IT'S A MIRACLE!" What happened? I healed the sick indoor environment, stepped back and let the house heal the systems of the body that were adversely affecting the people inside the house. I changed the nanoscale messages and signals and now the home transmits new instructions to the receptors of the brain and body. The chemical releases that were instructed to stay on by the anxiety-producing signals of the contaminated environment were deactivated, and all of the systems of their bodies were on the path to restoration.

Home Environmental Medicine (*the new paradigm of the Healthcare industry*) is fascinating and complex but not incomprehensible. No, it's not magic. It's Intuitive, Scientific, Technical, Hygienically-sound, Philosophical, Psychological, Philanthropic, Artistic and to some, a bit Mysterious. The main thing that you need to keep in mind is that you are always in an environment and you are always receiving and responding to signals conveyed in them. Everything is environment, and the elements, whether seen or unseen, are either producing or altering signals to the receptors in the human brain and body. It is also important to know that the contents of your indoor environment will end up inside of your body.

Without a doubt, the revamped dynamics of that former disastrous space, now free of the destructive, caustic environmentally-induced triggers, created a bridge of high synergistic wave energy linking the patient to the caregiver in a shared mind-separate bodies phenomenon that produces optimum patient outcomes. Additionally, everyone who enters the space thereafter will access this synergistic healthy energy. Now that I've given you some general information about the workings of HEM let's get to that typical first question that so many people have asked.

The most asked question is: *Where did you learn how to do this?*

I answer this question by taking a quick tour that retraces my exciting journey:

It was 1992 and after working for a decade as an accomplished architectural/engineering draftsman, I found myself facing the infamous pink slip. The U.S. was in a recession and the structural engineering firm that I was working for in Washington, DC "abolished my position." Money was scarce and building design firms were not hiring. I had skills and success in eight different disciplines in the building design industry but faced the peculiar paradox of being overqualified for all of them. I had 10 years of professional experience, a wealth of knowledge, finely-tuned technical skills and I was willing to teach. So I applied for a teaching position. There were two positions advertised at a state run drafting institute, however, I was informed that my application was one of a hundred that they received on the first day. One hundred people grabbing after two jobs? I decided it was time to make a shift. I knew I had to *dig a new well* (that's a metaphor for finding an alternative source of income to support myself). I used my artistic talents and worked as a freelance graphic artist by day and a part-time sales position in a men's clothing store in the evenings.

After a few months in this routine, an opportunity to help someone came. A domestic employer of my neighbor asked me if I would take over the cleaning of her home for pay. Her cleaning person recently quit and she desperately needed help. The lady was afflicted with a horrible rare skin disease called Scleroderma. She suffered the amputation of the tips of both thumbs, both pinky fingers, the tips of both big toes and the tips of her pinky toes. I was moved with great compassion by her unfortunate reality. She was a friendly lady, she still worked, but could not endure the excruciating pain she experienced when attempting to do almost anything requiring the use of her finger tips. The fact that her home was now overwhelmed with filth compounded her misery. I said to myself, "it's not going to kill me to help this poor lady" twice a month, so I agreed to help her.

The first day I worked for her I overheard her raving about my work to someone on the telephone. "WOW!!! Look at my chandelier!! It wasn't this clean when I bought the house, and I bought it brand new...WOW!!!!" She went on raving, "there's a young man cleaning my house...you should see my house!" I noticed a dramatic positive change in her demeanor by the time I finished cleaning the whole house. I didn't cure her disease, but her energy had clearly been elevated by my work. I was satisfied with my finished product and noticed *my energy was elevated at the end of the day too.* That observation put my journey into motion. How this phenomenon would translate into the new paradigm in the field of medicine as a healing art would evolve after many years of hard work.

My commitment to several thousands of single-handed intensive cleaning sessions became a meditation and education filled with lots of sweaty, drenched days of pure drudgery, challenges, more drudgery, observations, more drudgery, compassion, experimentation, more drudgery and developments. I knew I was in an esoteric realm of training and that I was becoming a *master* in every respect and aspect of this dynamic craft. My labors, techniques and developments continued until *the problem* presented itself. The problem? Yes, the problem that this 22-year journey would solve finally arrived. And now, after 22 years, let's take a look at the quality of indoor home environments and its effects on total community health.

Typically, before patients are discharged from hospitals or rehabilitation facilities, a discharge plan is designed. This plan is coordinated by the patient, caregiver, case manager, social worker, therapist, physician, nurse, and home care agency. Each entity performs a very specific function towards the recovery and care of the patient. The outpatient home is typically cleared of obstructions and tripping hazards. Unfortunately, many of the homes of seniors, people with disabilities, and the sickly in our communities are in appalling conditions. Their homes suffer from long-term maintenance neglect and are a contained collection of third-hand-smoke residue, pesticides, bioaerosols, surface bacteria, incontinent waste matter and clusters of dust particles all which tax and erode the systems of the body.

I was astonished by my survey results of ten major hospitals in the Greater Washington, DC Metropolitan Area. 10-out-of-10 said that indoor air quality and environmental healthiness was not on the checklist for patient discharge. Later that year, I found myself vacuuming one pound and three ounces of dust from the bedroom of an 84-year-old woman who was receiving in-home care from a nurse. So, here is the disconnect, while the National Institute for Occupational Safety and Health (NIOSH) conducts research and makes recommendations for the prevention of work related injuries and illnesses; and the Occupational Safety and Health Administration (OSHA) implements and governs the standards for safety, indoor air quality (IAQ) and the hygiene of hospitals and public facilities, there is no such governance over private homes in the community.

So, what's been going on? Patients from contaminated homes have been discharged from hospitals and rehabilitation facilities right back into their contaminated homes. Next, an in-home healthcare practitioner is assigned – in many cases as a live-in nurse or aide – to this environmental and occupational health trap.

The matrix dynamics of filthy home environments are as complex as the brain and systems of the human body; however, in many instances they are subtle. Nonetheless, they have proved to be responsible for chronic diseases, blood disorders, inflammatory diseases, lung infections, lymph-node and brain damage, stroke, heart damage, immune system damage and recurrent hospitalizations. It's time to remove all in-home outpatients and their care providers from harm's way.

Home Environmental Medicine is the new paradigm of the In-Home Outpatient Rehabilitation Industry.

Gregory Hunter – c. 2016

About Greg

Gregory R. Hunter, affectionately referred to as "The Incredible Gregory Hunter," (Mr. Incredible for short), is the Founding Owner and CEO of Hunter Cleaning Services of Takoma Park, Maryland. He is regarded by many as a renaissance man because of his broad interest, diverse talents, and unconventional and innovative thinking. The most outstanding fun-fact about Gregory's human package is his left and right brain hemispheres work in synchronization and in a state of coherence. This makes him highly intuitive, a visionary artist on one hand and highly analytical and technical minded on the other. His high physical, mental and spiritual energy plus his technical skills, makes his life dynamic and colorful. These attributes have enabled him to be his authentic self.

Gregory never fears a challenge or being different, because he's a "champion" and "underdog" at heart. Some have said, "as soon as you think you have him figured out, he shows you something else." Boredom is a concept that he cannot relate to. People fascinate him and bring rich experiences. When he's not engaging in a debate or probing the world of a teenager, he enjoys solitude in meditation, yoga, reading and art. Gregory is an indigenous American born in Washington, DC, with the advantage of city and rural experiences growing up. This widened his perspectives on regional cultures and nuances of life style. His international ventures broaden his understanding of people in context. Gregory is a health enthusiast, mindful of nutrition and is careful about what he eats. Learning and sharing ideas and information in diverse areas ranging from nanoscience and mechanics to telepathy keeps his world in an interesting place. It would not be unusual to find Gregory engaged in dialogue with a five-year-old child or a tycoon.

On the opposite end of his spectrum, he delves into the sciences and business strategy books. Theater, jazz concerts under the stars, stand-up comedy, and British detective films hold his attention as does a conscious Hip Hop artist or a DJ who has mastered his craft. Gregory can be found running a marathon, jogging through town or just walking down the road observing nature. At times he's unavailable because he's writing storyboards or mixing tracks for his next video creation. Gregory's clients love him and he serves them until death. With over 300 personal client relationships, Gregory has received a unique personalized education that included a private tour of the West Wing of the White House and insights on Stroke Rehabilitation.

Gregory is a member of Grass Roots Organization for the Well-being of Seniors GROWS/MC, a member of the DC Senior Resource Group, the Aging Life Care Association (Mid Atlantic Chapter), was a guest on DCTV's Shirley Tabb and Case Management Show (services for seniors segment), and is a member of the DC Tobacco Free Coalition.

Get the complete book and white papers on Intensive Cleaning and Home Environmental Medicine at:

- http://www.intesivecleaning-homeenviromed.com/
- http://homeenvironmentalmedicine.org/

You may also connect with Gregory at:

- huntercleaningservices@hotmail.com
- fb.me/mr.grhunter9
- www.twitter.com/@huntercleaning8
- http://www.dcsrg.com/maryland/takoma-park/hunter-cleaning-service
- https://www.youtube.com/c/huntercleaningscv8
- www.youtube.com/watch?v=gojLAeJWdEw

CHAPTER 37

THE POWER OF EMOTION!

BY DR. HANK SEITZ

Brian Tracy talks about how our thoughts are only activated and will only manifest when we have the FEELING behind the thought! We charge our thoughts by having the emotions, excitement and the passion of our desires.

Most of us have been taught to hide and conceal our emotions, being taught by those who had good intentions, but did not understand the power of our emotions. Before we came here we knew that we would have a guidance system that would lead us on our glorious, happy and lighted path. This guidance system is our emotions that guides us with divine wisdom and with just two simple types of feelings, good or bad, wanted or unwanted.

The bad feelings tell us that we are not on our path and they act as 'bumper cars' in our lives, keeping us from straying off our path of joy, abundance and freedom. The good feelings tell us that we are aligned with our genius and our amazing ability to be who we were born to be, magnificent creators using our thoughts and emotions! This is why it is all about us feeling good!

THE FIRST STEP OF ALL CREATION

In the past five years, all of science, including quantum physicists, molecular biologists and neuroscientists, agree that the creative process starts with thought, your thought. Most of us have once again been told, with all good intentions, to focus on what is not happening the way we want and to go out and face the problem and fight against anything that we don't like. Since our thoughts initiate our future experience, the more that we fight against what we don't want will only create more of what we don't want!

The more we are 'facing reality' the more of this reality we will experience, for whatever we focus our attention on must and will expand!

Most that focused their attention on the unwanted create more of the bad we experience in our lives. Whenever we are focused on something unwanted we can immediately know this is not what we want simply by paying attention to the way we feel.

I have had many people come to me and complain about their lives, their unloving spouse, their poor health and their poverty. When they do, I show no interest and they ask, "Why don't you have empathy for what I am saying to you?" And I respond, "I shall not join your pity party for this will create even more things in your life that you do not want."

To live a deliberate life, we must think deliberately and to do this we need a reference point to determine the wanted direction of our thoughts. The contrast of experiencing the things we did not want births the thoughts of what we do want, and provides us the reference point from which we can stand tall and state what we do want.

For example, if a business deal goes south, think about how you want your business deals to play out from now on. If your left knee is hurting, think about your right knee which feels fine, and then ask for your left knee to feel as good as your right. It is this asking in which we will receive and all of our dreams will come true. Ask and we shall receive. The question becomes, "What are you asking for?" as it is in your thought that comes what you do receive. Most of us become fixated on the business going south or our left knee hurting and then we get more bad business and more aches and pains!

If I am thinking about the unwanted I shall receive the unwanted. *As I change my thinking and only think upon the wanted, it is then only possible to have the wanted.* This then will make you feel good, and there is nothing more important than for you to feel good!

THE SUCCESS BLUEPRINT

"The Success Blueprint" within "The Power of Emotion" offers this powerful and life changing action to take and that is to begin telling your new story about how you desire your future to be! *As you tell the new story of your life with your thoughts, your words and your actions that are tied to your positive emotions, your new vision shall appear in your life.* In every moment, about every subject, you have the choice to focus either positively or negatively. In every particle of the Universe and every moment in time and beyond there is that which is wanted or that which is unwanted. There really isn't any good or bad but rather your own creation of what you want or what you don't want. . .   your own making of what you want or the lack of it with any subject under the sun.

In every subject then there are only two perspectives; what you want or the absence of what you want. You can tell in each of these moments, by the way you feel, which choice you are focused on and you have the freedom to change this choice instantly! This is why you are in the center of the Universe for what you ask for is acted upon by the energy or emotion of the Universe.

You can choose happiness or sadness, health or illness, abundance or poverty, empowerment or disempowerment and it is all your choice.

The things in this world that we don't want birth the desires of what we do want. As you start thinking about the things that you do want, you shall start to have them flow into your life. I have had a broken neck in a car accident and healed myself through the power of my thoughts. You can have a loving and supportive spouse, good health, the Universe's abundance and everything else you want, as you think about what you want with the power of your emotions.

Here are some ways to change your thinking from what you do not want to what you do want that will ignite your emotions:

Move from thinking and saying: –

- "I am sad." to "I am wanting happiness."

- "I can't do this." to "I can do this."

347

- "I don't feel good." to "I do feel good!"

- "I don't have enough money." to "I am wanting more money."

- "I am fat." to "I am slim, trim and fit."

- "I don't get along with people." to "I attract harmonious people."

- "I don't have a lover." to "I want a lover."

- "I can't afford that." to "I think I might get that!"

As you read these statements you can feel how the first part did not make you feel good and the second half of the statement made you feel good. Where we typically get 'tripped up' is from our upbringing that tells us we need to face reality and "tell it like it is," rather than think about what you do want and forget facing reality and instead state to yourself, **"I no longer face reality, I CREATE REALITY!"** It is this belief that we have to fight against and face things that are responsible for more miscreating and more disallowing of the wanted things than all other things put together. Once we start thinking on what will be, on how we want the future and to start calling it the way we want it, so will we also feel good and be guided by our emotions, our guidance system to everything that we want. This is now your new story that shall create the new life that you want.

YOU CAN OVERCOME AND CREATE ANYTHING

We are the creators of our own life experience! 99% of all the things we create is not done through hard work, our actions, or even by what we are saying. *We create by the virtue of the thought that we are offering.* It is our MENTAL FOCUS that is the starting point to all of creation and everything that you are experiencing in your life. All action and speaking has a corresponding thought vibration and all thought that you offer, whether from your memory, from another's thought or a combination, in this very moment, is attracting another similar thought. This is called the "Law of Attraction" and it is your current thought that shall then attract a vibrational match to another thought.

Every day our society tells us that this is not true. Every athlete will tell you that it is their 'hard work' that secured their achievements. But the starting point to everything, including 'hard work', is to think about what you want first. *This positive thought combined with emotion will then lead to inspired action.* Since we make it all up first in our minds, we can be successful, achieve much and be a top performer, and we can do it easily and quickly. We just need to tell ourselves the way we want it! "I want it easy and quick," and it shall come to you easily and quickly.

As you choose better-feeling thoughts, speak more about what you do want and less about what you don't want, you will begin to see changes in your life and will tune in to your broader and wiser self. From this broader perspective, you will see a spectacular view of life and start attracting more and more of the things you do want.

A successful process that I have shared with hundreds of companies and thousands of people in the past 21 years is the "Joy Shop." This is where you can overcome anything and create anything wanted in your life. The process starts with the "Joy Shop", a couple of pages of good feeling thoughts, which I wrote. The "Joy Shop" is read first thing each morning and will raise your point of thought attraction to begin calling forth better feeling thoughts. In this heightened state of mind, you then write down three things, each of which will come to you easily and quickly:

1. **Write down what you DESIRE and want.** You can start out with, "I am wanting to have a long, healthy, happy and prosperous life!" Other teachers have taught not to use the words "I want" but this is if I am 'begging,' versus when you state "I am wanting," you are commanding the Universe to yield to your desire and there is nothing more than for the Universe to give you what you are asking for!

2. **Write down what you APPRECIATED in the past 24 hours.** You will be amazed at how many things played out the way you wanted them. The things to appreciate can be as simple as a smile to a miraculous and 'out of the blue' event was attracted to you.

3. **Write down the way you want your day to turn out.** I call this pre-paving your day. It is as though you are paving a highway of the way you want your day to be. It can cover things from how your travels flow smoothly to how your important meeting was fantastic

with everyone in the room feeling good! Call it the way you want it, not the way it has been or the possible bad outcomes, but only the way you want it and everything will start playing out that way.

By thinking and then feeling in your "Joy Shop" each morning, I guarantee that you will have a better day the first day you do this, and your life will get better and better to the point of taking your breath away, so inspired and glorified in the way you have now deliberately created your life the way you want it.

TAPPING INTO YOUR POSITIVE EMOTION

All of science has agreed in the past five years on the three steps of creation that include:

- Step 1. It is our THOUGHT that starts the entire creative process.
- Step 2. This thought then creates a vibrational ENERGY. This energy is our emotions, our feelings and why Brian Tracy has pointed out that nothing is created without our feelings.
- Step 3. This energy then creates what the scientists call MATTER, what we would call our life experience of being, doing and having. In all three steps, along with everything in this Universe, it is all ENERGY, it is all EMOTION!

Your thought is energy, your emotion is energy and your creations are energy.

The miracle that you are rests in that you have the power with your thought to mold the energy of the Universe into whatever you please. This is why you are indeed the source of all your abundance, you are the source of the Universe's abundance and it is all up to you to allow this abundance in and have it the way you want it.

Since we are guided by our emotions, positive emotions will make us feel good and this then indicates that our thoughts must be in line with what we want. We in essence have two minds, one being our analytical mind and what some call our lower mind, and the other our divine mind what some call our higher mind. As we tap into our divine mind we tap into only positive thoughts that then creates positive emotions.

In Napoleon Hill's and my book "Think, FEEL and Grow Rich", Napoleon talks about tapping into this divine mind where all possibilities and all solutions rest. He shares a delightful story about how he would call into his mind a committee made up of many famous and brilliant people, including Abraham Lincoln, where he would tap into their mental capacity and receive counsel from those wise people who have walked before us. Brian Tracy also talks about how to sit each day in silence for at least a half hour, if not an hour, and in this silence one can tap into this creative intelligence.

You too can tap into this divine intelligence that will tap you into the positive emotions of the Universe. It is the essence of good feeling thoughts that lie within you that you can tap into as you quiet your lower or analytical mind and allow your higher and divine mind to come forth. The amazing step and all that is necessary is for you to sit quietly each day for just 15 minutes, breathe deeply and then ASK for your analytical mind to become a reflection of your divine mind.

These thoughts will raise your emotions to a point that will attract everything that you have wanted into your experience.

You will tap into your genius, your will process information instantly and receive the answers and solutions easily and quickly to all of your desires. So, now, go out and feel good with the power of your emotions, and raise your point of attraction to all that you desire.

About Dr. Hank

Dr. Hank Seitz is a passionate man who helps others using a time-proven success formula that taps into their unlimited potential, while guaranteeing specific and measurable business improvements. He was a General Manager with Procter & Gamble (P&G) for 15 years, managing a billion-dollar business in the Southeast United States. He developed a Success Formula for business success and used this process first with P&G and sales grew by 21%, and costs dropped by 34% in less than a year, while helping his people personally tap into their brilliance.

He left P&G and began his own consulting practice in 1995, with his first client being P&G. Since then, he has served as an advisor to the Board of John Deere and helped Coca-Cola, IBM, Chase Bank, and hundreds of other large and small companies and entrepreneurs. All have achieved measurable business results and at least a 300% ROI. Dr. Hank has a passion to help businesses grow and people to attain their greatest potential. He has helped hundreds of companies and thousands of people tap into their magnificence and achieve greater professional and personal achievement, along with using his productivity and hiring analytical system that increases productivity on average by 30% and retention by 50%. He has a degree in Business from the University of Wisconsin - Madison, and is a Behavioral and Talent Certified Analyst, with his PhD in Mental Science.

He is certified to administer the world's most statistically accurate and valid diagnostic tools that provide precision accuracy of people's behaviors, motivations, business acumen and talents. He is the creator of "Top Performers", a time-proven process that guarantees to increase your business, or your investment is returned in full!

Sixteen years ago Dr. Hank broke his neck in a car accident and was in a coma where he was asked if he wanted to "stay or go" and he chose to stay. He opted not to have surgery to put a rod in his neck and instead put his faith in a great power. He was told he would have chronic pain for the rest of his life and once again he called upon his higher power and is now pain free and enjoying good health. From this he learned how all of us can overcome any obstacle in our lives and achieve all of our dreams by thinking good feeling thoughts, and by only focusing on what we want and what we dream of being, doing and having.

Dr. Hank owns his consulting and coaching firm "Guaranteed Measurable Results." He is a Partner in Ultima Real Estate with 380 agents in Texas, and has a factoring company that provides cash for companies that are in business, doing business. He has been called "The Spiritual Teacher" and likened to Santa Claus, carrying priceless gifts for others to enjoy as he helps people make their dreams come true!

Please connect with Dr. Hank on:
- Website: www.DrHank.biz
- LinkedIn: http://www.linkedin.com/in/DrHankSeitz
- Facebook: http://www.facebook.com/DrHankSeitz
- Twitter: @DrHankSeitz
- Email: DrHank@DrHank.biz
- YouTube: http://youtube.com/DrHankSeitz

CHAPTER 38

ENDEAVOR TO PERSEVERE

BY HEATHER PRICHARD

Perseverance... How far are you willing to go without giving up on a goal or commitment? This is a question I was asked at the young age of 26, by a mentor of mine. I had just opened my first real estate company. That question made me stop dead in my tracks and think about limitations. Most all of the limits we have are limitations we have put on ourselves. As a certified Zig Ziglar International business/life coach, I have noticed many people are most tempted to give up on a goal right before they hit a huge breakthrough. This is a critical time to have a purpose larger than yourself that can help you keep pushing through tough times, climb those mountains, or even break through ceilings of achievements.

When it comes to overcoming obstacles, I am your girl! I have been blessed to own several very successful companies and sell companies that I have built. I am currently working toward the $100 million mark in my sales career of over 15 years. Most of all that I have accomplished are my two children, who are both now amazing, successful, young adults.

Although success has been for the taking in my life, none of this came easy. Along the way I have experienced divorce, financial challenges raising two children as a single Mom, challenging corporate partnerships, economic downturns, and some major health problems. With that in mind, these obstacles and the success stories I have achieved in life have made me who I am today. I won't say that I wouldn't trade the challenges for anything, because there are definitely some that I would. I would say that I did grow and have acquired priceless knowledge along the way.

I learned the lesson of perseverance at a very young age. It all began on a cold January morning in 1992, I was a young woman and seven months pregnant with my first baby. I had been experiencing some back pain and some other strange symptoms, but my Doctor thought it was my body adjusting to going into the latter part of my pregnancy. Then one night, I stood up out of bed and fell to the floor. When I started trying to get up I couldn't move my legs. I found myself pregnant, on the floor of my small apartment and paralyzed from the waist down. That day, in the early dawn of morning, life as I had always known it changed in the blink of an eye. I was rushed to the hospital and was immediately admitted into ICU. My vital organs were shutting down, the paralysis was moving up my lower extremities, and I was in excruciating pain.

The doctors were grasping at anything they could to determine what was happening to me. They guessed from spinal meningitis to a stroke. After many exams and an MRI, they took me back to my little ICU hospital room. The nurses then gathered my husband and my family. A doctor I had never met walked in wearing full surgical attire. He rushed over to my bedside and told me I had an (AVM) Arteriovenous Malformation in my spine. He said it had ruptured and was hemorrhaging. At the time, I had no idea what he had said. I was just relieved that he had found what was happening so that he could make me better and I could get to walk out of that hospital.

With a quiet innocence I asked the neurosurgeon, "After the surgery, will I be able to walk again?" With almost a chuckle in his voice he responded, "Heather, you will not ever walk again. You be lucky to live through the surgery. I give you a 50/50 chance and your unborn child less than 5% of living. An AVM rupture in the spine is very rare. I can't even find a case study on one to review. I will do everything I can to save your life. Now, say goodbye to your family because we will be taking you to surgery immediately." When I looked up through tear-filled eyes, I saw my family on their knees crying with disbelief. Saying goodbye to my family that day was one of the hardest things I have ever done.

I woke up seven hours later in recovery. After surgery, the doctors kept me sedated for a week or two. Every time I woke up I wanted to ask if my baby was still alive. I didn't know. I couldn't see or speak due to the medication, but I could hear and think clearly. Finally, one day I could speak! I asked my nurse "Did my baby live through the surgery?"

356

Her eyes looked up at me with shock and sincerity and she replied, "Oh honey! YES! Your baby is fine! You didn't know that? I'll let you listen to your baby's heartbeat!"

Hearing that precious sound of life in my tummy was the sweetest sound I had ever heard! I knew at that moment everything was going to be okay. I knew I was alive, my baby was alive, and that was the most important thing. Everything else would just have to come one step at a time. And that's exactly what happened! I knew the road ahead of me wasn't for the faint of heart, but I knew that the strength within me was stronger than this paralysis or anyone's prognosis of the outcome.

I soon started physical therapy. The therapist didn't want to try to help me walk because they didn't believe I would ever walk again either. Their goal was to help me learn how to live as a handicapped person. I quickly realized that our goals didn't match. I had set a goal that I was going to walk before my baby did. It was time to have a talk with my doctors. Although they didn't believe it would ever happen, they did begin to encourage my therapist to work with me. It took a lot of blood, sweat, and tears, but through the support of my family and lots of faith in God and belief in myself, I walked before my baby did!

Emotionally and physically, it was the hardest thing I have ever overcome. Nothing about it was easy. There were nights I would lay there and cry all night long. I was scared for my future and the unknown. I would fall asleep sobbing and soon wake up to recognize that fear would create the opposite result of what I envisioned for my life. I would go to therapy for hours at a time and leave in a dead sweat from trying so hard, but not able to move one single muscle. Guess what though, I would get up and do it again the next day! And again the next day and the next day and the next day! That my friends, is perseverance. I was steadfast in accomplishing my goals despite of the level of difficulty. There were days, and there are still days, that I feel like a failure because I didn't accomplish what I had set out to accomplish. Failure is an event, not a person. This is when I reevaluate my goals and keep on keeping on! When you do, results follow!

Despite all the people who didn't believe in me, God put the right people in my life that did believe in me and surrounded me with love and support. He will do the same for you when you need someone to be your cheerleader or to lean on when you feel weak. Although I was so appreciative of everything my doctors had done for me, I didn't believe them. I believed in the vision I had for my life. My vision wasn't raising my baby from a wheel chair. I had a vision of walking her into her first day of kindergarten. A vision of taking her on vacations and walking on my own two feet. A vision of walking her into a bridal store to pick out her wedding gown, which I did just a few months ago. That is what I focused on. I focused on my vision, my goal, and the end result I wanted. This lesson has helped me through life in every area, personally and professionally.

I live in a region that depends on oil and gas for our economy. Being a real estate broker and the owner of a real estate company in my home town in West Texas, I have had to learn how to adjust to the market changes. I have been through several downturns in the oil and gas industry over the years. There have been some years that people in our community have lost everything. There have been other years that our community has been abundantly blessed. Either way, I do not let the economy determine my level of income. There is always a way to adjust to the market in any area, no matter what political or economic challenges you are facing. Delivering high levels of customer service during the good times is the best way to keep the phone ringing when the times gets tough. Offering unparalleled service and putting my clients interest before my own is the way I have built my business. This is when people come to you instead of your having to go to the people.

My children, Brittany and Caden, are now young adults. Brittany recently got married and is a physical therapist that works with pediatrics. Caden, my son, will be graduating college in 2017. I am the blessed bride of the best man I have ever known, Kit Prichard. Over the past couple of years I have embarked on a dream I have always had. The dream to help people take their life from a stage of stability to success and living a life of significance. This is where I help people 'Be, Do, and Have' more than they ever imagined possible.

I am honored to carry on the legacy of one of my all-time favorite mentors, Mr. Zig Ziglar. Zig Ziglar was the mentor for the mentors! He touched over 250 million people during his career as a motivational speaker and best-selling author. When Mr. Ziglar went to be with our father in heaven, his family wanted to carry on his legacy. As a Platinum

Certified Speaker/Trainer for Zig Ziglar International, I am honored to take his message, values, philosophies, beliefs, knowledge and proven systems to the world.

My goal for my speaking, training and coaching business is to bring leadership back to the great United States of America! Friends, let's bring leadership back to our children, to the workplace, and to the home! It can start with you. I know you are already a leader because you purchased this book and you are reading it! I hope my story of perseverance has encouraged you to continue toward your goals and dreams or maybe even to start dreaming again.

Referring back to the question of "How far are you willing to go before giving up?" I haven't given up. . . ever. I never will. Although I have built a speaking and training business that I take across the county, I'll never stop selling real estate. I think it is a part of my DNA now. (Giggle, giggle). Many people have given up on their sales career when the going gets tough. Trust me, there are days I have asked myself why I am in the real estate business. I think in sales we all have days like that. The beauty is that if we don't give up, sales is a career where we can make an unlimited amount of money. We can earn what we put into it, and in some cases even more when we build a large enough referral base. If you are in sales and are feeling challenged, I encourage you to get a coach, start with a fresh set of goals and get back to the basics of business.

As a wise man I know says, people won't always remember what you say, but they will always remember how you made them feel.

About Heather

Heather Prichard is a Motivational and Keynote Speaker and Texas Real Estate Broker. She is also a Zig Ziglar International Platinum Presenter, Keynote Speaker, Trainer, and Coach. Heather carries Zig Ziglar's systems across the nation and has the honor to share his principles and philosophies with corporate America.

Heather Prichard has built and sold multiple companies. She is currently working toward a milestone of selling over $100 million in real estate transactions. Her expertise includes residential, commercial, and farm and ranch real estate. Heather is currently the owner of three highly successful businesses in the fields of business and personal development, financial services, and real estate. She has been in the real estate business in Texas since she was 24 years old. She has served on many boards and has received many achievement awards throughout her successful career.

Heather's passion is to help others live fuller lives, and she accomplishes this by bringing proven systems to businesses and individuals across the nation. Heather has trained and coached CEO's, managers, medical professionals, national insurance companies, real estate professionals, corporate executives, property managers, and many small business owners. The areas of her expertise include Sell by Design, Essential Presentation Skills, Goal Setting and Achievement, Building Winning Relationships, and Building the Best You. As a Certified Ziglar Coach, Heather also offers one-on-one coaching to her clients who are looking to enrich their lives professionally, personally, financially, and spiritually.

Success didn't come easy for Heather. She has overcome many challenges and struggles along the way. As a young woman and seven months pregnant, she had an AVM rupture in her spine. She was paralyzed from the waist down, with doctors leaving her with no hope to ever walk again. Heather learned very quickly that her mindset was going to affect the outcome. She set a goal to walk before her daughter did, and she reached that goal within a year!

Success wasn't an option for Heather. Considering she raised two amazing children as a single mom, it was a necessity.

A note from Heather…
My entire life I have had a dream and a vision to help and support others in achieving their goals. I believe that in life we rise by lifting others up. I feel abundantly blessed to be able to train and support others to push through challenges and be the best version of themselves. Above all I have accomplished in life, the greatest achievements are my two children who are now successful young adults. My daughter Brittany is a physical

therapist, and my son Caden is a college student studying computer science. In 2011, I became the blessed bride of Mr. Kit Prichard.

I believe that our faith, hope and love will get us a long way in life. Mindset, dedication, and our self-beliefs will get us the rest of the way. I have the experience and dedication to help you or your employees not only meet your goals, but break through ceilings of achievements and exceed your expectations.

If you are interested in my business coaching program, you can visit my website at: HeatherAPrichard.com. Through the Ziglar Coaching I offer my clients, I have been able to help many professionals achieve results they never thought possible. If you are a business owner looking to grow your team, I also offer tailor-designed sales presentations for groups in a corporate setting. You can get more information on the training events I offer on my website at: HeatherAPrichard.com.

To book an event for your business or organization or for one-on-one coaching with Heather Prichard, please visit her website:

- www.HeatherAPrichard.com.

CHAPTER 39

IDENTITY AND LIMITING BELIEFS

BY KASH GUIDRY

In today's society, we have the highest obesity rate ever recorded. In fact, the 36% is double what it was in 1980—which is alarming to say the least. According to the Boston Medical Center, an estimated 45 million Americans go on a diet each year and spend a whopping $33 billion annually on weight loss products. We also have more weight loss products, diet programs, dieticians, more gyms and fitness centers than ever before. But we are fatter than ever. How can this be? Another interesting statistic is that approximately 97% of dieters gain all of their weight back over the 18 months following their weight loss.

So is it because all the diets and weight loss products are ineffective? I mean, to leave the majority of everyone who partakes in their weight loss journey back at the starting point after they have reached their target goal just seems crazy to me.

Here's the truth, there are many yoyo diets out there that consist of low carbs and there are some that consist of eating extremely low calories, around and under that 1,000 calorie a day mark. Those diets are all about the quick fix, meaning initial weight loss but ultimately slows your metabolism down due to muscle loss and lack of food causing your metabolism to slow down as a survival mechanism.

But there are those who lost weight through proper dieting and exercise, and still gain all of your weight back after they lost it. And lastly you have some who simply can never stick to a diet long enough to even reach the target goal. I can assure you, if you can relate to this, there's an underlying enemy working against you that you are not even aware of. By the end of this chapter you will have a clearer understanding on why the dieting process in general has never been a success for you!

Over the past 13 years I have been fortunate enough to work with over 5,000 clients from over 45 different countries. People from all different walks of life. People with all different types of goals. From those who needed to lose as much as 200 pounds to those who just won their fight with cancer and need to gain 30 pounds. I've worked with diabetics – Type 1 and Type 2 – and those who are trying to come off blood pressure and cholesterol meds. I've worked with postpartum mothers trying to lose baby weight, obese children and I've worked with world champion athletes.

Many of the clients who have come to me have already had experience dieting before. Some have had success, others very little. As I consult with these clients, I get familiar with their past and what happens when they reach their goal and then gain everything back, and the ones who never seem to be able to stick to a diet. I consult with people that have hired world class trainers, purchased every type of diet plan possible, tried all the latest diet pills and still they find themselves back at square one. The right diet is very important, but even a so-called "Perfect Diet" will never work if you never change your very own BELIEF SYSTEM about the dieting process and your own capabilities.

How you see yourself, meaning your IDENTITY, and what you associate with the dieting process are the two most intricate factors for your getting results and keeping them. If you don't change your belief system about how you see yourself and what you associate with dieting, you will never get the results you're looking for and you will continue the vicious cycle of losing weight and gaining it all back again and again.

Let's dive in a little deeper.

MOTIVATION

Everything we do requires motivation, and I mean everything. From getting up out of bed in the morning to brushing your teeth, to going to the movies, to those we hang around and date, and to the foods we eat, motivation is required.

The two driving forces of motivation are PAIN and PLEASURE. Everything you do, consciously or unconsciously, it's to either avoid pain or to gain pleasure. Now here's the kicker, who decides what is painful and what is pleasurable? YOU DO!

What you associate with Pain and Pleasure all comes from the meaning you give things. One of my favorite quotes ever is from the great Tony Robbins: "Nothing in life has any meaning except the meaning we give it."

How you perceive things and what meaning you give it all comes down to your past experiences. If you have tried dieting a few times and lost a few pounds initially but gained everything back, you will likely link Pain to dieting and are unmotivated to diet again. And come January or Springtime, you already have the end result built up in your mind, and it's not a successful one. So what happens? Do you stay on track and follow through? No, you don't, from the moment you get started it's only a matter of time till you will fall off the deep end and binge. Each time leaves you associating even more pain with dieting – to the point you may never diet again. The crazy thing is the only reason you attempted to diet in the first place is due to the pain and discomfort you were in, so that Pain Motivated you to start, but because you link too much pain to the process, like having to give up certain things you love. This is all too painful for you. You rather have the immediate PLEASURE of having the food of your choice, and when you want it.

Those who are able to stick to eating healthy and make a lifestyle out of it don't associate pain to the process. They focus on the pleasure they are receiving and will receive – like looking good, fitting into smaller clothes, more self-confidence, improving their health, and the personal power they get from being disciplined. Until you change your beliefs on the dieting process, you will never take consistent action and you will always find an excuse. I don't care how many diets you try, how many trainers you hire, you will never follow through. There's another underlying force that needs to be altered if you want to get the body you want and most importantly, keep it.

IDENTITY

The belief that can be your best friend or your worse enemy is your IDENTITY! How you see yourself. There's a huge difference between feeling like you're overweight because you let yourself get out of shape, and believing that you're a fat person. Because believing that you're a fat person, and you are meant to be fat due to your genetics, and then to accept it, it will now become your Identity. From then on, even if you start to diet and get results, it's only a matter of time before you go right back to where you see yourself. And it will happen every single time you attempt to diet. How you see yourself can keep you from having the relationship you want and the career you want. Everything goes back to your Identity. I would encourage you not to take this lightly unless you want more of the same results you have been getting.

You must realize that the strongest force in the human personality is to always remain consistent on how we see ourselves. If you see yourself as an alcoholic, you will always resort back to drinking. If you see yourself as a procrastinator, you're going to always procrastinate. And those are just a few examples. There's hundreds of examples in many areas in life. And these beliefs are holding us back every single day.

Most people don't even realize when this shape in their Identity began. Much of the time it has everything to do with the environment they were raised in, and also what their current environment is today. Most adults who struggle with having the Identity of someone who is fat, probably started way back before they can even remember. Maybe they grew up in an overweight family that was never health conscious, they ate fast foods and candy and many other different types of unhealthy foods. They always saw their parents overweight and eating poorly, so at a young age it was embedded in their subconscious mind that its normal and acceptable to be this way.

There's a great story that I always use when I'm speaking at seminars when it comes to the topic of Identity and how your environment can shape you to walk the same path or motivate you to do the exact opposite, it's the story of "The Two Sons with a Bad Father."

There were these two brothers in their 30's, one was a drug addict and a drunk who was consistently abusive to his family. The other one was a successful businessman who had a wonderful family and was respected in society. People were curious to know why two brothers from the same parents, raised in the same environment, could turn out so differently. The first one was asked, "How come you do what you do? You are a drug addict, a drunk, and you are abusive to your family. What motivates you?" He said, "My father."

They asked, "What about your father?" The reply was, "My father was a drug addict, a drunk and he beat his family. What do you expect me to be? That is what I am."

They went to the brother who had his life together and asked him the same questions. "How come you do what you do? Your life is well put together and you are successful with a wonderful family. What's your source of motivation?" His reply was, "My father."

"When I was a little boy, I use to see my dad drunk and doing bad things to me and my family, I made up my mind then that I didn't want to turn out like him. He is my biggest motivation!"

That story is a perfect example of how your surroundings will motivate you and shape your identity one way or another. You can either mimic your surroundings and be just like your circle of influence, or you can have the awareness and decide you don't want your life to turn out the way theirs did. This is definitely a harder obstacle due to the power of your circle of influence, as you usually become what you hang around, but it's not an impossible task. You get to decide. You can either lead and hopefully your peer group follows, or if it gets to a point where you can't possibly resist eating poorly and being overweight due to those you hang around, maybe you need to spend time with others who have similar goals as you do, or even better, those who are on a higher level.

Your Identity sets the meter on what you expect for yourself, your STANDARDS. And that's what you will always get. No one who expects very little from their finances, their relationships, and their physical appearance somehow gets a great career, a great marriage, and a healthy, lean body. *Remember, your lowest level of belief represents your highest level of achievement.* If you believe in your mind that you are destined to be fat and it is impossible for you to be lean due to your genetics, whether you realize it or not, you have programed your subconscious mind to always give you that result. And it will. Once you take on something as a belief, and you make it real, you will act automatically going forward without even realizing you are doing so. You will be on autopilot; what you say, what you do, and what you don't do is all acting on habit, which is nothing more than a conditioned response all because of what you have programed and conditioned yourself to believe, and each day continuing to engage in self-sabotaging actions – leaving you unhappy, defeated and embarrassed.

THE POWER OF THE SUBCONSCIOUS MIND

Your subconscious mind is millions of times more powerful than the conscious mind. It is the rudder that steers the ship. It is where all your beliefs and experiences throughout your life are stored. As I mentioned earlier, the way you perceive anything is all based on experiences in your past, and the meaning you give it. Whether it happened to you, or you witnessed something that happened to someone else, from then on you will have a certain perception of that experience, and that will alter your actions going forward.

The *subconscious mind* is a super computer that automatically responds to situations we deal with all throughout the day and is based on previous stored information. It works without the approval of the conscious mind. Although the conscious mind thinks it's in total control, it's not. Here's a good example; have you ever been on your drive in to work, and you just happen to be on a very important phone call. Ten minutes later you show up at your destination and you don't even recall the drive there? That's your subconscious mind in control. It's no different than when you back out the driveway, you don't have to think of every little step, your subconscious mind does it for you.

Studies have shown that for the average person, over 90% of their time is being run by the subconscious mind, not the conscious mind. However, some people are being run by the subconscious mind as much as 99% of the time. This makes perfect sense why most people never change their ways. Outside of something dramatic happening to them, they never find the leverage to change.

The scariest part about the subconscious mind is that it cannot tell the difference between what's actually real or not, it only believes what you see it to be true or not true. If you tell yourself over and over and over again that 2+2 = 7, eventually you will believe it. If you have had a few bad experiences with diets or believe you can't get lean due to your genetics, you will believe it. You will make what you want to be real, whether it is or not. It's your decision.

What we think about we bring about, and no matter what failed attempts you have gone through in your past with dieting or anything for that matter, doesn't mean that's what lies ahead for you. If you want the future to be different than your present, you must change your belief system about your abilities and take massive action. It's the same thought process that got you to today, to a place of unhappiness as it pertains to your physical body, health and appearance, or anything else, for that matter. Your belief system can't be the same if you expect to make your future different.

You must change your mindset before you can change your body!

CHAPTER 40

MOMENTOLOGY MANIFESTO

BY MALAIKA SIMMONS

In order to properly build anything, you must have a plan. In order to get to a destination, you must have a roadmap. Zig Ziglar once said, "if you wait for all the lights to turn green before starting your journey, you'll never leave the driveway." You must understand that building a successful career, business, or life for yourself is no different. If you are reading this, you are in search of something more. You are in search of the road to success, but no one told you that you are already on it. Look up, look around, and notice where you are right at this moment. That is Momentology. It is the study and practice of operating 'in the now,' succeeding from where you are, with what you have, right now. In my book, *The Momentology Method: Stop Waiting, Start Winning*, I describe how I came to realize I was all I ever needed to win, and what you can do *TODAY* to see success in your life *NOW*. Not in ten years, not when you finish your degree, not when the kids go to college. Today is the day.

The *new* goal is to recommit every day to forging ahead in a positive direction. That is the most difficult part of the deal. You CAN do whatever you want to. You CAN achieve great things. You CAN live a phenomenal life. All you have to do is recommit yourself to greatness (in small doses) every single day for the rest of your life. Easy? No. Possible? YOU HAVE NO IDEA!

You must become what I call a momentologist. You will study, observe, and appreciate the present. Jim Rohn said, "Success is nothing more than a few simple disciplines, practiced every day." In this chapter I will tell you the things that I have found to be key in the journey to success. It starts with you. In this moment, every moment, moment-by-moment, you will observe your situation. You will focus on the now and become aware of your actions, thoughts, and feelings. This is not an easy journey, but it is well worth your time. I'll explain how to begin to peel back the layers to prepare you to meet yourself through awareness, gratitude, and expectancy. It is necessary to reach that deeper part of yourself that holds the truths that you've been hiding from you. It's like a fuzzy dream that you try to hold on to. The harder you try, the fuzzier it gets. It will begin to unfold... you just have to wake up.

AWARENESS

Awareness is the first step to fully practicing and winning with the Momentology Method. If you are reading this book, you have already begun. You *feel* like there is something you don't know, and you *desire* to know more. There are several stages to awareness. There is an awakening, that calls you to challenge or reveal your beliefs, and requires faith in maintain those beliefs.

(i). *Awakening:* That moment when you realize there is more to this thing called life. You may not be sure exactly what it is, but it is definitely...more. Now what do you do? You realize there is more you need to do, to become what you want to be. Success is addictive. The more you learn about it, the more you want to know. The more successful you feel, the more you'll be motivated to take on bigger and better things. The awakening may not occur overnight however. It's easier to stay stuck in our old limiting ways. Complacency is like a warm, comfy blanket of security. Adopting new ideas and habits can be like pulling the covers back on a chilly morning. You may not want to do it, but once you do, the crisp cool air invigorates you. Don't give in to the temptation to return to the status quo of the fuzzy blanket! Question everything. *Read* about success, *talk* about success, *listen* to successful people, and surround yourself with positive and inspiring messages. You are a work in progress. Stop fighting you and start forging you. The successful, 'take-on-the-world' you, is waiting.

(ii). *Belief:* You may have grown up in a very religious family, or maybe they were very spiritual, bordering on hippy-crazy. Like many people, you may be someone that believes in God, but does not go to church. You may be an atheist. Whatever your religious affiliation or non-affiliation, you believe something. Belief is the act of thought following a doctrine. Newsflash: even if you believe in "nothing", your doctrine tells you that there is no higher power to worship or acknowledge. What I challenge you to believe in, is **you**. This can actually be harder than believing in deities. You may think you have proof that you aren't capable of success. There's that failed marriage, business, attempt at college, or that job you got fired from. Get rid of these limiting beliefs. You are as ABLE to succeed as the next human. You are not lacking in ability, you lack knowledge. It is knowledge of self. You just don't KNOW (believe) you can succeed, therefore you do not succeed. Or more likely, you BELIEVE you will fail. Either way you are grossly misinformed.

(iii). *Faith:* Like belief, faith is highly misunderstood. Belief is WHAT you know to be true, faith is KNOWING that what you believe is true. Theologian and philosopher Augustine said that, "Faith is to believe what we do not see, and the result is to see what we believe." There is immense power in faith. Things will go wrong, plans will fall apart, but you've got to go through it, to see that you've done it. You can't see your footprints until you have taken the steps. Know that when you turn around, the evidence of your steps (your work) will be there.

What to do in this moment: Buy a CD, or a book, or sign up for a webinar on building a success blueprint (wink, wink) and simply listen, take it in and breathe. What you need to do most in this moment is be aware that you are about to change. Feel the knowing. Knowing comes from understanding. The definition of understanding varies from: 1). Having a mental grasp, to 2). Being in agreement, to 3). The ability to apply concepts. I'd argue that all three require a deepness, a stillness, and an acknowledgment of the belief that you are ALREADY SUCCESSFUL.

GRATITUDE

Gratitude is the second pillar and the underpinning to having all that makes you a success. It is in the deliberate acknowledgement and thanksgiving for all that you already have, that you begin to see the world for what it really is. There is so much to be grateful for at any given time. Gratitude makes you happy. Think about anytime you have said thank you and REALLY meant it. You were happy right? It *felt* good to receive whatever it was that you were getting. The more you are grateful, the more you will have to be grateful for. It is a wonderful system. The more you are grateful, the more you will see that you DO have things going for you. It is easy to complain about what you think you don't have, and how *everyone* else seems to have it. Money, fitness, health, luck (that's my favorite) all belongs to others, right? Do you have a car, a home, ten toes, two functioning lungs, both arms, both legs, can you walk, did you eat today, do you drink (fairly) clean water, have (any) clothes to wear, and lastly do you ever drink Starbucks? If you can answer yes to at least three of those, and ESPECIALLY if you said yes to the last one... Congratulations! You have a great deal to be thankful for.

(i). **Determination:** This is actually deciding that you will do what you say you'll do. It is about making a conscious decision to be successful. Many people think they have done this when they say, "I want to make a lot of money." Not by a long shot. You are successful the moment you DECIDE to be a success. There are a series of things that happen. You begin to take conscious steps in the general direction. Course correct if necessary. You decide in no uncertain terms that you will do what you dream. We generally know what we SHOULD be doing, we just don't do it. Decide and SAY you will do it. Not that you'll *try*. You will DO it. Do not concern yourself with how.

Pick up a pen, hold it in the air. Now *try* to drop it. Hey! What happened? It fell to the floor? As Yoda said, "Do or do not. There is no try".

(ii). **Fear:** Recognize the difference between healthy and needed cautious excitement, what some would even call anxiousness, and fear which is debilitating and comforts your limiting beliefs about what you can or cannot accomplish. We are often far too specific in our fears, which means we spend too much time on them and they expand. When you think about being happy and successful, what do you say to yourself? Do you say you want "a good job?" Do you want "a lot of" clients? Perhaps. What about things you worry about? Why do we say, I need $422.00 for this late bill, or I need to lose 25 lbs., or I hope my car doesn't break down on Highway 66? Try to pinpoint exactly what you want and do not be afraid to THINK BIG.

What you can do in this moment: be kind to yourself and others. Henry Wadsworth Longfellow said that, "...affection never was wasted." This is true for yourself and for others. In kindness to others you will see that there is goodness in the world and it will come back to you. When you are thankful for all that you have, you will see that you have enough, you are enough, and you will want to give. Pay for someone's toll, their coffee, buy a bag of groceries for the food bank, or donate school supplies. Tutor or mentor someone who needs it, sign up for Toastmasters and say hello to the world, one conference room at a time. Know that the very act of thinking that you are successful brings about the people and circumstances that make it true.

EXPECTANCE

The last pillar is expectance. Expectance comes from knowing. What you focus on expands. You get in life what you think most about. If you fill your moments with worry, doubt and fear, you will receive the strife you dream up for yourself. Expect greatness. Expect to win. This can be difficult for those of us who are not necessarily born competitors, but it is a skillset you must work to improve upon. It is not as difficult as you might think. True success comes not from competing, but from creating. If you have properly prepared and positioned yourself, and you are working from an authentic space, you can expect that good things will come of it.

(i). ***Persistence:*** Once you decide what you want to do, or be, or have, you must call upon what many call "will power" to stay on task. I prefer to rely on habit. Repeating certain behaviors will reform your mental DNA. The GSD (GET STUFF DONE) gene is not naturally operational in all of us, and sometimes requires a booster shot to get it to function properly. Refocus, reclaim, and rejoin the effort to become successful. If you continue to hit the mental restart button whenever you feel you have missed the mark, you will slowly change your habits to missing the mark less often. You will start to see little wins, which will encourage you to stay focused for longer periods resulting in bigger wins. It doesn't matter how far you've come or how far you've yet to go. True success is measured in minutes, not miles. Acknowledge and accept the win (no matter how small), and move on.

(ii). ***Action:*** The quickest way to dispel fear is through action. Do not give in to fearful thoughts which breed procrastination, but disguise themselves as "preparation." Prepare, position, and proceed, then repeat.

Create your own manifesto, define your destiny and create your greatness one moment at a time. Use the guardrails if you must, but move forward.

WHAT YOU CAN DO IN THIS MOMENT:

Stop expecting to blink your eyes and your wishes to be granted! Momentology is not about things happening in an instant. It is about moving through life with purpose, awareness, gratitude and expectancy. Enjoy and appreciate every moment. There are no coincidences. The Law of Cause and Effect states that the life you live today is the result of the things you thought or did yesterday.

REMEMBER, WHETHER OR NOT YOU EXPECT TO FAIL, YOU ARE CORRECT!

About Malaika

Malaika Simmons, author of *Momentology: Stop Waiting, Start Winning*, the companion eBook, *Through the Looking Glass: See Yourself In the Moment*, co-author (with her 6-year-old daughter) of the children's chapter book series, *Shiloh B.*, and creator of The Momentology Method®, used to be very busy. Then she discovered that when you add a little brilliance to your "busy," you get balance. Manage life in moments. That's what the Momentology Method® is all about. Learn to accept the "now." Realize that all you need to be successful you already have within you. Many of us just need help bringing it to the surface.

Malaika has almost 20 years of experience in corporate policy, training, program and project management roles, with degrees in research and psychology. There was, however, always something spinning in the back of her mind. More. There's more to do. There's more to be. There's more to life. She began searching, and a pattern emerged. She realized that she was all she needed to be successful. The clues were in her education and excellence-focused upbringing. As a child, Malaika was encouraged to be curious about the world, and always sought to challenge her environment.

Malaika was often told in school to "stop day-dreaming." She would finish classwork early and stare out of the window or doodle. One day, she looked through the Yellow Pages (pre Google) and found a publisher for her book of poems. She left him a message on his answering machine (yes, it was actually a machine). His return call startled her mother, who wondered why a grown man was calling the house for her 9-year-old daughter. Malaika would later win writing awards and she wrote, directed, and starred in plays in junior and high school. She was TV anchor for her high school news show. A scholarship to Temple University had her starting college courses before she graduated high school. Then life happened, and she stopped dreaming and started surviving.

One day, as a grown up still trying to figure out what she wanted to be when she grew up, she met someone. On July 5, 2009 she met Shiloh Brooklyn Simmons. As she held her new baby girl in her arms, she knew her life would never be the same. Her "mini me" became her motivation.

Malaika found her calling and her cause. Through studying philosophy, neuroscience and psychology, she discovered a way to teach others what had been given to her. She uses her proprietary Momentology Method to help busy, driven women move from feeling stuck and spinning their wheels to feeling accomplished and taking charge of their journey – by leveraging the skills and knowledge they already possess. She was also selected as one of America's PremierExperts™, and is President of the Fair Lakes Toastmaster's club.

Malaika Simmons, author, speaker, personal and executive coach, is creator of the Momentology Method®, and founder of The Momentology Institute (www.momentologyinstitute.com). To subscribe to her weekly e-spire (email inspiration) visit: www.malaikasimmons.com.

Connect with her online at:
- malaika@malaikasimmons.com
- www.twitter.com/MalaikaSimmons
- www.facebook.com/themomentologymentor
- www.momentologyinstitute.com
- www.malaikasimmons.com

CHAPTER 41

WHAT'S IN YOUR MARKETING SUCCESS TOOLBOX?

BY MONICA HOLMES

As HR Director of a mid-size corporation, it was Sam Anderson's responsibility to figure out the best HR software application to move his company into the 21st century. No more paper forms and drawers and drawers of files stored off-site. The cost savings for no longer having to pay for off-site storage would be reinvested in new software. The question was, 'Which system is the best?' How did Sam make his choice? What would you do to help him make the choice?

First, he inquired of other HR directors what software system they used. He spent a great deal of time researching online. He read marketing materials that had come his way. He narrowed it down to two companies. Sam knew this was a large purchase for the company and he had a lot riding on making the right choice.

One of the companies was EnjoyEmploy. They maintained a consistent marketing plan that provided Sam with the information he needed. Sam had a problem to solve and was interested and ready to make a purchase. (If Sam was not eager to solve a problem, he would not be interested in purchasing from EnjoyEmploy or anyone else.)

EnjoyEmploy had started to build a relationship with Sam by maintaining their marketing campaign every month of the year. Marketing is not a hit-or-miss proposition for any successful business. Your marketing campaign is a most important tool in your success toolbox.

Once Sam made a decision to buy—step one in the purchasing paradigm—he began to search for information to solve his problem.

Step two is Sam's search for more information. To assist him with his search, EnjoyEmploy kept their brand and product line in Sam's radar. They sent a mailer every month. They made sure their special offer was on both the front and back of the mailer. Sometimes Sam was too busy to look at both sides. But no matter which side was up, it kept EnjoyEmploy's name, brand, and special product offer in Sam's mind. Sam saw their brand each month. It's as if they were listed in Sam's address book.

EnjoyEmploy maintained their content marketing campaign every month of the entire year. Monica, their marketing manager, had it noted on her calendar every month. She knew that when a client wants to or must buy, EnjoyEmploy's name, brand and product will be familiar to them.

Throughout the year, Monica phoned Sam to see where he was in the purchasing paradigm. Again, it pays off to keep your brand and product in the back of the client's mind.

Monica sprinkled social media throughout the marketing campaign to continue to:
- Build EnjoyEmploy's brand
- Encourage engagement
- Generate social conversations and leads
- Assist their customer service program

Even though it's difficult to find new content that creates a buzz, she knew it was essential to keep a social conversation going. Many potential sales leads may never go to a website. Monica used photographs, links, and open-ended questions to optimize social media presence. Sam was able to post questions and concerns and get an immediate response.

Monica knew that social media provides a venue for customers to become part of the latest story. Sam saw that EnjoyEmploy sponsored a contest to examine the target usage of their network and then focused on what optimized their social media impression.

Monica understood social media was a great place to share customer success stories so Sam could identify with like users of their product.

Sam identified with one customer's personal story about the problems EnjoyEmploy's software solved for them. Stories are much more persuasive than facts.The story moved Sam to see how EnjoyEmploy could solve his company's problems. That's not something that statistics or facts can do: move your leads to make a purchase.

The EnjoyEmploy always-on brand hashtag solicited many comments, funny stories, or innovative uses of their product. This allowed Sam to get answers to questions he had, some he didn't know he had and ask. Sam watched their videos. It made it easy to learn more about EnjoyEmploy's culture and customer service practices. This was a great way to capture clients who don't like to read.

Sam was part of an EnjoyEmploy product launch via social media and felt like he was in on the fun. Product launches are one of the three most common uses of social media, according to Glenaster Insights. Monica helped EnjoyEmploy sell a result, not a process. EnjoyEmploy rose above the social media that's just hullabaloo, and kept their audience engrossed with appropriate content.

Sam knew that Mike, his supervisor, would soon be asking him what HR and financial management system he had chosen. This moved Sam to step three of the purchasing paradigm. Sam was ready to compare the top two products. EnjoyEmploy had also been following up their monthly mailer with a monthly e-newsletter. Monica used this different type of communication to capture those clients who don't look at snail mail. Some clients looked at both. Monica hit a double!

The content of the e-newsletter included EnjoyEmploy's product offerings on the top half and sprinkled throughout the entire e-newsletter. If the client just looked at the top half, their brand and offer was always visible. Included were brief comparisons to other products so that Sam was assisted in eliminating like products. EnjoyEmploy added subtle decisions throughout the copy to move Sam closer to purchasing their product.

Sam thought about his meeting with Mike that was looming and made his decision: EnjoyEmploy. Sam now needed confirmation that he had selected the best product that met the organization's needs. When Sam contacted EnjoyEmploy, Monica had a series of white papers and case studies ready. Sam was looking for affirmation. The three white papers provided:

1. A detailed deep dive: a description of the features and benefits of the EnjoyEmploy product Sam was interested in. Monica was sure to keep in mind busy professionals would appreciate ample use of subheads and easy-to-reference graphics.
2. A light and lively list of key points and answers to questions EnjoyEmploy has learned through their testing and their customers' implementations.
3. A real life success story that shows Sam how EnjoyEmploy solved another organization's problem.

This is how EnjoyEmploy helped Sam confirm that their product was the best solution.

White papers and case studies are an important part of EnjoyEmploy's marketing strategy. This further helps Sam to see he was making the right decision purchasing their product.

Sam met with Mike. He was able to clearly outline why EnjoyEmploy met their needs and move their HR and financial management processes into the 21st century. Sam was ready to take step four of the purchasing paradigm.

Monica knew not to leave any money on the table in EnjoyEmploy's marketing campaign. Monica pulled out all the stops and offered a tiered approach of product packages. She applied Perry Marshall's 80/20 principle, and offered a variety of product packages to offer just the right thing for a wide range of clients. Some will only want to spend $39.99 and others will be ready, willing, and able to spend $3,999.99. These offers were available to be sent out at any time to improve EnjoyEmploy's bottom line.

It sounds really easy, right? Monica made sure that she was consistent. Constant contact is key to strong, successful marketing campaign. She made sure to:

- Get the mailers to the printer prior to mailing the same day every month.
- Find the best way to use social media to keep the buzz going.
- Send out the e-newsletter the same day every month.

- Develop white papers to promote the features and benefits, answer common questions, and ensure all graphics, claims and photographs are true representations of the product.
- Create case studies that clearly detail other clients' success stories.
- Follow-up so clients have a real person in the mix.

About Monica

Monica Holmes is a first generation American. German was the language spoken in her home. While her parents and relatives spoke and understood English, it was a difficult language to entirely immerse themselves in. All through school she found herself explaining such nuances as:

- Words that sound alike and yet are spelled very differently. For example, 'right' and 'write.'
- Words that have many different meanings such as 'run,' 'set' or 'hand.'

Her grandmother could speak English but often words that she seldom heard made no sense to her. Monica found herself explaining the meaning in a variety of ways until she understood their meaning. Thus began her love of language, words, and writing.

Her best friend lived across the alley. Every day of summer vacation they would ride their bikes to the library. They checked out lots of books, put them in their bike basket and then rode to the Uptown drug store. They would sit at the counter and enjoy a cherry coke. Every evening Monica would read as many of those stories as she could. The next day she become a character in the next set of new books. The library was one of her favorite places. It still is today.

Monica's bachelor and master's degrees are both in Communication relating to business and organizations. Her first job was working for an insurance agency at the time when companies moved to using email and voice mail. Monica knows what it's like to have the security of a job and then suddenly technology takes over and the entire organization's mission statement and way of doing business changes. Monica has over twenty years in - depth experience in instructional development, project management, technical writing and training.

Monica enjoys starting a new story and working through to a happy ending. She is first-rate at learning new technologies and 'translating' the new processes in a wide variety of ways using:

- Project management expertise including maintaining implementation and training plans, training schedules, manuals, metrics, and communications documents,

- Experience writing a wide variety of training and support documentation including test scripts, user guides, support documents, on-the-job handouts, cheat sheets, glossary of terms, FAQs, updates as new versions are released, and as–is and to-be business process flow charts.

- Multitasking abilities to ensure appropriate follow-up of client needs, solutions and best practices additional training support for each audience.

- Flexibility to step in to assist other teams to meet project deadlines and test new functionality

- Change management strategies in the project management cycle

These are skills that Monica has acquired working with clients such as Fermilab, Morgan Stanley, Motorola, Exelon, Siemens Building Technologies, Blue Cross Blue Shield and USCC. Monica knows the importance of asking questions, learning from content experts and doing in-depth research to quickly add value to a successful project.

Connect with Monica at:
- monicaeholmes@yahoo.com
- 630.483.7107

CHAPTER 42

SECRETS TO SUCCESS IN REAL ESTATE INVESTING

BY MICHAEL JORDAN

When millions of people around the world huddled over television sets clamoring about the downfall of the economy in Detroit, a select number of investors ran like the wind—towards the very metropolis that residents, politicians and corporations were running away from. It was in that environment that I jumped into the market of real estate investing and changed my life forever.

Building wealth through real estate requires patience and commitment to core principles. In my experience, the single-most important factor for success in real estate investing is realizing that every investment is essentially part of a greater cycle, and that the handling of this cycle will undoubtedly orchestrate its performance and results. In this chapter, I hope to highlight the secrets that have helped me make millions at an early age, and the proven strategies that I have utilized to safeguard my assets. There are industry leaders that claim to have the secret steps to success, and guaranteed results for their proven methods. What I believe is that the secrets to success revolve around proper due diligence, utilizing proper resources, and establishing a power-team of individuals.

The potential to make millions from scratch is real, and every step has the potential to boost or sabotage the performance of an investment. I have personally experienced the mind-numbing dread of losing enormous profits due to lack of attention to detail, but I have also relished in the surplus yields of an investment with brilliant results. What I have learned is that with a good work ethic and the right organization, anything is possible. Having a general game plan and a system to handle the variables that will arise in the lifecycle of an investment is crucial to a profitable experience. Knowing market trends, popular neighborhoods, and the use of a reliable tenant screening system will keep your investment property performing the way you intend it to. Buying a home, renovating it, and placing a tenant seems simple enough, and it really can be!

When the drastic turn of the economy in 2008 left countless homes in urban Detroit under foreclosure, the real estate market presented many opportunities for interested investors. Less than ten thousand dollars allowed one to purchase a home that at one point had been valued at over one hundred thousand dollars. News headlines of investors flocking to blindly purchase homes from banks and property developers at deeply slashed prices took over the media. Buyers of these homes were often greeted with surprises—past-due bills, long-term squatters, previous homeowners refusing to leave, and a homeless population with nowhere else to go. From there, the long and necessary process to restore order began.

It was through the mess of homes in need of renovation that investors like myself found great opportunity. While some neighborhoods were showing signs of neglect, the best areas in the city were still buzzing with safe and friendly communities. It was in those thriving areas of Detroit that I invested heavily. I invested my own capital into homes that showed signs of promise and appreciation. In addition, I invested in quality-screened tenants whom most often were ex-homeowners with stable employment, but had a lack of available funds to purchase homes of their own. The combination of good tenants looking for a safe haven and quality dependable neighborhoods made for an investor's paradise, and my business flourished greatly. I recognized that although some of the lowest priced homes in Detroit were available for purchase, the vast majority of the cheapest homes available were nothing more than endless money-eating pits.

Recognizing the difference between price and value of an investment property is critical to yielding significant returns. Market trends fluctuate, and you should use that to your advantage to get the best deal possible. Although a low price may sound right, the actual value and location is what an investor should be more interested in. Value is influenced by the appreciation potential of the home and the general neighborhood attraction, among other factors. Back taxes, past-due utility bills, failed city inspections, liens on a home, and even unkempt nearby homes can serve to drastically reduce the value of a home - sometimes resulting in a net loss of capital upon purchase. In the worst-case scenario, an unknowing investor can purchase a home (or group of homes), which has been previously condemned for demolition. This is exactly why research and having a complete understanding of the market is important. One of the most common mistakes that the average real estate investor commits is not putting enough time into planning their investment. I have spent a great amount of time helping investors see past deals that present unrealistic profits. Just because the price looks right, does not necessarily mean that the deal is a real-life formula for success.

Decent working-class neighborhoods, with homes that attract responsible tenants, have proven advantageous to my investors and myself - even though they hold solid (as opposed to inflated) returns on investment (ROI). Neighborhood comparisons should always be made, as some homes will look great on paper, but in reality have lower than projected actual value. Neighborhood vacancies, slow response of city services, and general blight can drive down the value of a beautiful home with endless potential. Conversely, an "ugly home" in a great neighborhood can be spruced up cosmetically and structurally to dramatically increase its sales potential and overall appreciation potential. Neighborhoods with minimal abandoned homes and a "community-feel" often serve as the most attractive investment markets with desirable appreciation potential. Familiarizing yourself with the home you are buying, along with its history and comparable properties, will help to avoid a profit-dwindling situation. Do your homework, and truly know where your money is going!

Not utilizing a team of experienced professionals to help guide one's success is an enormous mistake that an investor can make. A power-team is necessary in order to delegate, manage, and verify the crucial functions of your investment. One tip I give to anyone who is starting in this industry is to keep notes on the professionals they meet. Some of the most valuable partnerships and joint ventures I have made have been with individuals months or even years after I had initially met them. At an early age, I realized that simply putting a name and phone number into my phonebook without the details on where we met, what they do for a living, or how they can potentially help me, was as useful as throwing a bucket of water into the ocean. Every time I meet an individual at an event, meeting, or even if I am shopping at the mall, I always utilize the small section on my phone's contact form that most people look over. Even if I am not able to use their abilities and resources at that moment, I may get to a point in my life when I will. For example, at one point in my career, I was primarily involved in the construction industry. Naturally, I met a good number of people who worked in related trades. Whether the individual was a competitor, client, or businessman in a totally unrelated field, I always kept notes on how I may be able to work with that individual in the future. What field were they in? Where, how, and when did I meet them? What was the attitude I received towards building wealth and success with this associate? Did she or he seem like the type of person that I could get along with? As silly as some of these things may seem, no one can remember everything about everyone they meet, and the possibility that your business may require a service from someone whom you have met in the past is real. Keep good notes on all your contacts, because in this evolving market, you can never know for certain what avenue the business will take.

Once those relationships are in place, it is imperative to strengthen them. I take pride in always keeping my word – something that may seem so simple, but realistically is hard to do. It is important to deliver on all aspects of a relationship – from clear expectations, unwritten standards of respect, and handling business matters in the best interest of all parties involved. I make sure that the individuals I deal with know I am dependable and honest. That makes them more comfortable in their business with me, and helps to establish trust all-around.

After the right system is assembled, success only depends on keeping the course. Due diligence in the business of property investments goes further than relying on limited resources to help turn your investment property into a cash cow. There are many moving parts in the machine that is an "investment property," but with a solid game plan, the possibilities are endless. I can never say it enough: putting together a team of trusted colleagues with a diverse skill set will keep your investment's lifecycle smooth and profitable. It is imperative that as an investor and leader, you know the strengths and weakness of your team and delegate appropriate responsibilities to them. By the same token, do not mistake movement for progress – just because someone seems busy, does not mean they are producing quality work. Checks and balances must be in place. Under no circumstance should you feel alone in your venture. If you do, it is only because someone from your team is not pulling his or her weight.

Knowing the different levels that your investment property can perform at is as important as any factor in your investment. Maximizing the performance of your investment is paramount to success (profit), while having clear and predetermined plans for dealing with the circumstances that arise will aid in the efficiency of the investment's life cycle. From tenants to toilets, it all should flow smoothly. Established screening systems for neighborhoods, renovation crews, tenants, and even property management companies will help you, the investor, capitalize on your money. Making millions through real estate without a proper plan to protect your wealth is just as silly as making a deal with one eye closed. I always initiate a business deal by not only considering the potential profit, but also by focusing on the worst-case scenario and situations that could happen other than what I had planned. By ensuring that I can accept the worst case scenario and live with it, I can be sure that my investment will be a successful one. By owning real estate that can offer a monthly return on my investment and that has the potential to appreciate, I can be sure that I am spending money and building wealth wisely.

My motivation, organization, and success in building great relationships have led me to become a millionaire at an early age. It was not always a smooth ride, and there were many speed bumps along the way. However, I never lost sight of my end goal or my determination to be the best. Attaining the status of one of the top property developers in Metropolitan Detroit has granted me countless opportunities to help others reach their financial goals. From small-scale, first time investors to equity groups and investment funds, I believe that the principles for success are universal, and I give the same advice to everyone. Success in business is the result of motivation, organization, and using the right relationships to ensure stability and wealth. Life is full of opportunities, and I urge anyone who desires to be successful to take advantage of everything presented to them with an open mind, and understand that success only occurs when preparation meets opportunity.

About Michael

Michael Jordan is a venture capitalist who has succeeded in many different avenues of business, most prominently the rental home real estate market. Born and raised in the suburbs of Detroit, with a father who worked both in the automotive industry and in construction, he discovered from an early age the stability of an economy centered on industry.

A student athlete on full scholarship playing basketball at the University of Detroit Mercy, Michael started his first business at the age of 19. Following two years of NCAA tournament play, Michael's passion for success through business overtook his desire to play professional sports. It was at that time that he transferred to the University of Michigan to pursue a degree in Business Management.

During his first semester at the University of Michigan, Michael realized the potential to make money by being an expert networker and a professional in the construction and real estate market. His attention shifted and he became wholly invested in growing his business and achieving the success of his mentors (most of whom were twice his age). Like many of those around him, he believed in the strength and potential of Real Estate Investing.

His natural-born passion to compete and succeed, along with his lifelong dreams of success on the basketball court, fueled a competitive drive to set high standards for himself and his companies. His first venture in real estate focused on the construction of new homes in Metropolitan Detroit. While in the process, he began to buy packages of properties in and around the City of Detroit, which he converted into economical, high quality rental homes. Due to an increase in demand for quality homes in Detroit and the number of homebuyers looking for residual income, Michael capitalized on the tangibility of Detroit homes as secure investments. By building a trusted team and continuing to invest into the city's neighborhoods, Strategy Properties became a key provider of rental homes in Michigan and many other states across the nation.

Michael currently resides in the hometown of Henry Ford, Dearborn, Michigan, with his beautiful wife and daughter. He hopes that through his business ventures, he will develop non-profit organizations structured to service those in need. The work ethic and dedication that his father instilled in him at an early age continues to drive Michael to reach and surpass his greatest ambitions.

Michael's desires are to continue the development of investment homes services, and to evolve with the ever-changing housing market. Being fluid in an economy that will undoubtedly fluctuate is one of Michael's greatest attributes to his success, and he promotes this ideology as a pillar of success in any business venture.